FEAR, WAR, and the BOMB

MILITARY AND POLITICAL CONSEQUENCES OF ATOMIC ENERGY

by
P. M. S. BLACKETT

WHITTLESEY HOUSE · McGraw-Hill Book Company, Inc.
New York and Toronto

FEAR, WAR, AND THE BOMB

This book was published in Great Britain under the title: MILITARY AND POLITICAL CONSEQUENCES OF ATOMIC ENERGY

PUBLISHED BY WHITTLESEY HOUSE

A DIVISION OF THE McGRAW-HILL BOOK COMPANY, INC.

PRINTED IN THE UNITED STATES OF AMERICA

PREFACE

THE origin of this book was an attempt to find a rational basis for a policy for the United Kingdom in relation to atomic energy. As one of the members of the Advisory Committee on Atomic Energy, set up by the British Government in August, 1945, I was officially concerned with the formulation of such a policy; but after the hopeful start represented by the Attlee-Truman-King Declaration in November, 1945, and the setting up of the United Nations Atomic Energy Commission in the following January, I found my views diverging more and more widely from those of my colleagues.

The conviction gradually grew in my mind that the policies of Britain and the United States—for, in essentials, the two seemed the same—were following paths which were as unrealistic in their military basis as they were likely to be disastrous in their political consequences.

Analyzing the main source of my disagreements with my colleagues, I found them to lie, firstly, in a different view as to the probable effect of atomic bombs on wars between great continental powers; and secondly, in a different estimate as to what was and what was not practical international politics in the world of today.

In the summer of 1947 I began, at first with the object of clarifying my own views, to write an account of the probable influence of weapons of mass destruction on warfare, using the abundant published material about the course of the late war and allowing for the expected improvements in weapons. It was not possible, however, to stop there. For it seemed clear to me that where our policy had gone wrong was in failing to base the plans for the control of atomic energy not only on realistic military thinking but also on realistic political thinking. So it seemed necessary to write an account of the campaign for control, with the object both of bringing to the surface its implicit military assumptions, and of attempting to forecast the effect of setting up such a control system on the future relations between the major Powers. What finally drove me to complete this heavy double task was the belief that it was precisely through the artificial separation of the political from the military consequences of atomic energy, that Anglo-American policy had gone astray.

In the early spring of 1948 the Advisory Committee on Atomic Energy was abolished, and so I no longer had any official responsibility in relation to atomic energy. I decided, therefore, to elaborate what I had written into a book for publication.

During the necessary extensive reading in the voluminous literature on atomic energy, many aspects of the problem came to light which were new to me; these led to corresponding shifts in my own views, and so may have resulted in discrepancies in emphasis between the different chapters. The main material on which the argument is based consists of official and semi-official reports, together with the more easily accessible articles by private individuals. In however many respects my views may differ from those of the American atomic scientists, I have found their periodical, *Bulletin of Atomic Scientists*, an invaluable compendium of the most important literature, both official and unofficial; the existence of such an atomic reader's digest greatly lightens the task of anyone attempting to understand the history of the campaign for control. No attempt has been made to use material from the daily press of the world, except in so far as isolated articles or clippings have come accidentally to my notice. Two official American reports—*A Program for National Security* (*Compton Report*) and *Survival in the Air Age* (*Finletter Report*)—which have become available to me recently are discussed in Appendix V.

When the book was finished I found I had signally failed to write a recipe for action which would be likely at the present time to commend itself to the political taste of a majority of my countrymen. But for this the state of the world, not I, must take the blame. Moreover, this lack may be all to the good, for the world has perhaps already had a plethora of recipes in the field of atomic energy, but too little diagnosis and too little understanding. If this book contributes to the latter it will have served its purpose.

I wish to express my gratitude to the many friends who have read the typescript at the various stages of its completion and have profoundly assisted me in the elucidation of the intricacies of this complex subject by their detailed advice and by their often pungent criticisms.

CONTENTS

1. INTRODUCTION

UNDERLYING all discussion of proposals for the control of atomic energy lies the problem of how the invention of atomic bombs affects warfare. It is always difficult to foresee the effect of an important new weapon on the art and practice of war, because of the complexity of the reactions which it brings into being. Though it is especially difficult to foresee quantitatively the effect of atomic bombs, because of their technically revolutionary character, it is particularly important to attempt to do so. For the appropriateness of any proposals for the control of atomic energy will depend on the estimate made of the effect of atomic bombs on the course of future wars. It is clearly essential to make these estimates of the future not only in as quantitative a form as possible, but in relation to concretely imagined war situations involving the existing nations in the world today, taking into account, as far as is practicable, their social, industrial, geographical and military diversities.

There has often been a widespread skepticism about the application of numerical and statistical arguments to situations as complex as modern warfare between existing nations; and so a tendency has existed to rely on purely qualitative arguments about war conceived in the abstract. Though a statistical argument about a possible real war may be just as false as a qualitative one about an abstract war, this is no reason for neglecting to acquire all possible numerical facts about the past, before the attempt is made to predict the future. As was aptly said a century ago by Charles Babbage: "Nor let it be feared that erroneous deductions may be made from such facts; the errors which arise from the absence of fact are far more numerous and more durable than those which result from unsound reasoning respecting true facts."

When an important new weapon is invented, one finds opinion as to its effectiveness lying anywhere between the two extremes of what may be called the radical and the conservative views. The radical view, that the new weapon (be it crossbow or atomic

1

bomb) has revolutionized warfare and made all other arms obsolete, is usually supported by a few military enthusiasts and by many amateurs.[1] On the other extreme lies the conservative view, popular in most military circles, that each new weapon is only one more new weapon, and will eventually be absorbed, as in innumerable cases in the past, into the practice of the military art, without essentially changing its character. Somewhere, of course, between these extremes, the truth must lie.[2]

Though the radical view is widely held to be true of the atomic bomb, in view of its exceptional destructive power, no serious suggestion appears to have been made by any major Power that atomic bombs are such uniquely powerful weapons as to make possible a reduction in the size of its armed forces as a whole. The two opposing views, the radical view that the atomic bomb is a revolutionary weapon, and the conservative view that it is just another weapon, are nicely married in the thesis, said to have been expressed by a well-known American general: "Of course, the atomic bomb is a revolutionary weapon, but far from being a cheap weapon, or from having made other arms and weapons obsolete, a still larger Army, Navy and Air Force is needed to hold the bases from which the atomic bomb is to be used."

There seem to have been many people who were so deeply impressed by the results of dropping two atomic bombs on Japan, that they came to believe that the use of even a few atomic bombs would decide the course of future wars. If this were true, it would indeed seem rational to single them out from all other weapons and armaments for special treatment. If, on the other hand, one concludes from an analysis of the past that even a large number of atomic bombs will not by themselves decide the course of future

[1] "The atomic bomb has almost certainly relegated all other weapons of modern war—tanks, battleships, guns, rifles, and trained conscript masses—to the museum." Sir William Beveridge, *The London Times,* August 14, 1945.

An able and very balanced statement of the effect of atomic bombs on warfare, and an effective criticism of Sir William Beveridge's statement was given by Rear-Admiral Thursfield in *The London Times* of August 15, 1945.

[2] "It is obvious that men make wars. The corollary that men lose wars is a truism that is often forgotten. The popular tendency at the moment is to identify all man's military achievements with the machine. The aeroplane, the tank, the battleship, radar and the atom bomb amongst others are all credited by various proponents, with having been the decisive factor in winning the war for the Allies. It seems to be felt, in some quarters, that given enough atom bombs, any power could guarantee for itself ultimate victory in a future war. But the story of Germany's defeat in World War II convincingly destroys such theories." Milton Shulman, *Defeat in the West* (London, 1947).

wars between Great Powers, and that there exist other weapons of comparable power, then the problem of the control of atomic energy becomes part of the problem of general disarmament.

The evidence which will be presented in later chapters shows that many of the proposals for the control of atomic energy, in particular the Lilienthal and Baruch Plans, appear to have been based on a superficial appreciation of the effectiveness of atomic bombs in wars between Great Powers. In the writer's view almost irretrievable harm has resulted from this error.

In order to assess the effect of atomic bombs in future wars, it is clearly necessary to start with as sound and as detailed a knowledge as it is possible to attain of the part which atomic bombs and other weapons of comparable destructiveness have played in the past. Since only two atomic bombs were used in the second World War, and then only at a very late stage and under very special circumstances, it is by no means sufficient only to study what happened at Hiroshima and Nagasaki; on the contrary, it is essential to study the war as a whole and to attempt to assess the part played by other arms. Of primary importance is the study of the effects of ordinary bombing with high explosives and incendiaries, for the effects of these are in many respects closely similar to the effects of atomic bombs.

Now the significant fact of the bombing offensive against Germany is the huge weight of ordinary bombs which were dropped without leading to a decisive failure of either production or civilian morale; and this offensive took place at a time when Germany was engaged in a vast land battle in which she had already been decisively defeated and had already suffered enormous losses in manpower and equipment. As will be shown in Chapters 2 and 3, three million tons of ordinary bombs were dropped by British and American aircraft in the European and Pacific wars. Since one atomic bomb of the 1945 type produces (as will be shown later) about the same material destruction as 2,000 tons of ordinary bombs, it is certain that a very large number of atomic bombs would be needed to defeat a great nation by bombing alone.

The fact that the scale of normal bombing was so much greater than the scale of atomic bombing makes it essential to base predictions about the future on an historical analysis of the observed effects of the huge normal bombing offensive, and not only on the effects of the two atomic bombs. Statistically the former campaign provides a much larger and so more reliable "sample" from which to predict the future.

Owing to the lively controversy of the years since the first World War as to the relative merits of different methods of using air power, the Allied bombing offensive in the second World War has been far more scientifically documented than most other aspects of the war. Published documents and reports are available from which it is possible to assess with considerable accuracy the part which long-range bombing played in the final defeat of Germany and Japan. It is a significant fact that the excellent and comprehensive reports of the bombing of Germany and Japan, published by the United States Strategic Bombing Survey, have had only a limited circulation in America and have neither been reprinted in England, nor attracted press attention. This lack of notice, especially in England, is certainly connected with the contents of the reports, which prove the surprising ineffectiveness, as judged by their impact on German morale and industrial production, of the bombing attacks on German cities which constituted such an important part of the British war effort. In startling contrast is the enormous publicity lavished on all aspects of the atomic bomb, and of its effects at Hiroshima and Nagasaki. Important as these effects were, there is a serious danger of false conclusions being deduced from them, unless the very special circumstances of the close of the war against Japan are borne in mind, and the lessons of Hiroshima and Nagasaki are supplemented by those of Berlin, Hamburg, Dresden and the sixty other German cities which were severely damaged by ordinary bombs.

The attempt to estimate the effects of atomic bombs in future wars from the effects of normal bombing in the European war has been criticized on the ground that the atomic bomb is so revolutionary a weapon that no useful lessons can be learned in this way. It must be emphasized, however, that, easy as it is to err in judgment in this as in other fields of knowledge, there is no reliable way of attempting to predict the future—and all rational policy-making involves a prediction about the future—except by attempting to understand the past. Much space in this book is, therefore, devoted to a detailed study, in as numerical a form as possible, of the history of the bombing offensives of the last war, and of the part they played, in comparison with the other military operations, in securing the final defeat of the Axis Powers. Admittedly the study is far slighter than could be desired, but as is inevitable in the real world of affairs, policies have to be determined and executive decisions taken on the best available evidence; they cannot wait till historians have said their last words—if they ever do. So, if charged with superficiality in analysis or with the inadequacies of his facts, the writer can legitimately make the claim of the detective in the well-known story: "He told . . . the truth, and nothing but the truth; not the whole truth, which after all nobody ever tells, if only because there is not time."

The most important deduction that must inevitably be drawn from this analysis is that any future war in which America and Russia are the chief contestants—and this clearly is the only major war which needs serious consideration—would certainly not be decided by atomic bombing alone. On the contrary, a long-drawn-out and bitter struggle over much of Europe and Asia, involving million-strong land armies, vast military casualties and widespread civil war, would be inevitable. It is one of the main themes of this book that the acceptance of this thesis undermines the logical basis for the plans for the control of atomic energy which have been recommended by a majority of the member nations of the United Nations Atomic Energy Commission.

The conviction appears to be widespread, particularly in America, that any future major war is likely to take the form primarily of a campaign of mutual destruction of the cities of the contending nations. Though this belief may possibly prove to be well founded, it appears to have arisen in part from what now appears to have been a failure to understand fully the military and political lessons of the late war, and in part also from a psychological reaction to the historic fact that it was Britain and America, two nations which normally consider themselves among the most humane and peace-loving in the world, which first made use of this fearsome weapon of mass destruction. The theme that the Soviet Union may be expected to launch a surprise atomic bomb attack on all the big cities of the United States as soon as she is technically able to do so, and that such an attack might inflict tens of millions of casualties in a night, is implicit in much American contemporary thought. It is clearly assumed, for instance, in the Report of the President's Advisory Committee on Universal Training,[3] and the report[4] of the President's Air Policy Committee.

Senator Brien McMahon[5] said to the U.S. Senate:

> It would not be necessary for an enemy to destroy our cities in order to destroy us. By the use of radioactive particles, or death dust in combination with disease germs, every living thing in our cities could be annihilated and the cities themselves left standing and empty of resistance to an invader.

Dr. J. R. Oppenheimer[6] wrote:

> The pattern of the use of atomic weapons was set at Hiroshima. They are the weapons of aggression, of surprise, and of terror. If they are ever used again, it may well be by thousands or by tens of thousands . . . But it is a weapon for aggressors and the elements of surprise and terror are as intrinsic to it as are the fissionable nuclei.

In contrast with these views we have the opinion of the military historian, Liddell Hart:[7]

> An important lesson from the experience of warfare is that aggressors—unless they are merely barbaric hordes—tend to rely on improved use of conventional weapons, and to avoid widespread destruction, whereas the incensed victims of aggression tend to be far more reckless. That is a natural tendency—because aggressors are calculating. They plan to achieve their gains with the least possible damage, both to themselves and to their acquisitions, whereas the victims of aggression are driven by an uncontrollable impulse to hit back regardless of the consequences. That tendency has been demonstrated afresh in the war just ended. Hitler, during the time when he had immensely superior bombing power, was remarkably reluctant to unleash it fully against his opponents' cities, and repeatedly sought to secure a truce in city-bombing during the peak-days of his power. Neither we nor the Americans, when they came into the war, were restrained by any such calculating considerations

[3] President's Advisory Committee on Universal Military Training, *A Program for National Security* [*Compton Report*] (Washington, 1947).
[4] President's Air Policy Committee, *Survival in the Air Age* [*Finletter Report*] (Washington, 1946).
[5] Reported in *Bulletin of Atomic Scientists* [*B.A.S.*] (Chicago) July, 1947.
[6] J. R. Oppenheimer, quoted in Bernard Brodie (Editor), *The Absolute Weapon*, p. 73 (New York, 1946).
[7] B. H. Liddell Hart, *The Revolution in Warfare*, p. 85 (New Haven, 1947).

about the ultimate effects of unlimited devastation. We were dominated by the impulse to destroy Nazism whatever else was destroyed in the process.

It will be one of the objects of this book to weigh the degrees of truth in these divergent viewpoints. Whether or not the prevalent grim prophecies are likely to be fulfilled, there is no doubt that they are widely believed, especially in America; as a result, a state of intense public alarm has been created, which is little conducive to clear thinking about the complicated issues confronting the world. "Without the elimination of an atomic armament race by international control, the two worlds which are shaping up now will not be merely two competing economic systems, but two camps of enemies armed to the teeth and *watching each other's preparations in hysterical anguish*"[8] (Author's italics). There is much evidence to support the view that the prevalence of such "hysterical anguish" has been an important factor in causing the present deadlock in the negotiations on control, by making any control system which does not offer something near perfect security appear valueless.

Neglect of the broad lessons of the second World War is not the only charge that can be levelled against much contemporary discussion of atomic bombs; another serious lapse, in the writer's view, has been the failure to take fully into account the role that atomic energy may play as a source of industrial power, especially in countries such as the Soviet Union, which before the war had a much smaller per capita energy production than the United States of America. It will be shown that the marked tendency in America and to a less extent in Great Britain, to play down the possibilities of atomic power has an understandable origin in the already adequate, or nearly adequate, supplies of energy from coal, oil and water power, in these advanced industrial countries.

When we come to consider the implications of the United Nations Atomic Energy Commission's (A.E.C.'s) plan for the control of atomic energy, we shall find that it could, and in all probability would, have led to a slowing down of, or even to calling a halt to the exploitation by Russia of atomic energy for industrial purposes. The theme that atomic bombs are so dangerous that

[8] Editorial in *B.A.S.*, August, 1947.

humanity should be prepared to forego the advantages of atomic power in order to save itself from destruction by atomic bombs is being energetically propagated today in America. The well-established, but often forgotten, fact that the standard of living of the citizens of a country is closely dependent on its supplies of energy, makes it evident that a nation which already has achieved a high energy production, and so a high standard of living, is likely to be much less interested in increasing its energy supplies than a nation with a lower energy supply and so a lower standard of living.

Only on the basis of such detailed analysis of the tactical and strategic consequences of atomic bombs, and of the possible social and industrial consequences of atomic power, can one enter usefully into a discussion of the rival American and Russian plans for the control of atomic energy. These plans have now been under continuous and bitter discussion ever since they were first put forward in the early summer of 1946, by Mr. Baruch and Mr. Gromyko. Since the essentials of the American proposals have received the support of the great majority of the members of the Atomic Energy Commission, and indeed of the United Nations Assembly itself, it is this plan which will be subjected to the closest study.

This study must clearly take two forms. It must involve a detailed discussion of both the origin and the probable consequences of the plan. The first is a matter of historical discussion, and the second involves a prediction of the future. Just as the analyses of the military lessons of the last war have often been superficial and misleading, many predictions about the future working of proposed methods of control of atomic energy can easily be shown to have often been far too removed from contemporary facts to be a safe guide to rational policy-making. The American plan was hailed by the more restrained in most of the Western world as a great contribution to world peace, or as one of the most generous political gestures of all time, and by the more enthusiastic as a seven-league stride into Utopia. Russia's rejection of the plan has earned her unlimited abuse, and has been widely held to have been a major cause of the rapid deterioration in the relations between the Great Powers during the last two years. If the argument of this book has validity, some of these judgments require modification.

Among the several points of difference between the majority of the nations on the A.E.C. and Soviet Russia, the question of whether the veto should operate in relation to matters concerning atomic energy was probably decisive in producing the final deadlock. Mr. Baruch, in putting forward the official American proposals in June, 1946, placed great emphasis on the necessity of revising the Charter of the United Nations so as to free the infliction of punishment for violation of an atomic energy agreement from the limitation imposed by the unanimity rule. The Soviet Union energetically opposed any such alteration.

In April, 1948, the deadlock on the A.E.C. became so clear that the discussions were effectively brought to an end, thus terminating for the time being the attempt to obtain international control of atomic energy. It is of interest to note that, shortly afterwards, United States Secretary of State Marshall told[9] the House of Representatives Foreign Affairs Committee that he was opposed to any scheme for amending the Charter. He was in favor of abolition of the veto in the pacific settlement of disputes, but the veto was necessary where acts of aggression were concerned. He is reported to have added: "We do not want our manpower and our strength committed by a two-thirds vote."

If this statement was meant as a serious statement of policy, it would seem to imply a reversal of the view expressed in the Baruch Plan that the application of sanctions against a violator of an atomic energy agreement should not be subject to the veto. However the subsequent attitude of the American delegation does not confirm this interpretation. It seems therefore that a serious inconsistency exists between Mr. Marshall's statement and the official American policy.

2. AIR POWER IN THE EUROPEAN WAR (1939-1945)

EVER since the first World War, acute controversy has raged over the effect of air power on warfare. As a result, the strategic bomb-

[9] *Manchester Guardian*, May 6, 1948.

ing offensive by the Anglo-American air forces in the second World War has been the subject of particularly detailed study. Much use will be made in this chapter of the admirable analyses carried out by the United States Strategic Bombing Survey. Details of these reports and some statistical results derived from them are given in Appendix I.

In the 1920's and 1930's the controversy centered mainly on whether air power should be used primarily (*a*) to operate *tactically*, in support of, and in close relation with, the operations of land forces, or (*b*) to operate *strategically*, far into enemy territory against targets such as factories, military installations, etc., independently of the progress of other military operations. A widely held belief during this period was that the increased aerodynamic performance of bombing aircraft, combined with improved navigational methods, more accurate bombsights and strong defensive armament would give the bomber such a marked ascendancy over the defenses, as to make possible the destruction at long range of specific military and industrial targets far into an enemy country, on such a scale as drastically to weaken the enemy's will to resist. Enthusiasts even maintained that a great nation could be induced to surrender by the exercise of air power alone.

As will be shown in detail later, the practice of attempting to defeat an enemy by deliberately destroying his cities arose out of this strategic conception of the use of air power, when the experience of actual war conditions had shown that it was not possible to hit specific small targets. What came to be called "area" attacks, "terror" attacks or, more often and less correctly, simply "strategic bombing" came into being as a technically debased form of the original conception of long-range attacks on specific military and industrial targets. We will now consider the actual policies of the big Powers, both as judged by their preparations for the war and by their actual practice during the war.

There is ample evidence that the German Air Force was designed primarily to fill a tactical role, and in particular for close cooperation with land forces, though during the course of the war it was actually for a time used for area attacks unrelated to any land battle. The actual history of the war shows clearly that the decisive successes achieved by the German Air Force resulted

10

from its tactical use, while its use for area attacks was a failure. The G.A.F. provided invaluable assistance to the German armies in their triumphant advances over most of the continent of Europe, by the support it gave to the land battle[1] with dive bombers (mainly Junker 87's) and by attacks, farther behind the lines, on military establishments, transport, etc., with longer-range aircraft (mainly Heinkel III and Junker 88's). It thus came about that, except for the destruction of parts of Warsaw, Rotterdam and Belgrade by air operations close ahead of their troops, the German advance over Europe took place without indiscriminate attacks on cities.[2] So, when the German occupation forces took over Poland, France, Belgium, Holland, Norway and Greece, they found relatively undamaged cities and relatively unimpaired industrial systems.

That the main role of the G.A.F. at the time of the Battle of Britain was to attack specific military and industrial targets is clearly seen from Hitler's operational orders issued on August 1, 1940, for the invasion of England.[3] The emphasis on not unneces-

[1] "It is quite clear from all the evidence that Hitler and the German Staff thought essentially in terms of land warfare. They failed to understand air power even more completely than they failed as regards sea power." Lord Tedder, *Air Power in War*, p. 45 (London, 1948).

[2] "The threat of destruction by aircraft of a city about to be attacked by the army was a normal part of Hitler's technique, and when the threat failed to induce capitulation the destruction was carried out. The timing of such a threat in relation to the advance of the land forces is shown by the case of Prague in 1938, where we have available an account of Hitler's interview with the Czech Premier Hacha on 14 March. He was told from the very outset that there was no question of negotiating, that he had to accept decisions already formed, and sign a document of surrender which had been prepared beforehand, that Prague would be occupied the next morning (German motorized detachments had already in fact crossed the Czech border . . .); and that if the least resistance was offered, the most terrible destruction would be wrought in Prague by the Luftwaffe (a forecast of Warsaw, Rotterdam and Belgrade). Hacha fainted and was given injections." Lewis B. Namier, *Diplomatic Prelude,* p. 68 (London, 1947).
There is no doubt that Hitler, by such threats, made the world think that the strategic destruction of cities was an integral part of the German techniques of war. This made it comparatively easy later on for a British Government and the R.A.F. to sell to the public the idea this was the correct strategy to adopt.

[3] "For prosecuting air and sea war against England, I have decided to carry on and intensify air and naval warfare against England in order to bring about her final defeat. For this purpose I am issuing the following orders:
1. The German Air Force with all available forces will destroy the English Air Force as soon as possible. The attacks will be directed against airborne aircraft, then ground and supply organizations and then against industry, including the manufacture of aircraft equipment.
2. After gaining temporary or local air superiority, air attack will be continued on harbors, paying special attention to food storage depots in London.
In view of our own intended operations, attacks on harbors on the south coast must be kept down to a minimum.

sarily destroying the British ports which Hitler hoped to use is worth noting, as is also the stated intention to reserve terror attacks to be used only as reprisals. The heavy area attacks on British cities which started early in September, were announced as reprisals for British air attacks against German cities. A full history of these events, by which to judge finally the legitimacy of this claim, is not available, but it will be shown later that the available evidence does, on the whole, support it. The heavy area attacks on English cities and especially on London were much more destructive than the contemporary British attacks on German cities, but brought no decisive gains to Germany, and they were stopped in May, 1941, owing to the preparations for the invasion of Russia.

Confirmation of the view that the G.A.F. was not designed for strategic area bombing is found in Air-Marshal Sir Arthur Harris' book, *Bomber Offensive*. In his account (*p. 86*) of the Battle of Britain he writes as follows:

> They had in fact no strategic bombers at all, since their whole force of over a thousand bombers was designed for army co-operation work and was only used for attack on cities when not required to support the German army. Even in daytime it was fitted only to carry out the work of a tactical air force, not strategic attack.

During the war with Russia, area attacks on Moscow and other major cities appear to have been attempted at the outset. They failed to achieve any decisive success and seem to have been abandoned after a few months in favor of operations in close support of the land fighting.

Hitler did not embark again on heavy indiscriminate attacks on cities until the spring of 1944, with the introduction of the new V1 and V2 weapons. Since there was at that time only a partial defense against the V1, and none against V2, these attacks only ceased with the capture of the launching sites by the Anglo-

---

3. Attacks on warships and on merchant shipping will be of secondary importance to those against enemy air power, except when specially favorable targets present themselves. . . .

4. The intensified air war will be so planned that adequate forces may be diverted at any time to opportunity targets. Moreover fighting strength must be maintained at disposal for Operation Seelöwe.

5. I am reserving terror attacks as reprisals.

6. Intensification of air war to begin on August 5th, 1940. . . ." Shulman, *Defeat in the West*, p. 47.

American invasion of France. Though technically successful, they had little effect on the progress of the war as a whole. Hitler, however, probably considered them potentially decisive weapons, which could lead to the defeat of England.

The balance of evidence certainly justifies the conclusion that Germany neither originally planned, nor ever seriously attempted to execute, at any rate till very late in the war, a policy of attempting to defeat her enemies by air power alone.[4]

The Russian view of air power seems to have approximated closely the German, in the sense that it was envisaged mainly as a very important adjunct to military operations; the Soviet Air Force was designed accordingly. Few long-range bombers were either made or used,[5] but large numbers of fighter and fighter bombers were employed in support of the Army. The decision to concentrate on large numbers of small fighter and ground attack types, rather than on smaller numbers of long-range bombers, was probably one of the important factors which enabled her in the end to repel the German armies and eventually to drive them back. The Russian policy throughout the war, like the original German policy, did not include deliberate large-scale area attacks on the residential areas of cities far behind the lines. Many of the cities occupied by the Russians in their final advance westward were certainly destroyed, some in actual fighting, many more by systematic German demolition, but few by Russian bombers.

In the Soviet-Finnish War of 1939 to 1940, large Russian air forces were employed against only weak air opposition—a situation in which decisive area attacks on cities would have been very

[4] A detailed analysis of the German theory and practice of air warfare is given by Liddell Hart in *The Revolution in Warfare,* and by Asher Lee in *The German Air Force* (New York, 1946).

An account of the German Air Force by a German air officer, Generalleutnant H. J. Rieckhoff, has been published under the title *Trumpf Oder Bluff?* (Zürich-New York, 1945). A detailed discussion of air strategy and tactics is given which includes an appraisal of the validity of Douhet's theory of victory by the strategic use of air power. Rieckhoff sums up the German air staff view (*p. 104*) in the statement that Douhet's theory was applicable against states such as France, Poland, Czechoslovakia and England, but that it was considered as quite out of court against Russia. ". . . dass aber gegenuber Russland von einem strategischen Einsatz der Luftwaffe keine Rede sein konnte." This view amounts to stating that the use of air power strategically can be decisive against a relatively weak Power but not against a major Power.

[5] "None of us ever learned very much about Russian bombers. Apparently Soviet factories concentrated on the production of fighters, attack planes, medium bombers and observation ships. Heavy bombers were seldom seen, and a Russian raid on Berlin or the Ploesti oil fields of Rumania was rarely reported." Walter Kerr, *The Russian Army,* p. 138 (New York, 1944).

easy to carry out. That they were not carried out is indicated by the official Finnish figures[6] of the total number of civilians killed by air raids during the thirteen weeks of the war. The number was 646. As the Anglo-American forces found in their air offensive against transport and military targets in France in 1944, it is impossible to avoid killing a considerable number of civilians in this type of operation. But the very small numbers killed in the Finnish war shows that the Soviet air forces did not systematically make area attacks on civilian populations. An American journalist,[7] writing in the *New York Herald Tribune*, said: "In so far as the war in the air is concerned, it is true that the Red Air Force never tried to exterminate the civilian population in Finland."

The only detailed analysis of Russian air strategy available to the writer is an apparently well-informed book written in Swedish in 1944 by Sven Hermann Kjellberg and published in Zürich under the title *Russland im Krieg*. Kjellberg believes that the Soviet military authorities made a rather abrupt change of policy about 1936, involving the abandoning of long-range bombers in favor of short-range bombers and fighters mainly designed for cooperating with the Army. He believes that, prior to 1936, Russia possessed some 2,000 efficient long-range bombers, which, according to his estimate, was more than all other European Powers, including Germany, put together (*p. 226*). Kjellberg suggests (*p. 229*) that this change may have been the result of the rearmament of Germany and her consequent reemergence as a major military Power. The interpretation that one must put on this change of policy, is that the Soviet Command considered strategic bombing effective against a weak Power but not against a strong Power. At the opening of the Russian-German war in 1941, it is clear that Russia made use of few long-range bombers,[8] but of very large numbers of fighters and of heavily armed and armored attack planes (Stormoviks). Probably 50 per cent of all Russian planes were at that time of this latter type (*p. 237*). Kjellberg considers that, when the tide finally turned in Russia's favor after Stalingrad, it was to a considerable extent the use of aircraft of these

[6] William P. and Zelda K. Coates, *The Soviet-Finnish Campaign, Military and Political, 1939-40* (London, 1942).

[7] Quoted by Coates, p. 102.

[8] The only heavy area attack by the Soviet air force mentioned by Kjellberg is that on Talinn in September, 1944, shortly before its capture by the Red Army.

types which made possible the subsequent almost unbroken Russian military advances. It is clear that very large numbers of light bombers and fighter aircraft were available.

Essentially the same view of Russian air strategy is held by General Sir Giffard Martel, head of the British Military Mission in Moscow from 1941 to 1943. In his book, *The Russian Outlook*, he says of the Russian Air Force: "By far the most important part of the Air Force is the Army Co-operation Command. In fact, this contained the greater part of the Russian Air Force. There was also a long-range bomber command for use against targets which were beyond the operational zone of the Army. . . . It was never very large and was often used to assist the Army Co-operation Command on targets in the fighting zone." With the Russian experience in view, General Martel expressed the following opinion:

> It can be argued with much reason, however, that we would have won the European war more quickly and efficiently if we had put rather more weight on cooperation between the Army and the Air Force from the start, instead of depending so much on the power of air bombardment alone.

Of the major contestants in the war, it seems to have been the British who first planned and put into operation a campaign of strategic bombing with the intention of attempting to achieve a decisive result by the use of air power alone. That this was not an improvised policy to meet a war emergency, but a long-range policy decided many years before is clear from published material. For instance, Liddell Hart, writing of the period after the war of 1914-1918, says:[9]

> The Royal Air Force propounded the view that the bomber would be the decisive factor in any future war, and would suffice in itself to produce a decision—by destroying the industrial resources of the opposing Power. That view came to be associated with the writings of the Italian, General Douhet, but had long been a primary article in the R.A.F. creed before Douhet's theory had gained currency.

A useful analysis of some of the more extreme views of the air power enthusiasts, in particular Brigadier-General Groves and

[9] Liddell Hart, *The Revolution in Warfare*, p. 15.

Major Seversky, is to be found in a recent book by Admiral Sir Gerald Dickens.[10]

So it came about that, at the outbreak of the war in 1939, the British bombing force, small and weak as it was at the start, had been designed and trained for the purpose of strategic bombing and not for tactical cooperation with the army. In the early summer of 1940, when an attempt was made to use this force strategically against Germany, it was found to be almost completely ineffective. The aircraft available, mainly Blenheims, Hampdens and Wellingtons, were too vulnerable to fighters and anti-aircraft fire to attempt day raids,[11] and their navigation, target identification and bomb aiming were too inefficient at night to hit specific military or industrial targets. "Night photographs taken during June and July of 1941, show that of those aircraft reported to have attacked their targets in Germany only one in four got within five miles of it, and, when the target was the Ruhr, only one in ten. The proportion of total sorties, including those aircraft not reported as having attacked the target, was of course much lower."[12]

At what date the first official decision was taken to embark on a large-scale bombing offensive against German cities with the explicit object of dehousing the working population and of destroying their morale is not quite clear. Air-Marshal Harris states[13] that it had been made[14] before he became Commander-in-Chief of the Bomber Command in February, 1942:

> The German defences were so strong that it was impossible to operate regularly or with sizeable force by day, so that all our main operations were confined to the hours of darkness. But at night the bomber crews were hardly ever able to find their targets even

[10] Admiral Sir Gerald Dickens, *Bombing and Strategy* (London, 1947).

[11] "It had been thought that, though the bomber could not by its very nature be as fast as the fighter, yet it could cope with the fighter provided it had sufficient speed and effective defensive armament. The heavy casualties suffered by the raids off Kiel and Wilhelmshaven (1939), showed that this was not the case and from that time on till late in the war the great bulk of our bomber operations over Germany were at night." Tedder, *Air Power in War*, p. 34.

[12] Sir Arthur Harris, *Bombing Offensive*, p. 81 (London, 1947).

[13] Harris, *Bombing Offensive*, p. 73.

[14] Lord Tedder writes of this decision: "When early in 1942, Bomber Command was given the directive specifying the principal industrial cities of the Ruhr as first priority targets, the operations to be 'focused on the morale of the enemy civil population and in particular on the industrial workers,' this was clearly a common denominator target system—the enemy war industries were to be attacked by demoralizing the workers." *Air Power in War*, p. 98.

though, before I took command, it had already been decided (it was a decision with which I had nothing to do) that all our main attacks should be against large industrial areas, which meant of course, large industrial cities as a whole.

Returning to the earlier period of the war, we note that the first attack by British bombers on a German town appears to have been on Hanover in May, 1940. At that time the official communiqués described such raids as against military targets; but the figures already quoted for the accuracy, or rather inaccuracy, of the bombing over a year later, make it certain that the bombing in these early raids must have appeared to the Germans as completely indiscriminate. Hitler, after several warnings, replied by initiating the "Blitz" attack on London on September 7.

Liddell Hart writes of these events:[15]

> The German's departure from this code (i.e. of avoiding attacks on civilian populations independent of military operations) can hardly be dated before September, 1940, when the night bombing of London was launched, following six successive attacks on Berlin during the previous fortnight. The Germans were strictly justified in describing this as a reprisal, especially as they had, prior to our sixth attack on Berlin, announced that they would take such action if we did not stop our night bombing of Berlin. Moreover, it must be admitted that, notwithstanding their overwhelming bombing superiority, they took the initiative a few weeks later in proposing a mutual agreement that would put a stop to such city bombing. Moreover, several times they discontinued their attacks when there was a pause in the much lighter British raids, thereby showing their desire for a truce to the inter-city bombing competition. The significance of these tendencies lies in their evidence, not as to German "humanism," but as to their long term realism.

This "realism" had clearly both a military and a political aspect. City bombing was clearly thought by Hitler in 1940 to be inefficient militarily, but also to be undesirable politically as a weapon against England; for he still hoped that England would capitulate and even join his planned war against Russia. Hitler's mass extermination of some seven million Jews and Eastern Europeans in the death camps at Maidanek, Oswiecim, Belsen, etc., and the deliberate destruction of hundreds of towns and villages in Russia showed that his reluctance to embark on area bombing of cities

[15] Liddell Hart, The Revolution in Warfare, p. 72.

in 1940 was in no way derived from any reluctance to kill civilians or to destroy cities, but rather from carefully weighed considerations of political and military expediency based on the actual circumstances of the time.

It is interesting to note that James M. Spaight, late Principal Assistant Secretary at the Air Ministry, in his book, *Bombing Vindicated*, published in 1944, also concludes that the German air attacks on British cities, starting in September, 1940, were in fact a reprisal for our attacks on German cities in May, and that his own belief was that they would not otherwise have been undertaken.

It is further worth recalling that Spaight, who must, from his former official position, be held to have written as unofficial spokesman of a strong body of Service opinion, claimed the credit to Britain for introducing as a main strategic policy the area attacks on cities. "It has been the British way of using air power which has revolutionized war."

It is interesting to compare the scale and results of the British and German bombing offensives from August 1940 to May 1941.[16] During this period British bombers dropped some 20,000 tons of bombs on Germany; that is, at the rate of about 2,000 tons per month. In the light of information now available, the effect on German production was so small as to be quite unmeasurable; it was certainly less than 1 per cent. The number of civilians killed was less than 3,000; that is, less than 0.15 persons killed per ton of bombs dispatched. The number killed each month was about 300.

The German reply to these attacks started in September, 1940, and continued until May, 1941. In these nine months 50,000 tons of bombs were dropped on Great Britain, killing 40,000 civilians. That is, 0.8 people were killed for every ton of bombs dropped, or five times as many as in the British offensive against Germany. The monthly weight of bombs dropped on England was 6,000, or three times that of our offensive. The monthly casualties in the United Kingdom from the German attacks were about 4,500 killed, which was about fifteen times the German casualties produced by the British attacks.

[16] See Table 2, Appendix I.

Thus, looking at the first period of the war as that ending in June, 1941, with the start of the German attack on Russia, we see that the British attacks on cities had an almost negligible effect on the German war effort and were replied to by a German attack about three times as heavy in weight and over ten times as heavy when measured in casualties and probably also in industrial damage.

With the benefit of wisdom after the event, the same criticism can be levelled against the inception of the British bombing offensive, in 1940, as can be levelled against so much of the early British war strategy. Such weak opening moves as the mining of Norwegian waters in the spring of 1940, and the move into Greece,[17] appeared to have had some psychological value at the time in satisfying the desire for some offensive action, but they were militarily so unsound that their actual effect was to precipitate a much heavier and effective counterblow by the enemy, which Britain was ill-prepared to meet.

Underlying the staging of the British bombing offensive in 1940-1941 and the enthusiastic expectations it aroused, was a gross underestimate of the weight of bombs required to have a decisive effect on the economy and morale of a determined nation; since the estimate turned out to be wrong by a factor of at least fifty, it constitutes one of the greatest numerical blunders of military history.

Though 1942 saw some increase in the scale of the British bombing offensive, it was not till the early months of 1943 that it reached the weight of the German attack on England in 1940. This increase was due to the coming into service of a considerable number of new four-engined heavy night bombers (Lancasters, Halifaxes and Stirlings) and the American day bombers (Fortresses). From then to the end of the war, the weight of attack on Germany increased rapidly to an average rate of 100,000 tons a month in 1944 and 1945; that is, fifty times that of the initial British offensive in 1940 and 1941.

[17] "An astonishing and ironic revelation regarding the campaign in Greece has been made since the war by the Greek Commander-in-Chief, General Papagos. The Greeks actually asked Britain not to send help, feeling that it would be too small to be effective but enough to attract the Germans like a magnet. Britain insisted in order not to lose face. The whole episode now appears a sorry tale of political strategic frivolity, and the British Government did not deserve to get off as lightly as was the case." Cyril Falls, *The Second World War*, p. 91 (London, 1948).

By the spring of 1942, the British War Cabinet had planned an all-out bombing offensive against German cities with the object of dehousing a large fraction of the German working-class population, in the hope that this, and the consequent effect on civilian morale, would so reduce production as to cause a collapse of the enemy war effort.

Some aspects of the complex origin of this first modern example of a planned campaign of mass destruction as a method of winning a major war have already been discussed. Of primary importance was the low ebb of the Allied military positions, with a large part of European Russia overrun, with Rommel near Egypt, and the formidable nature of the problem of getting a foothold again in Europe. A bombing campaign seemed the only offensive action open to the Western Allies. It was inaugurated, not with careful calculation of its probable effectiveness, but as a result of a failure to find a satisfactory answer to the question "What else can we do?" The choice of cities, rather than industrial and military targets, was dictated, as in 1940, by the inability of night bombers to hit anything smaller. Only in the last eighteen months of the war was the technique of night bombing so improved, largely by radio aids and target marking devices, as to make possible the precision bombing of "point" targets.

The American report writes as follows of the objects of this campaign:[18]

> With the appointment early in 1942 of Sir Arthur Harris as Chief of the Bomber Command, the picture changed; for he regarded area bombing not as a temporary expedient, but as the most promising method of aerial attack. Harris and his staff had a low opinion of economic intelligence and were skeptical of "target systems." They had a strong belief in Germany's powers of industrial recuperation and doubted that her war potential could be significantly lowered by bombing. At the same time, they had a strong faith in the morale effects of bombing and thought that Germany's will to fight could be destroyed by the destruction of German cities. Under Harris' forceful leadership, the great area offensive was launched in the summer of 1942, to continue through subsequent years until April, 1944. The first thousand-bomber raids on Cologne and Essen marked the real beginning of this campaign.

[18] *United States Strategic Bombing Survey 3* [*The Effect of Strategic Bombing on the German War Economy*], p. 2 (Washington, 1945).

Before and up to the second quarter of 1944 the great bulk of R.A.F. tonnage (60 per cent of the total dropped in 1942 and 1943) was concentrated on area raids.

The analyses of the results of the bombing offensive which are quoted in Appendix I show that Harris was correct in assuming that Germany's power of industrial recuperation was likely to be great, but was wrong in supposing that her will to fight would be broken by the destruction of her cities.

The American bombing policy was rather different, since U.S. aircraft were designed as day bombers and so were strongly armed for defense. The intention was to attack "point" targets, such as aircraft factories and oil installations. Area attacks on cities were, in general, undertaken only when weather conditions prevented the finding and bombing of "point" targets. In the first phase of the offensive, up to the Schweinfurt raid in October 1943, the Fortresses went mainly unescorted and in close formation, relying on the defensive power of their guns. When losses due to enemy fighters got too serious, long-range fighters (Lightnings and Mustangs) were used as escorts. In the last phase of the war, when the German Air Force had almost ceased to exist, Fortresses again could safely fly unescorted. From early 1944 to the end of the war, a major part of the American effort and a very considerable part of the British effort were directed to transportation targets, railways, marshalling yards, locomotive repair facilities, etc.

An important advantage of the American day operations over the British night ones lay in the far greater toll they took of enemy fighters and so the far greater contribution they made to the winning of air superiority over the German territory.

The combined Anglo-American bombing offensive—with the British night bombers attacking mainly industrial and built-up areas, and the American day bombers attacking, where possible, factories, industrial installations, etc.—was formally adopted at the Casablanca Conference in January, 1943, as a major part of the Allied war strategy. This conference authorized an enlarged scale of air attack on Germany with its objective "the destruction and dislocation of the German military, industrial, and economic system and the undermining of the morale of the German people to the point where their capacity for armed resistance is fatally weakened."[19] A public expression of this policy was given by Winston Churchill: "Opinion is divided as to whether the use of air power could by itself bring about collapse in Germany and Italy. The experiment is well worth trying, so long as other methods are not excluded."

The results of this bombing offensive, as analyzed by the American Strategic Bombing Survey, are summarized in Appendix I. The remarkable and unexpected result was the discovery that German total war production continued to increase till the summer of 1944 in spite of the very heavy bombing. *Chart 1* shows the actual production of German war industry (Curve B), together with what, it is estimated, it would have been in the absence of the area bombing of cities (Curve A). In addition, the total of bombs dropped is shown in Curve C. The rapid fall of production (*Chart 2*) which started in August, 1944 (when the Anglo-American armies were already in Paris, and the Russian armies had freed the whole of their homeland and were well into Poland) was due not to the destruction of factories or the demoralization of the civilian population, but mainly to the success of the air attack on the German transport system, which impeded the flow of coal, food, etc., and to the shortage of oil.

Certain industries which were singled out for special attack were markedly affected rather earlier. Synthetic rubber and aviation gasoline started to decline rapidly after March, 1944. On the other hand, aircraft production continued to rise until mid-1944 (*Chart 3*).

It will be noticed that more aircraft were produced by the United Kingdom than by Germany in every year of the war till 1944, when for the first time the German production was the larger, in spite of the bombing. Part of the rapid increase of German production in the last years of the war was due to increasing concentration on single-engined fighter types, whereas a large part of British production was of four-engined bombers: the total structure weight of British aircraft production remained greater[20]

[19] *U.S.S.B.S. 1 [Overall Report, European War]*, p. 3 (Washington, 1945).
[20] "During the last quarter of 1944 German monthly fighter production was very considerably higher than the combined British and American fighter production." Tedder, *Air Power in War*, p. 42.
The reason why the operational strength of the G.A.F. steadily fell was due to the destruction of aircraft on the ground and when landing and taking off, and to the

Chart 1

GERMAN ARMAMENT PRODUCTION AND WEIGHT OF BOMBS DROPPED ON GERMANY

A. Estimated German production in absence of Area Bombing
B. Actual annual production (1940 equals 100)
C. Total tonnage of bombs on all targets

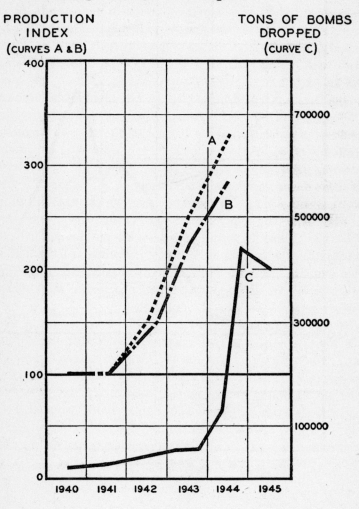

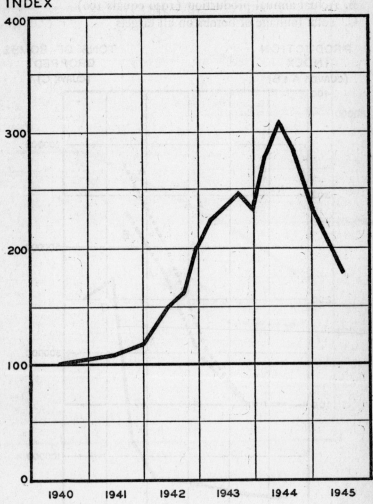

Chart 2

GERMAN ARMAMENT PRODUCTION

(1940 equals 100—*Kaldor*)

Chart 3
ANNUAL PRODUCTION OF BRITISH AND GERMAN
AIRCRAFT: ALL TYPES

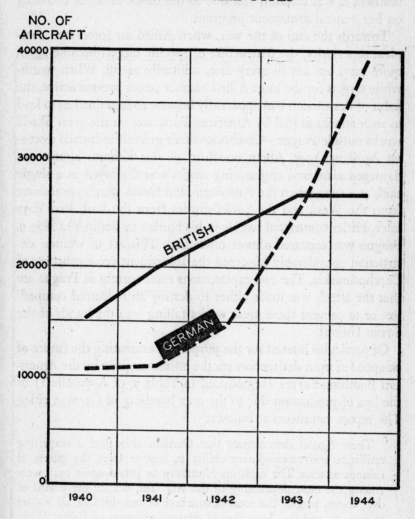

than the German even in 1944. The five-fold increase of German tank production between 1941 and 1944 is even more startling (Table 5, App. I). However the causes of Germany's defeat are assessed, it was certainly not due to the direct effect of bombing on her general armament program.

Towards the end of the war, when Allied air forces had complete superiority, the destruction of specific targets became again quite easy, but not in every case, militarily useful. When worthwhile targets for the huge Allied bomber forces became scarce, the habit of destruction had apparently become so ingrained as to lead to such attacks as that by American Fortresses on the great Skoda works outside Prague—Czechoslovakia's greatest industrial asset—on April 25, 1945. About one-third of this hitherto almost undamaged arms and engineering works was destroyed in a single raid, at a time when the American land forces were approaching from the West, and the Soviet armies from the East. Five days later, Hitler committed suicide in his bunker in Berlin. On May 9, Prague was captured almost unscathed. This act of wanton destruction considerably hindered the subsequent reconstruction of Czechoslovakia. The two explanations most current in Prague are that the attack was made either to destroy an industrial competitor, or to prevent these great works falling into the hands of the Soviet Union!

Of particular interest for the purpose of estimating the future of weapons of mass destruction are the estimates given by the American Bombing Survey (reproduced in Table 7, of Appendix I) of the loss of production due to the area bombing of German cities. The report comments as follows:

> These figures demonstrate that German cities had a surprising resilience and extraordinary ability to recover from the effects of ruinous attacks. The raids on Hamburg in July-August 1943 were among the most devastating of the war. Yet, despite the deaths of over 60,000 people, the total destruction of one-third of all houses in the city and the disruption of normal processes of living, Hamburg as an economic unit was not destroyed. It never fully recovered from the bombing, but in five months it had regained 80

---

shortage of oil. The bomber offensive was effective in reducing the strength of the G.A.F. when it was directed against airfields, oil installations, transport, but apparently ineffective when directed against airplane and engine factories.

per cent of the former productivity, despite the fact that great areas of the city lay, and still lie, in dust and rubble. As in the case of industrial plants, when it was found much easier to destroy the buildings than the machines in them, so also it is much easier to destroy the physical structure of a city than to wipe out its economic life. (*U.S.S.B.S. 1*, p. 72)

The reasons for the very surprising resilience of German industry under the Anglo-American bombing offensive are of great interest and have been analyzed in detail, for instance, by Nicholas Kaldor.[21] One of the contributing causes was the fact that the German economy, in spite of the huge commitment of the war on the Eastern Front, was not till quite a late date working at full capacity. Single shifts were almost universal, women were not mobilized, and arms output in general was limited by demand, not by production capacity. As a consequence, there was much slack in the economy which could be, and actually was, taken up to compensate for the effects of the bombing. So convinced was Hitler in the autumn of 1941, during the battle for Moscow, that the war was effectively won, that large cancellations of armament orders were made. Germany never, in fact, waged total war.

A major success of the bombing offensive was the precision attack in 1944-1945 on transportation targets and specific industrial targets such as oil installations. The American and British contributions to these operations were about 75 per cent and 25 per cent respectively. In addition, there were some cases when heavy bombers were successfully used in a tactical role. Amongst these were the bombing of the coast defense batteries shortly before the Normandy landing, and the saturation bombing of a small area at St. Lô which preceded the American breakout of the Normandy beachhead. The mass attack on German cities (which was the main British contribution, both in planning and execution), though technically a success in the final stages, must be considered a strategic failure in that it affected German production remarkably little. Over 80 per cent of the area attacks were by British night bombers.

During 1943 and 1944 a very marked increase took place in the fraction of night bombers which found their target and in the accuracy of the actual bombing. This was due to a number of

[21] Kaldor, *Review of Economic Studies 1945-1946*, p. 33.

causes, which included the use of new radio and radar navigational aids, improved bombsights, better training and the development of ingenious methods of target marking by flares dropped by a specially trained "pathfinder" force. These developments have been described in detail, for instance, in Air-Marshal Harris' book on the bombing offensive, as well as in various official publications. An important factor was the liberation of France in the summer of 1944, which made available forward airfields from which Allied fighters could operate much closer to the centers of German industry, and which allowed the setting up of forward radio navigational stations able to guide British bombers accurately farther into Germany. As a result of these developments, much of the night bombing in the latter half of 1944 and in 1945 attained a high precision, allowing successful attacks on small targets. The American Bombing Survey sums this phase up as follows:

> Not until the war in the air had been won, and the landings in the Mediterranean and France successfully accomplished, were the heavy bombers free to exploit the victory in the air and attack in full force the centers of oil production, the centers of transport and other sustaining sources of military strength within the heart of Germany. . . . The greatest single achievement of the air attack on Germany was the defeat of the German Air Forces (*Ibid.*, p. 10).

The air offensive against oil production played a most important part in the winning of air superiority by the decisive limitation it set to German air operations. Though aircraft were in good supply, the fuel to fly them was not.

It is important to remember that the air superiority, as measured by operational strength, of all the Allies over Germany in 1944-1945, when this air offensive took place, was very great. On the Western Front, Germany had 2,473 fighters and 209 bombers, compared to the Anglo-American strength of 4,573 fighters and 2,682 bombers, of which the majority were four-engined.[22]

The oil and transport offensives achieved very important military results without inflicting much general destruction; the area bombing of cities gave very small militarily useful results and inflicted enormous general destruction on Germany. The former

[22] Tedder, *Air Power in War,* p. 42.

offensives demanded precision attacks; and, as has clearly been shown, these became only possible at a late stage of the war when the Allies possessed a large degree of air superiority and had advanced bases near the German frontier, to enable radar navigational methods to be more effectively employed and fighter escorts to extend their range farther into enemy country. On the other hand, the area bombing, which was originally adopted just because of the inability to do precision bombing, did little to help win the war and greatly increased our difficulties afterwards.

The night bombing offensive of the R.A.F. was an attempt to exercise air power decisively without defeating the enemy air force and without winning air superiority over enemy territory first. This attempt failed. The later successes of the bombing offensive were made possible by the gradual winning of air superiority over Germany, and this was achieved in large measure by the destruction of enemy fighters in the American day raids. It would be almost true to say that in 1943, when the bombing offensive began in earnest, the success of a raid should have been estimated more by the number of enemy fighters shot down than by the amount of industrial damage produced.

It is clear that the effect of a strategic bombing campaign is dependent on the degree to which the economy of the attacked country is already strained by the demands of a major war effort on land. The effect of the Anglo-American air offensive would have been still less if Germany had not been heavily committed to a vast military campaign on the Eastern Front from June 1941, and on the Western Front from June, 1944.

In spite of the great developments of air power, it is clear that Germany's defeat in the second World War, as in the first, was brought about primarily by her huge losses in manpower and matériel incurred in the land battles, particularly on the Eastern Front. A clear indication of this is seen from the figures of the German casualties up to November, 1944 in the various theaters of war, as shown in Table 1 of Appendix II.

Of the three million killed and missing, about 75 per cent were lost in the war with Russia; that is, up to November 1944 three times as many men were lost on the Eastern Front as in all other theaters of the war. These figures confirm the view expressed by

Shulman[23] in his analysis of the cause of Germany's defeat, as seen from captured documents and interrogation of the German generals. "The furnace in which the defeat of German armies was forged was the vast Russian theater. There, two-thirds of the total German armed strength was constantly engaged and systematically destroyed."

Contrary to what is often said, it is thus clear that the strategic bombing offensive contributed very little direct help to the Soviet campaigns until the spring of 1944. Appreciable indirect help, however, resulted earlier from the diversion of German fighter squadrons from the Eastern Front to the defense of the Reich. Air-Marshal Harris writes: "The strategic consequence of bombing Germany may be summed up in a few simple figures: in 1941, when the Germans invaded Russia, the German army had the support of well over 50 per cent of the whole German Air Force. At the end of 1943, the German Army had the support of less than 20 per cent of the whole German Air Force."

Air power played, of course, a decisively important role in all the great land battles of the war. This was as true of the Soviet advance westward as of the Anglo-American advance eastward. Both the decisive fronts—the Russian front after June 1941 and the Western front after June, 1944—were the scene of intimate cooperation of air and land forces. The brilliant Anglo-American campaign which liberated France, and then drove on into the heart of Germany, was enormously facilitated by the almost complete command of the air enjoyed by the Allies, and the air support to the land forces provided by large numbers of fighters and fighter-bombers. In addition, the attack on transportation targets in 1944 and 1945 with over 700,000 tons of bombs was a decisive success by producing a progressive interruption of the whole German transport system.

In the light of the knowledge we now have of the enormous weight of bombing required to produce an important effect on the war economy of a major power, it is possible to make some estimate of what might have happened had Germany or the Soviet Union adopted the policy of diverting a large part of their aircraft production and air effort to long-range strategic bombing.

[23] Shulman, *Defeat in the West.*

It is clear that, up to the time when France capitulated, such a change of policy on the part of Germany would have been detrimental to the German campaigns. On the one hand, such a diversion would have been at the expense of the brilliantly effective cooperation between the German Army and Air Force; and, on the other, it would have led to no compensating advantage, as the campaigns in Poland, France, the Netherlands, and Norway were far too quickly won for strategic bombing to be necessary or even useful.

Very similar considerations apply to the Soviet air policy. The diversion of an appreciable fraction of the U.S.S.R.'s total air effort to strategic bombing would have led to extremely small returns in comparison with the consequent reduction in the strength of her combat and close support types, which played a vital role in all the major land battles, and which in the last two years of the war gave her air superiority on the Eastern Front.

It is generally agreed that Hitler's first step towards ultimate defeat was his failure to invade England in 1940. This was mainly due to his inability to defeat the R.A.F. fighters, and so to gain air supremacy over the southern coast of England. This failure to achieve air supremacy was due to lack of sufficient fighters, both for direct offensive combat with the R.A.F. Fighter Command, and also to escort his bombers in their attacks on airfields, etc. If Hitler had built more long-range bombers and fewer fighters, he would have been still less able to invade England in 1940. Wing-Commander Asher Lee writes: "Had the Luftwaffe been twice as big in 1940, as well it might have been, if it had concentrated after 1937 on the production of Messerschmitt 109's and Junker 87's, at the expense of the heavier Junker 52's and Heinkel III's, then it might have been the major instrument of successful invasion of the British Isles."

In the light of what we have learned from this analysis, let us turn back to British air strategy before 1939. We know that the Battle of Britain was won by only a small margin, owing to the shortage of fighters. The skill and gallantry of R.A.F. fighter pilots and the technical brilliance of British fighter aircraft and radar stations just succeeded in saving the country from the results of having deliberately diverted so much of its limited air resources

31

to preparations for an ill-conceived and ill-planned campaign of offensive action. While the decisive battle was being fought in the air over southern England during the memorable August and September days of 1940, the R.A.F. long-range strategic bombing force was carrying out attacks on Germany, which were as provocative as they were ineffective, and which were soon to bring far heavier retaliation—measured in killed or in industrial and civic damage—than that which Britain was inflicting on Germany. Almost the only militarily useful action carried out at this time by British heavy bombers was the attack on Hitler's invasion fleet; however, this could have been more successfully done by aircraft of shorter range and higher performance.

3. AIR POWER IN THE PACIFIC WAR

A DETAILED account of the part played by the Air Force in the Pacific War is given in the *United States Strategic Bombing Survey*.[1] The Japanese forces achieved their rapid advances over the Philippines, Burma, Malaya and Indonesia by the coordinated action of relatively small forces of highly trained naval, military and air units.

> Allied air power in the Philippines, Malaya and the Dutch East Indies was virtually eliminated, mostly on the ground, in a matter of days. Those enormous areas, once local Allied air power had been eliminated, were laid open to occupation in a matter of weeks, at a total cost of less than 15,000 Japanese soldiers killed, and with the loss from all causes of 381 Japanese planes. (*U.S.S.B.S. 4*, p. 1)

In such a rapid and victorious advance there was neither need for, nor was there the time in which to carry out, a strategic bombing offensive. Manila, Rangoon, Singapore all fell relatively undamaged into Japanese hands. What bombing of cities there was, as at Rangoon, was done close ahead of the attacking troops. Japan had no need to destroy the cities which she knew she could capture intact. Even if this had not been the case, it is probable that

[1] *U.S.S.B.S. 4* [*Summary Report, Pacific War*] (Washington, 1946).

she would not have destroyed these cities even if some military advantage seemed likely to accrue. For Japanese political policy towards the occupied areas was to fan anti-White feeling and Far Eastern Asian solidarity. In this they had great success, to be seen in the rise of the originally pro-Japanese nationalist movements of Indonesia and Burma. It would have been a most foolish act of the Japanese to have attacked the civilian Asian populations, whom they saw—and saw correctly in many cases—as allies against their American and British enemies.

It is important to note that Japan's opening stroke of the war—the attack on Pearl Harbor before the declaration of war—was not an area attack on the civilian population of a city, but a brilliantly successful attack on American naval and military power in the Pacific. Even so, it was amply adequate to bring into the war an America bitterly determined to defeat Japan.

In this connection it is of interest to study the overall strategic plan of the Japanese war leaders. The essence of their plan has been summarized by the American Survey in the following way:

(a) The threat of Russia on the Manchurian flank had been neutralized by the decisive victories of Germany in Europe, which might eventually lead to the complete collapse of the Soviet Union.

(b) Great Britain was in such an irretrievably defensive position that, even if she survived, her entire war-making potential would be spent in a desperate effort to protect her home islands.

(c) The forces which the United States and her Allies could immediately deploy in the Pacific, particularly in the air, were insufficient to prevent the fully trained and mobilized forces of Japan from occupying, within three or four months, the entire area enclosed within a perimeter consisting of Burma, Sumatra, Java, northern New Guinea, the Bismarck Archipelago, the Gilbert and Marshall Islands, Wake, and from there north to the Kuriles.

(d) China, with the Burma Road severed, would be isolated and forced to negotiate.

(e) The United States, committed to aiding Great Britain, and weakened by the attack on Pearl Harbor, would be unable to mobilize sufficient strength to go on the offensive for eighteen months to two years. During this time, the perimeter could be fortified and the required forward airfields and bases established. So strengthened, this perimeter would be backed by a mobile carrier striking force based on Truk.

(f) While the stubborn defense of the captured perimeter was undermining American determination to support the war, the Japanese would speedily extract bauxite, oil, rubber and metals from Malaya, Burma, the Philippines and the Dutch East Indies, and ship these materials to Japan for processing, to sustain and strengthen their industrial and military machine.

(g) The weakness of the United States as a democracy would make it impossible for her to continue all-out offensive action in the face of the losses which would be imposed by fanatically resisting Japanese soldiers, sailors, and airmen, and the elimination of its Allies. The United States in consequence would compromise and allow Japan to retain a substantial portion of her initial territorial gains.

Certain civilian and naval groups were familiar with the United States, its industrial and technological potential, and probable fighting determination when aroused. They expressed doubts about a strategy which promised no conclusion to the war other than negotiation, and which thus might drag out interminably with consequent risk of defeat. The Navy, however, was gravely concerned about its declining oil supply after the United States and British economic embargo of July 1941. Such civilians as were reluctant were overruled and went along with the more dynamic opinion.

None of the responsible Japanese leaders believed that within any foreseeable period of time Japan could invade the United States and dictate peace in the White House. Admiral Yamamoto's supposed boast that Japan would do so was in fact never made. These leaders furthermore felt that Japan's limited shipping would be strained to the utmost in providing logistic support for the plan adopted and would be wholly inadequate for any more ambitious program, unless the initial operations went unexpectedly well.

Pearl Harbor led directly to the Japanese defeat, because, though tactically successful, it could not be followed up. It left America with essentially unimpaired military and industrial resources free to prepare Japan's final overthrow. To have substituted for the actual attack on the American armed forces, a mass attack, say, on Honolulu, would have made the ultimate outcome still more certain. The Japanese military leaders were not so stupid as all that.

The Japanese expansive tide finally came to an end, meeting its first decisive check in the naval battle of the Coral Sea in May, 1942. Then, slowly at first, but gradually acquiring increasing momentum, began the return tide of the American counter-offensive in the Pacific and that of Stilwell and the British in Burma. In a series of bitterly fought actions, American Naval,

Army and Air Force units, cooperating intimately, gradually advanced, island by island, atoll by atoll, across the Pacific, ever closer towards the Japanese homeland. These brilliantly conducted operations provide admirable examples of the cooperation of all three arms and, in particular, of the essentially tactical use of aircraft, including heavy bombers. By the spring of 1945, the assault on the Japanese mainland became possible.

It is useful to consider the overall state of Japanese war potential in March, 1945, at the time of the launching of the heavy bombing offensive against the Japanese home islands. In spite of the remarkable expansion of Japan's industry in the years before Pearl Harbor, her industrial production at the outset of the war did not amount to more than 10 per cent of that of the United States. By the time of the start of the mass bombing of Japanese cities, the Allied counter-offensive had driven her back—either by direct conquests, by-passing or blockade—to the islands of the homeland. Her Navy had been reduced to insignificant proportions and her merchant marine had been destroyed or immobilized by blockade. American air supremacy was absolute over the remaining outlying Japanese-held areas and already partially achieved over the home islands.

> Oil imports . . . had been eliminated by April 1945. Crude oil stocks were virtually exhausted; refinery operations had to be curtailed; and stocks of aviation gasoline fell to less than 1,500,000 barrels, a point so low as to require a drastic cut in the field training program and even in combat air missions. Bauxite imports declined from 136,000 tons in the second quarter of 1944, to 30,000 tons in the third . . . by November, 1944, the overall level of Japanese war production had begun to turn down, including even the highest priority items, such as aircraft engines. (*U.S.S.B.S. 4*, p. 15)

From 1942 onwards, the Japanese merchant fleet declined continuously as a result of heavy losses, and at the end of the war it amounted to little more than 10 per cent of its original tonnage. Nearly nine million tons of shipping were sunk or so seriously damaged as to be out of action at the end of the war. Of this total, 54 per cent was due to submarines and 40 per cent to aircraft, including air-laid mines. The Japanese Navy at the beginning of the war consisted of 381 warships, amounting to 1,270,000 tons, to which an additional 816 ships, totalling 1,048,000 tons, were added during the war. The number sunk was 549, totalling 1,744,000 tons. Only some 200,000 tons were still afloat at the end.

After the liberation of the Philippines and the capture of Okinawa (March, 1945), oil imports into Japan were completely cut off; fuel stores had been exhausted; and the few remaining Japanese warships, being without fuel, were decommissioned or were covered with camouflage and used only as anti-aircraft platforms. Except for its shore-based Kamikazi air force, and surface and under-sea craft adapted for anti-invasion suicide attack, the Japanese Navy had ceased to exist. (*Ibid.*, p. 11)

However, at the time of the surrender some 5,400 suicide planes were still available.

It is the opinion of the Survey that by August 1945 even without direct air attack on her cities and industries, the overall level of Japanese war production would have declined below the peak levels of 1944 by 40 per cent to 50 per cent, solely as a result of the interdiction of overseas imports. (*Ibid.*, p. 15)

It is in the light of these decisive successes by the American land, sea and air forces that we must judge the effect of the bombing offensive on the Japanese home islands. The possibility of large-scale mass attacks on the cities of Japan waited on the provision of air bases within 1,500 miles of the target. Long-range bombing by B29 bombers started in a small way from the Marianas in November 1944, but only 8,000 tons were dropped by the end of February, 1945, and these were aimed at "point" targets such as aircraft factories, etc. The deliberate campaign of mass attack on Japanese cities did not start until March 9, with a devastating raid on Tokyo—the most devastating raid yet made, not excluding those with atomic bombs.

We can summarize the bombing offensive against the Japanese home islands from March 9, 1945, to the dropping of the first atomic bomb on August 6, by the following figures. Of the 660,000 tons of bombs dropped by Allied planes in the Pacific War, 160,000 (24 per cent) were dropped on the homeland. The monthly tonnage of bombs dropped increased from 13,800 in March to 42,700 in July. The number of civilians killed amounted to about 220,000; that is, about 1.3 killed per ton. About 100,000 tons of this total were dropped on sixty-six urban areas, and so come into the category of the use of a weapon of mass destruction; the remaining 60,000 tons were dropped on specific military and industrial targets.

Some 3,000,000 houses were destroyed either by the raids or by demolition to create firebreaks. About a quarter of the population of the cities fled or was evacuated, leading to a mass migration of some 8,500,000 people. Reduction of industrial capacity by the air attacks from their pre-raid values ranged from almost 80 per cent for oil refineries and aircraft engine plants, to 10-20 per cent for steel, light metals and chemicals.

The Survey states that it was not able to disentangle completely the effects of the area and the precision attacks:

> Even though the urban area attacks and attacks on specific industrial plants contributed a substantial percentage to the overall decline of Japan's economy, in many segments of that economy their effects were duplicative. Most of the oil refineries were out of oil, the alumina plants out of bauxite, the steel mills lacking in ore and coke, and the munition plants low in steel and aluminium. Japan's economy was in large measure being destroyed twice over, once by cutting off imports, and secondly by air attack. (*Ibid.*, p. 19)

On August 6, 1945, the first atomic bomb was dropped on Hiroshima and on August 9 the second on Nagasaki. On August 14 the Japanese Government surrendered unconditionally.

We can now summarize the events of the Pacific War that have special relation to the question of the use and efficacy of weapons of mass destruction in the following conclusions. The Japanese, in their brilliantly successful campaigns of 1941 and 1942 neither needed nor used weapons of mass destruction, but relied on highly coordinated operations of all arms directed against enemy forces and communications. In this campaign the invaders had reason to expect and actually obtained active support from a substantial fraction of the population of the invaded countries. Under these circumstances, tactics of mass destruction would have been highly detrimental to Japanese interests. It is interesting to compare these circumstances with those of the advance of the German Wehrmacht over Western Europe in 1940. Here, also, the invader expected and received aid from a certain fraction of the population of the invaded countries, and this, no doubt, constituted an added reason for not making use of weapons of mass destruction. There was, however, a difference of some importance between the two circumstances. In the Far Eastern war, the fact that the invaded countries were colonies led to a substantial fraction of the mass of the population, including most of the nationalist elements, siding with the invaders, whereas in Europe the aid received by the Nazis came from a small section of the population, without substantial mass support.

The Allied counter-offensive, from 1943 to March, 1945, consisted of a similar series of combined operations directed against enemy armed forces and sea transport. Till the latter date it was technically impossible to engage in heavy bombing of Japanese cities owing to lack of suitable bases. By March, 1945 Japan's defeat was certain, the decisive element being that her home islands were cut off from the rest of her short-lived empire, on which she relied for supplies. Japanese war production was dropping rapidly at the end of this period.

The all-out air attack on Japan from the Marianas, which began in March, 1945 accelerated markedly the rate of collapse of Japanese war potential and led, in the view of the Survey, to a high probability that Japan would have surrendered during the summer or autumn of 1945, even if the atomic bombs had never been dropped, and the Russian offensive in Manchuria had never taken place.

As has already been emphasized, this air campaign consisted of precision attacks on military targets, together with devastating attacks on cities, but it is not possible fairly to apportion the results achieved between the two. But attributing, as is legitimate, a substantial part of the effects to the area attacks, one can conclude that this campaign of mass destruction by air attack was the first fairly successful one in history. On the other hand, it is quite likely that victory could have been achieved without it.

The conditions under which this success was achieved need careful consideration. The first was the attacking Power expected no help from, nor had any sympathy with, the attacked population. The second was the attacking Power's overwhelming superiority in war production, which made it possible for the air offensive to be planned on a continually increasing scale. Thirdly, as a result of this superiority in air power, complete air supremacy was established over the target area, and there was little danger of a decisive counter-attack even on the advanced air bases from which the assault on Japan was being staged. Fourthly, the country attacked had already been decisively defeated in three years of bitter fighting and was on the verge of economic collapse.

4. THE ATOMIC BOMB AS A WEAPON

So MUCH has been written of the effects on Hiroshima and Nagasaki of the explosion of the two bombs, that it is only necessary here to survey briefly the main facts. The chief sources of information which will be used are the British[1] and American[2] official reports.

The attacks were launched from the island of Tinian by B29 aircraft carrying the bombs, accompanied in each case by one or two observation planes. The first bomb exploded at 8:15 a.m. on the morning of August 6 over Hiroshima.

> Most of the industrial workers had already reported to work, but many workers were en route and nearly all school children and some industrial employes were at work in the open on the program of building removal to provide firebreaks and disperse valuables to the country. The attack came forty-five minutes after the "all clear" had been sounded from a previous alert. Because of the lack of warning and the populace's indifference to small groups of planes, the explosion came as an almost complete surprise and the people had not taken shelter. Many were in the open, and most of the rest in flimsily constructed homes or commercial establishments. (*U.S.S.B.S. 5*, p. 3)

About 4.4 square miles of the city were completely burnt out.

The surprise, the collapse of many buildings, and the conflagration contributed to an unprecedented casualty rate. Seventy to

[1] His Majesty's Stationery Office, *Effects of the Atomic Bombs on Hiroshima and Nagasaki* [*British Report*] (London, 1946).
[2] *U.S.S.B.S. 4* and *U.S.S.B.S. 5* [*The Effect of Atomic Bombs on Hiroshima and Nagasaki*] (Washington, 1946).

eighty thousand people were killed, or missing and presumed dead and nearly an equal number were injured. The magnitude of the casualties is set in relief by a comparison with the Tokyo raid of March 9-10, 1945, in which, though nearly sixteen square miles were destroyed, the number killed was no larger. . . .

At Nagasaki, three days later, the city was scarcely more prepared, though vague references to the Hiroshima disaster had appeared in the newspaper of August 8. (*Ibid.*)

Thus when the bomb was dropped no raid warning was given and so only some 400 people were in the city's tunnel shelters, which had a capacity for about 30 per cent of the population.

Eyewitnesses in Hiroshima were agreed that they saw a blinding white flash in the sky, felt a rush of air and heard a loud rumble of noise, followed by the sound of rending and the falling of buildings. All also spoke of the settling darkness as they found themselves enveloped by a universal cloud of dust. Shortly afterwards they became aware of fires in many parts of the city. (*British Report,* p. 2)

The following table, extracted from *U.S.S.B.S. 5*, gives some numerical details of the effects of the two atomic bombs, together with the effects of the great fire raid on Tokyo in March 1945, and the average effects of a large number of other attacks on Japanese cities. The great difference between the casualties in the Tokyo

Effort and Results	Hiroshima	Nagasaki	Tokyo	Average of 93 urban attacks
Planes	1	1	279	
Bomb load	Atomic bomb	Atomic bomb	1,667 tons normal bombs	1,129 tons normal bombs
Population density per square mile	35,000	65,000	130,000	
Square miles destroyed	4.7	1.8	15.8	1.8
Killed and missing	70–80,000	35–40,000	83,600	1,850
Injured	70,000	40,000	102,000	1,830
Mortality rate per sq. mile destroyed	15,000	20,000	5,300	1,000
Casualty rate per sq. mile	32,000	43,000	11,800	2,000

raid compared with all subsequent raids with normal high explosives and incendiary bombs is to be ascribed mainly to the lack of warning and of preparation to meet this type of attack.

The plutonium bomb used at Nagasaki had a 15 per cent greater radius of destruction than the Uranium 235 bomb used at Hiroshima.[3] The lower casualties at the former city were mainly due to the uneven terrain, which shielded parts of the city from the effects of the bombs. The figures in the table show that the population density at Tokyo was much greater than at the two other cities; so, if an atomic bomb had been dropped on the former city, the casualties would have been two to three times as heavy as they actually were at Hiroshima.

The effects of the explosion are described in the following passage:

> At the time of the explosion, energy was given off in the forms of light, heat, radiation, and pressure. The complete band of radiations, from X and gamma rays, through ultra-violet and light rays to the radiant heat of infra-red rays, travelled with the speed of light. The shock wave, created by the enormous pressure, built up almost instantaneously at the point of the explosion but moved out more slowly, that is at about the speed of sound. The superheated gases constituting the original fire ball expanded outwards and upward at a slower rate. . . . The duration of the flash was only a fraction of a second, but it was sufficiently intense to cause third-degree burns to exposed human skin up to a distance of a mile. . . . In the immediate area of ground zero (the point on the ground immediately below the explosion), the heat charred corpses beyond recognition. (*U.S.S.B.S. 4*, p. 22)

Clothing or light buildings provided considerable protection from the flash. Penetrating gamma rays and neutrons affected the bone marrow of people near the center of the explosion, but the effects took several days to develop, death occurring soon after. Though these radiations are very penetrating, it was found that a few feet of concrete provided adequate protection even close to "ground zero." The majority of the casualties resulted from the collapse of buildings through blast, and from the subsequent fires, some of which were due to the direct effect of the radiant heat and some to the overturning of domestic stoves, etc., in the wrecked buildings.

[3] Paul Nitze, before U.S. Senate Committee on Atomic Energy, Feb. 15, 1946.

41

The blast wave which followed the flash was of sufficient force to press in the roofs of reinforced concrete structures and to flatten completely all less sturdy structures. Due to the height of the explosion, the peak pressure of the wave at ground zero was no higher than that produced by a near miss of a high explosive bomb and decreased at greater distances from ground zero. The blast wave, however, was of far greater extent and duration than that of a high explosive bomb and most reinforced concrete structures suffered structural damage or collapse, up to 700 feet at Hiroshima and 2,000 feet at Nagasaki. Brick buildings were flattened up to 7,300 feet at Hiroshima and 8,500 feet at Nagasaki. (*U.S.S.B.S. 4*, p. 23)

From the official reports we can obtain a clear picture of the overall effects of the two bombs on the life of the two cities.

Both at Hiroshima and Nagasaki the scale of the disaster brought city life and industry virtually to a standstill. Even the most destructive conventional attacks, the incendiary raids on Hamburg in the summer of 1943, and on Tokyo in the spring of 1945, had no comparable effect in paralyzing the communal organization. (*British Report*, p. 3)

At Hiroshima the effects are reported as follows:

Of approximately 90,000 buildings in the city, 65,000 were rendered unusable and almost all the remainder received at least superficial damage. The underground utilities of the city were undamaged except where they crossed bridges over rivers cutting through the city. All the small factories in the center of the city were destroyed. However, the big plants on the periphery of the city were almost completely undamaged and 94 per cent of their workers unhurt. These factories accounted for 74 per cent of the industrial production of the city. It is estimated that they could have resumed substantial normal production within thirty days of the bombing, had the war continued. The railroads running through the city were repaired for the resumption of through traffic on August 8, two days after the attack. (*U.S.S.B.S. 4*, p. 23)

At Nagasaki the results were rather different. Some 20,000 of the 57,000 houses were destroyed or badly damaged. The effect on industry is reported as follows:

Had the war continued, and had the raw material position been such as to warrant their restoration, it is estimated that the dockyard could have been in a position to produce at least 80 per cent of its full capacity within three or four months; that the steel works would have required a year to get into substantial production; that the electric works could have resumed some production within two months and been back at capacity within six months; and that restoration of the arms plant to 60-70 per cent of former capacity would have required fifteen months. (*Ibid.*)

Much has been written of the possibility of passive defense measures designed to reduce damage and casualties. All the evidence is that, except in the case of surprise attack, both damage and casualties could be reduced to a small fraction of what they were in Japan, provided that sufficient cost in capital investment and interference with many aspects of normal civilian life can be faced. The view of the American Survey is clearly stated thus:

The experience of both the Pacific and European wars emphasizes the extent to which civilian and other forms of passive defense can reduce a country's vulnerability to air attack. Civilian injuries and fatalities can be reduced, by presently known techniques, to one-twentieth or less of the casualties that would be suffered were these techniques not employed. . . .

The most instructive fact at Nagasaki was the survival, even when near ground zero, of the few hundred people who were placed in tunnel shelters. Carefully built shelters, though unoccupied, stood up well in both cities. Without question, shelters can protect those who get to them against anything but a direct hit. Adequate warning will assure that a maximum will get to shelters. . . .

Analysis of the protection of survivors within a few hundred feet of ground zero shows that shielding is possible even against gamma rays. Adequate shelters can be built which will reduce substantially the casualties from radiation. . . .

It appears that a few feet of concrete, or a somewhat greater thickness of earth, furnished sufficient protection to humans, even those close to ground zero, to prevent serious after effects from radiation. . . .

Men arriving at Hiroshima and Nagasaki have been constantly impressed by the shells of reinforced concrete buildings still rising above the rubble of brick and stone or the ashes of wooden buildings. In most cases gutted by fire or stripped of partitions these buildings have a double lesson for us. They show, first, that it is possible, without excessive expense to erect buildings which will satisfactorily protect their contents at distances of about 2,000 feet or more from a bomb of the types so far employed. Construction of such buildings would be similar to earthquake resistant construction, which Californian experience indicates would cost about 10 per cent to 15 per cent more than conventional construction.

Protection of personnel against the heat radiation is relatively easy, as quite a light covering of material will absorb most of the heat radiation.

A detailed analysis of the damage to different types of structure leads to the figures given in the following table, for the average radii and areas of damage for different types of buildings at Hiroshima and Nagasaki.[4] As an overall figure for an average town, we will take it that one plutonium atomic bomb causes severe damage over an area of eight square miles.

Type of structure	Area of severe damage (sq. miles)	Radii of severe damage (yards)
Reinforced concrete buildings	0.43	700
Heavy steel frame buildings	1.8	1,400
One-story brick buildings	8.1	2,600

A plutonium bomb produces a blast wave comparable to that which would be produced by the explosion of one lump of 20,000 tons of T.N.T.[5] From careful surveys of the damage, it has been calculated, however, that only a little over 2,000 tons of high explosive bombs—for example, ten-ton blockbusters—would be required to produce the same structural damage as one plutonium bomb. The reason why this figure is so much lower than the figure of 20,000 tons for the equivalent amount of T.N.T. when exploded in one mass, lies in the fact that such a very large explosion pulverizes nearby objects to a quite unnecessary degree; in fact, it "overhits" the central part of target area, and so wastes a large part of the energy.

The calculation runs as follows: "At Nagasaki, brick buildings within 6,000 feet of ground zero were structurally damaged. From surveys of damage by ordinary bombs we know that the corresponding distance for, say, a ten-ton high explosive bomb is 400 feet."[6] Hence the area adequately destroyed by a plutonium bomb is $(6,000/400)(6,000/400) = 225$ times that produced by a ten-ton bomb. Consequently, one plutonium bomb does about

[4] Ansley J. Coale, *The Problem of Reducing Vulnerability to Atomic Bombs*, p. 73 (Princeton, 1947).
[5] *British Report*, p. 4.
[6] *U.S.S.B.S. 5*, p. 33.

the same effective damage as some 2,250 tons of ordinary bombs properly distributed over the target. It is well known that the area damaged by a given weight of ordinary bombs varies rather little with the size of the bombs; for instance, roughly the same damage would be done by 200 ten-ton bombs, and 2,000 one-ton bombs.

A rather similar estimate of the number of ordinary bombs equivalent to one atomic bomb is given in the official documents submitted by the United States to the United Nations Atomic Energy Commission.[7] A plutonium bomb is estimated to do as much structural damage as 167 ten-ton blockbusters, each of which contains five tons of T.N.T. So on this calculation one atomic bomb is equivalent in respect of damage to 1,670 tons of ordinary bombs.

Actually the practice developed during the war of dropping a mixed load of high explosives and incendiary bombs so as to produce the maximum total damage and casualties. The American report calculated the equivalent mixed load as follows:

> On the basis of the known destructiveness of various bombs computed from the war in Europe and the Pacific, and from tests, the Survey has estimated the striking force that would have been necessary to achieve the same destruction at Hiroshima and Nagasaki. To cause physical damage equivalent to that caused by the atomic bombs, approximately 1,300 tons of bombs (one-fourth high explosives and three-fourths incendiaries) at Hiroshima and 600 tons (three-fourths high explosives and one-fourth incendiaries) would have been required at Nagasaki—in the target area. To place that many bombs in the target area, assuming daylight attacks under essentially the same conditions of weather and enemy opposition that prevailed when the atomic bombs were dropped, it is estimated 1,600 tons of bombs would have had to be dropped at Hiroshima and 900 tons at Nagasaki. To these bomb loads would have had to be added a number of tons of anti-personnel fragmentation bombs to inflict comparable casualties. These would add about 500 tons at Hiroshima and 300 tons at Nagasaki. The total bomb load would be thus 2,100 tons at Hiroshima and 1,200 tons at Nagasaki. With each plane carrying ten tons, the attacking force would have been 210 B29's at Hiroshima and 120 B29's at Nagasaki.

[7] Bernard Baruch [U.S. Representative], *The International Control of Atomic Energy: Scientific Information Transmitted to the United Nations Atomic Energy Commission, 1946, Vol. I*, p. 37 (Washington, 1946-1947).

In view of the unevenness of the terrain at Nagasaki, the figures for the Hiroshima bomb can be taken as the more typical.

A rough average of these various estimates gives us the result that one plutonium bomb is about equivalent to 2,000 tons of ordinary high explosive bombs as regards the structural damage produced.

It is less easy to give a reliable equivalence for the civilian casualties produced by atomic and ordinary bombing. These depend to a very large extent on the distribution of the people at the time of the attack between open places, ordinary houses, reinforced concrete buildings or specially constructed shelters, and so will be much greater for a surprise attack on an unprepared city than for an expected attack on a prepared city. It is not clear what assumptions as to these factors were made to obtain the figures quoted above, and it seems possible that this American report has underestimated the effectiveness of atomic bombs to produce civilian casualties in any but a very well prepared city. For instance, the March 9 raid on Tokyo with normal bombs killed some 80,000 people; that is, nearly the same number as at Hiroshima. But the population density in the former city was four times that in the latter, so, had the atomic bomb been dropped on Tokyo, one would have expected some 300,000 killed. To achieve this result with normal bombs would probably have required some 6,000 to 10,000 tons of ordinary bombs.

Lacking, therefore, a firm basis on which to revise the figures of equivalence of one plutonium bomb to some 2,000 tons of ordinary bombs given by the American Survey, we will adopt this on a provisional basis for further calculations, remembering that in some circumstances the figure may require considerable modification. In the case of possible surprise attacks at the outset of a war, the personal casualties would be higher than is indicated by this equivalence, but in a long-drawn-out war, when there is time for defensive preparation to be made, the figure may be taken as a rough numerical guide as to what may be expected to occur.

The B29 aircraft used in the attack on Japan are very vulnerable to contemporary fighters and certainly could not have been sent alone against a reasonably well-defended target. If Japan had, for instance, possessed an air defense system comparable with that, say, of Britain or Germany in 1943 or 1944, it would certainly have been necessary to send a large number of bombers to Hiroshima and Nagasaki, and probably also to have given them an escort of fighters.

The conditions of the air war over Japan in August 1945 must be remembered. Air supremacy over the target area had already been attained so that there appears to have been no effective fighter or anti-aircraft opposition. An additional cause of the lack of opposition to the atomic bombing lay in the fact that the Japanese had ceased to attempt to interfere with the reconnaissance flights that were a daily occurrence at that time. Thus, when three aircraft appeared on the morning of August 6, no attempt at defense measures was made.

It is the opinion of the Survey that, with present types of aircraft, a day offensive against a well-defended country could not be sustained on a large scale without control of the air; that is, with present aircraft not outside the range of fighter cover.[8] At any rate it is clear that had Japanese air defense been reasonably efficient at that time, it would have been necessary to send the aircraft which carried the atomic bomb, not by day and accompanied only by two observation planes as was done, but either by night, or if by day, then accompanied by a considerable number of other B29's to give mutual protection and to divide the defense.

Control of the air over the Japanese home islands was only achieved slowly and with difficulty. Of major importance in attaining this air superiority was the great deterioration that had taken place in the skill and training of the Japanese pilots. This had two main origins—the loss of nearly all the very highly skilled pilots with whom Japan had started the war, as a result of the bitter fighting of the previous three years, and the impossibility of replacing them owing to shortages, particularly of fuel, which drastically curtailed the training program.

It is not possible without further assumptions to estimate more than roughly the number of aircraft which would have been needed against strong defenses, but it is unlikely that the American air staff would have contemplated a day attack, say on a German city in 1943, from bases 1,500 miles away, with less than

[8] *U.S.S.B.S. 4,* p. 19.

47

50 B39's, if they had considered it possible at all. Looked at from this point of view, the statement in the report,[9] that the figures in the table on page 40 show "most strikingly the comparison between the striking forces needed for atomic and for conventional raids," must be understood as applying to the very special conditions of the Japanese War in August, 1945.

For in another part of the report we find the statement:

> The atomic bomb in its present state of development raises the destructive power of a single bomber by a factor of between 50 and 250 times, depending upon the nature and size of the target. The capacity to destroy, given control of the air and an adequate supply of bombs, is beyond doubt. Unless both of these conditions are met, however, any attempt to produce war-decisive results through atomic bombing may encounter problems similar to those encountered in conventional bombing. (U.S.S.B.S. 5, p. 29)

It is useful to pursue this point somewhat further, as it is of great importance for estimating the future. Consider, for instance, an imaginary raid on Germany in 1943 with fifty B29 aircraft carrying one or more atomic bombs. If all fifty aircraft carried atomic bombs, then, since one bomb can be taken as destroying about eight square miles of a city, the raid as a whole could destroy 400 square miles. No city in the world, with the exception of London and Los Angeles, approaches this size.

If the target were a moderate-sized city with an area of, say, eight square miles, then one atomic bomb would be ample to destroy it all, and it would be pointless to drop more. So, in this case, the raid of fifty aircraft, with only one carrying an atomic bomb, would be only some six times as effective as the same raid with no atomic bombs.[10] If the target were quite small, say, an isolated industrial plant, with an area of 1 square mile, then the fifty aircraft which would have to be sent would be able to destroy it with ordinary bombs. Thus no gain would accrue from the use of atomic bombs.

We can sum up the question of the relative number of aircraft sorties required to destroy a given target with high explosives

[9] U.S.S.B.S. 5, p. 33.
[10] Fifty B29's would carry 500 tons of ordinary bombs, whereas forty-nine with ordinary bombs and one with an atomic bomb would carry the equivalent of under 3,000 tons of ordinary bombs, giving a 1 to 6 ratio.

and ordinary bombs, by noting that this depends essentially on two factors: (*a*) the degree of the opposition, and so the total number of aircraft that must be dispatched; and (*b*) the size of the target. With negligible opposition, and any target with an area greater than, say, eight square miles, some 200 sorties by B29 aircraft with high explosive bombs would be required to equal the effect of one sortie with an atomic bomb. This was the case at Hiroshima and Nagasaki. Against heavy opposition, this equivalence is still maintained if the target is exceedingly large; but for smaller target sizes, the relative value of the atomic bomb falls off, till for quite small targets and very heavy opposition it offers little advantage over ordinary bombs. In this sense the special properties of the atomic bomb make it essentially a weapon for very large targets when used strategically. Since there are few targets large enough to bring out its full advantage, other than great cities, it tends to become inevitably considered as only a weapon of mass destruction. In the next chapter the tactical use of atomic bombs will also be considered.

5. FUTURE TECHNICAL DEVELOPMENTS

IN ORDER to assess the influence of atomic bombs on the course of a future war, it is necessary to estimate what changes are likely to occur by a given date in (*a*) the destructiveness of the bombs, (*b*) the methods of conveying the bombs to the target, (*c*) the active defense against the aircraft or rocket carriers, and (*d*) the passive defense measures which each country may adopt. These various factors will be discussed in turn; in general we will consider mainly advances that are likely to be achieved, firstly, within the next five years, that is, by 1953, and secondly within the next ten years, that is, by 1958. For the choice of these time scales there are certain definite reasons.[1]

[1] In the *Compton Report* (discussed in Appendix V), p. 12, we read: "As has been noted, we cannot safely assume that we will have sole possession of atomic explosives beyond 1951, although most scientists and engineers familiar with the production of the atomic bomb believe it will be 1955 at the earliest before an attack in quantity can be made against us."

It is clear that the only war in which atomic bombs are likely to be used is one in which the main contestants are the United States of America and the U.S.S.R. A period of five years from now is the latest possible date at which one could reasonably expect that the U.S.S.R. would not possess at least some atomic bombs. This is therefore the latest possible date at which a war between these two countries might occur with only one of them, America, possessing atomic bombs. The period of ten years is chosen as the latest date at which it is at all reasonable to attempt to predict the pattern of future events.

Much has been published on the future of all these four factors, but of especial importance are an article by General Henry H. Arnold[2] and two which give the American Army[3] and Navy[4] views. A critique[5] of the two latter papers has been given by Bernard Brodie.

There has been much discussion of the possibility of a "super bomb" probably using a nuclear reaction involving hydrogen or lithium initiated by the explosion of a plutonium or uranium 235 bomb. By this means scientists believe that an explosive power many times as great might be produced. However, this has so far not yet apparently been achieved, and its likely performance is still highly speculative.[6]

An increase in the explosive power of a bomb would yield increased results when the target is a large city, but it must be re-

[2] "Air Force in the Atomic Age"— Article by General Henry H. Arnold in Dexter Masters and Katherine Way (Editors), *One World or None* (New York, 1946).

[3] "The Effect of the Atomic Bomb on National Security." An expression of War Department thinking, submitted to Congress and reprinted in the *Army-Navy Journal*, April 12, 1947. Reprinted in *B.A.S.*, June, 1947.

[4] "Navy Department Thinking on the Atomic Bomb," *B.A.S.*, July, 1947. This summary of Navy thinking was prepared by Bernard Brodie after interviews with Admiral Nimitz and other senior naval officers. Brodie is a member of the Institute of International Studies, Yale University.

[5] Bernard Brodie, *B.A.S.*, August, 1947.

[6] For instance John J. McCloy, former U.S. Assistant Secretary of War, is reported as stating that ". . . there can be little doubt that within the next ten years, to be conservative, bombs (of the same type as those already used) of the power equivalent to 100,000 to 250,000 tons of T.N.T. can be made, something over ten times more powerful than the bombs dropped on Hiroshima. And if we can move to the other end of the periodic table and utilize hydrogen in the generation of energy, we could have a bomb somewhere around a thousand times as powerful as the Nagasaki bomb." *B.A.S.*, Jan., 1947.

membered that the present bombs[7] are already unnecessarily powerful for use against many small but important targets such as a single factory or a single large ship. On the other hand, even for a small target, the bigger the power of the explosive bomb, the larger the permissible aiming error. Very considerable military advantage would, however, be gained if atomic bombs could be made (a) of less overall weight, and (b) containing less fissile material. For a smaller or lighter bomb could be carried in a smaller and faster aircraft, or as the war-head of a V2 weapon of reasonable size. And a bomb with less fissile material would allow more—but less powerful—bombs to be produced. For many military purposes, much greater results could be obtained if either or both of these objectives could be attained. Almost certainly some advances in these directions will be made, but the known physical principles underlying the "critical size" of a bomb of fissile material make rather unlikely a great reduction in the minimum amount of fissile material in a bomb of anything like the present type.

No official figures have been given for the overall weight of the atomic bomb. It is only possible therefore to quote various apparently well-informed statements. Brodie writes:[8] "The gross weight of the bomb is still secret, but even if it weighed four to six tons it would still be a light load for a B29"; and also: "If it be true, as has been hinted, that the B29 is the only existing bomber that carries the atomic bomb, the fact might argue an even greater gross weight for the bomb than that surmised above." These statements seem to put the overall weight as lying between four tons and ten tons, as the latter is the maximum bomb load of a B29.

As no details have been published as to the actuating mechanism it is not possible to attempt to estimate to what extent the gross

[7] The most detailed account of the physics of the super bomb that has been published appears to be that by Josef H. Thirring in *Die Geschichte der Atombombe*, published in Vienna in 1946. Published physical data are used to estimate the energy release obtainable in theory by using the high temperature produced by a uranium bomb to initiate a hydrogen-helium, or a lithium-helium reaction.

Thirring points out that, since lithium is a common element, bombs with a much larger amount of fissile material would be more economical than is the case with scarce uranium. He envisages bombs with six tons of lithium as possibly giving one thousand times as much energy as simple uranium bombs. A bomb of this type, with its complicated activating mechanism, would certainly weigh considerably more than plutonium bombs. It is clear that super bombs will require larger carriers than ordinary atomic bombs.

[8] Brodie, in *The Absolute Weapon*, pp. 37 and 38.

weight of the bomb may be reduced in the future. This is of course a matter of great importance in view of the influence on the design of the aircraft or rockets to carry the bombs.

To allow for some increase in the explosive power of the bombs in the next few years, we will base our discussion on the assumption that the explosive force will be twice that of the one used at Nagasaki; that is, the improved bomb will be assumed to have an explosive power of some 40,000 tons of T.N.T. exploded in one place. Since the early atomic bombs produced about as much destruction as 2,000 tons of ordinary bombs, and since the area of destruction increases more slowly than the explosive force, we will assume that the improved bomb will have the same destructive power as 3,000 tons of ordinary bombs.

Though rockets of the German V2 type might possibly be built to carry an atomic war-head a distance of a few hundred miles, the technical problem of making such a rocket with a range of a 1,000 miles or more is very formidable. The view of the American Navy[9] has been expressed as follows: "For these and other reasons not here touched upon, it seems a wholly reasonable and safe assumption that rockets with atomic war-heads capable of thousands of miles of range are not to be expected for at least twenty-five years."

It will be remembered that the German V2 weapon had an overall weight of fourteen tons and carried a war-head of one ton a distance of 200 miles, with an average accuracy of about four miles. As a basis for the subsequent discussion of the strategic effects of atomic bombs, we will make the assumption that within the next ten years, that is, till 1958, rockets of the V2 type will not be able to deliver atomic war-heads a distance greater than a very few hundred miles, and that the mean aiming error at this range will not be less than a few miles.

Since no effective method of destroying rockets in flight has apparently yet been devised, and since none seems in sight, we will assume that there will be no such method within the next ten years.

Mention must also be made of the probable developments of pilotless aircraft, of which the German V1 was the first and, so far, the only type used operationally. The balance of advantage in dispensing with a pilot is always a very difficult one to estimate, as it involves gauging numerically the relative advantages of increased performance, in range or speed, or both, against the loss of the power of human intelligence to find the target or evade counter-measures. Undoubtedly there are circumstances in which a pilotless aircraft has some advantages over piloted aircraft, particularly at ranges of a few hundred miles. But at ranges of a few thousand miles, their greater vulnerability, due to their lower capability of taking evasive action, combined with the difficulty of guiding them to a target, would seem to make them nearly useless for attack on specific small targets.

It will be remembered that the German V1 weapon had an overall weight of three tons, and carried a one-ton war-head a distance of 200 miles at a speed of 350 m.p.h. The average aiming error was about five miles, that is, about one-fortieth of the range. Within three months of the start of the attacks, fighters and anti-aircraft fire shot down 80 per cent of those launched at London from the French coast.

The angular accuracy achieved with this weapon would be quite useless at ranges of 1,000 miles or so, as it would give an aiming error of some twenty-five miles. In fact, for all pilotless weapons, whether of the rocket or aircraft type, which are to be used at ranges of over a few hundred miles, some form of guiding seems essential, if a worthwhile accuracy is to be attained. But no such devices seem likely within the next ten years to be accurate enough to deliver an appreciable fraction of missiles into any target smaller than a large city at a 1,000-mile range.[10]

As a basis for our discussion, we will make the assumption that no type of pilotless aircraft or rocket is likely to be useful for attack, at a range of 1,000 miles, on such a small target as a single factory, or an atomic bomb plant, at least for very many years. As already shown in the table on page 44, the radius of action of an atomic bomb against ordinary reinforced concrete buildings is only 700 yards—an entirely impossible accuracy for pilotless weapons at great ranges. It is obvious that an atomic bomb plant would

---

[10] For a discussion of the problem of guiding long-range rockets, see article by General Arnold on "Air Force in the Atomic Age," in *One World or None*.

be specially strengthened so as to be almost completely immune to a bomb exploded high up, as the bombs were over Japan. If the height of explosion is decreased so as to increase the force of the explosion, the area over which the increased force is obtained is correspondingly[11] reduced.

Support for these views was given by Rear-Admiral Parsons, Director of Atomic Defense for the U.S. Navy,[12] to the effect that there is "no straightforward approach, based on scientific and engineering data available in early 1947, which would produce ranges with V2 type vehicles beyond a few hundred miles." Regarding "inter-continental supersonic missiles" as still in the stage of "unrealized blueprint ideas," Admiral Parsons deduced that "delivery of atomic bombs at ranges of 1,000 miles or more would require that they be carried in subsonic or transonic vehicles against which there are several means of defense, including jet-propelled fighters armed with rockets and jet- or rocket-propelled anti-aircraft missiles fired from the ground." He concluded that "against an alert and well-equipped defense, subsonic delivery would be costly and would require a large number of bombs in order to get home a decisive attack." This last sentence would perhaps be more accurate if the word "bombs" were replaced by "aircraft."

In spite of these arguments, one finds repeatedly statements which imply that successful long-range attack with pilotless vehicles against atomic installations are likely to be possible.

For instance we find the following remark by F. H. Osborn, Deputy U.S. Representative at the United Nations Atomic Energy Commission. "The airplane or rocket carrying atomic explosives is a conclusive weapon. It extends the range of power of those possessing it to the farthest corner of this planet."[13]

[11] According to R. E. Lapp (*B.A.S.*, Feb., 1948), the optimum height of explosion to give the maximum area of destruction on the ground is about 2,500 feet. Lapp points out that at Nagasaki, when the bomb was "exploded high in the air, about ten square miles of city were hard hit, whereas at Alamorgordo (New Mexico) when the bomb was exploded at low altitude, only three square miles or less were damaged to the same degree."

[12] Quoted by the *New York Times*, March 19, 1947.

[13] *B.A.S.*, July, 1947.

On the other hand we read in the *Compton Report*: ". . . the era of push-button warfare, in which inter-continental rockets with atomic war-heads wipe out tens of millions overnight, has not yet arrived. It is extremely unfortunate that the mistaken idea has been planted in so many minds that that era is now present."

From this analysis we conclude that certainly for ranges over 1,000 miles and probably also for ranges over 400 miles, the only vehicle for the delivery of an atomic bomb with adequate accuracy within the next ten years will be the conventional piloted aircraft. We have, therefore, first to consider the possibility of delivering atomic bombs with ordinary aircraft within the next five years at extreme inter-continental ranges of the order of 2,000 miles.

There are already in existence aircraft such as B36's and B50's which could just do such journeys and return, or could strike at still longer ranges if the crew were prepared not to return. It has often been argued from this fact that repeated military operations at such distances are possible. This is, however, far from certain, as it neglects (as did Douhet and his school) the possible parallel increase in defense measures. The view of the American Navy is clear on this point:

> The large subsonic bombing aircraft, on the other hand, operating at extreme range, and without a heavy fighter escort, cannot be considered a sufficiently reliable means of delivering scarce and expensive atomic bombs against a strong and well-alerted enemy. . . . The present technological trend is decidedly in favor of the defense as against the offense in ordinary strategic bombing. Means of detection and interception of subsonic bombing aircraft are making great strides. Guided, or homing missiles of the rocket type, fitted with proximity fuses, promise to give new potentialities to anti-aircraft fire. . . . Jet propulsion, permitting speeds far above those available to propeller-driven aircraft, is much more suited to short range fighter planes than to large, long range bombers, due to the tremendous and rapid fuel consumption involved in the jet principle. . . . At any rate, the present trend is the only one we can see in operation, and that trend decidedly favors—as against the recent past—the defense of large centers of population and industry.

Provided these statements are taken to refer to an atomic bomb offensive at really long ranges—for instance, at more than 2,000 miles, against a large and heavily defended country with very many essential targets widely spaced and many of them well inland, the conclusions are almost certainly true.

It is interesting in this connection to note the speed advantage of modern fighters compared with contemporary long-range bombers, as given in Jane's *All the World's Aircraft*, and other publications, from which the following figures are extracted:

Comparative Performance of Contemporary Fighters and Long-range Bombers

Bomber	Bomb load (lbs.)	Max. Speed (m.p.h.)	Cruising Speed (m.p.h.)	Max. Alt. (ft.)	Radius of Action [equals ½ range] (miles)
B29 Super Fortress (U.S.)	10,000	342	240	33,000	1,630
B50 (U.S.)	20,000	400	300	35,000	1,750

Fighter	Max. Speed (m.p.h.)	Cruising Speed (m.p.h.)	Max. Altitude (ft.)
P80A Shooting Star (U.S.) jet	558	500	40,000
P84 Thunder Jet (U.S.) jet	590	550	40,000
Mosquito NF36 (Br.) (Reciprocating)	415	276	43,000
Vampire (Br.) jet	540	450	50,000[14]
Meteor IV (Br.) jet	585	540	54,000

It will be seen that modern jet fighters now in service have a speed advantage of more than 150 miles an hour over the latest long-range bombers with reciprocating engines. This situation may change when long-range jet-engined bombers come into service. It is very probable, however, that the small short-range fighter will, in fact, maintain a marked speed advantage over the long-range piloted jet engine for some time to come.

There is a possibility that for a period of years the speed advantage of fighters over bombers may decrease to a small margin owing to the speed of both approaching that of sound—about 760 m.p.h. at sea level and 660 m.p.h. above 40,000 feet. This might occur owing to the difficulty both would have of passing beyond the speed of sound. But sooner or later—and probably sooner,[15] if newspaper reports are to be trusted—the fighter will go faster than

[14] A Vampire has recently set an altitude record of 57,000 feet.
[15] This is reported to have been achieved already. *New York Herald Tribune* (Paris edition), Jan. 10, 1948.

sound, many years before the large piloted bomber does; and then its speed advantage will be restored for a time in full measure.

It must not be forgotten that any new technical advance, whether in aerodynamics or in engine design, is generally incorporated earlier in small aircraft than in large, owing to the much longer period of development of a large aircraft. A reflection of this is seen in the table on page 56, where jet fighters figure prominently but no jet bombers. So it comes about that fighters are usually technically in advance of contemporary bombers. This is slightly offset by the possibility of fitting more elaborate gadgets in the larger aircraft, but not, in general, to any substantial extent.

Even, however, if the speed margin of fighters over bombers is maintained in the future, as it has been ever since the first World War, the problem of air defense does become much more difficult as the speeds of both bombers and fighters increase, owing to the reduction in time available for the warning system to operate and the interception to be achieved. To counter this effect of increased speed, an increased depth of defense is required. If, with present bomber speeds of around 300 m.p.h., a certain degree of defense can be achieved with a depth of defense of 150 miles, then, when bomber speeds rise to 500 m.p.h., a depth of defense of some 250 miles will give the same time available for interception. By depth of defense is meant the distance the attacking aircraft have to fly through radar cover before reaching vital targets.[16]

On weighing all these arguments, it is safe to conclude that within the shorter of our two periods, that is, within the next five years, piloted bombers with a range over, say, 1,500 miles, which can be expected to be in service in large numbers, will be so inferior in speed and maneuverability as to be extremely vulnerable to contemporary fighters, and probably also to improved anti-aircraft weapons. We conclude, therefore, that repeated deep penetration of a heavily defended territory is likely to be an expensive operation. This is likely to be true both by day and by night. For the development of air-borne radar has made the night fighter

[16] Lord Tedder has recently written: "Very greatly increased bomber speeds will immensely increase the difficulties of providing adequate warning and effective interception, and indeed the fighter's superiority of speed over the bomber (upon which its effectiveness in defense primarily depends) may well dwindle to almost nothing." But no time scale of this development is indicated, nor is it indicated when the advent of the super-sonic fighter should restore its advantage.

nearly as efficient as the day fighter. So in this period we must conclude that effective inter-continental air war is not possible.

In the latter part of our period, that is, from 1953 to 1958, the prospects are not quite so clear. It is possible that the speed advantage of fighters will be drastically reduced. But it is also possible that new and improved defense measures will be developed. So it is likely that, certainly till 1953 and probably also till 1958, any long-range bombing campaign must be carried out in very great force. For all the experience of the war shows that, both by day and night, losses can only be kept down to acceptable limits by sending large forces of attackers. In air war there is still safety in numbers. If day attacks are made, fighter escorts will be essential, thus limiting the range to that of the fighters. If the attacks are by night, the problem of target finding in the face of heavy opposition and enemy use of decoys, etc., remains formidable, even with all the latest navigational aids.

These arguments, so far, refer to the attack on targets at long range, say, over 1,500 miles from the air bases. However, the possibility of adequate defense falls rapidly as the distance between air base and target becomes smaller, since smaller and faster aircraft can be used and the time available to the defenders for interception becomes less. In fact, a bomber of short range, say, 500 miles, carrying an atomic war-head, might have a performance not very far below that of a contemporary two-seater fighter.[17] This consideration emphasizes again the extreme importance for the attacker of obtaining bases as near as possible to the essential targets, and for the defenders of keeping the air bases available to the attacker as far away as possible. The more atomic bombs available to the attacker, the more difficult, of course, the task of defense; but as soon as the defender has atomic bombs also, they may well prove very effective for a counter-offensive against the attackers' forward air bases.[18]

The relative cost of a fighter and a bomber is of importance. Since the cost of an aircraft is roughly proportional to its weight, and since a long-range heavy bomber weighs over 100,000 lbs., compared with the 10,000 to 20,000 lbs. of a fighter, a nation which

[17] Compare the performance of the Mosquito fighters and bombers in 1943-1945.
[18] The contrary view that there is no value in having more than a certain number of bombs has often been expressed but has been convincingly refuted by the military.

wanted only fighters could produce between five and ten times as many as an enemy nation with the same industrial resources could produce of bombers.

In the event of the outbreak of war between two continental Powers, one must reckon, therefore, with the possibility that a nation which had adopted a defensive policy, and had not used its aircraft production resources on long-range bombers, might have at its disposal a first-line strength of many thousands of fighters. Against such a country a long-range bombing offensive would have to be launched on a huge scale to have a good chance of decisive success. If the lessons of the last war can be relied on, the essential conditions for the success of such an offensive against targets deep in enemy territory would be the previous winning of at least a measure of air superiority over the enemy country. And this could only be achieved by very large numbers of fighters operating from near-by bases, so making the operation essentially a short, not a long-range one.

The interesting point arises that a country which had adopted the defensive policy of concentrating on fighter types for defense against bombers would thereby have at its disposal a very large force of aircraft also suitable for cooperation with a land campaign either offensive or defensive in character. For the experience of the war showed that fighters and fighter-bombers are of great value for this purpose. It will be remembered from the analysis in Chapters 2 and 3 how decisively important, in all the major land campaigns of the late war, was the support of large forces of fighter-bomber aircraft.

An estimate of the scale of an atomic bomb attack which would have to be launched on a major continental Power to have an important effect on its power to wage war can be made by noting the loss of territory and of industrial capacity by the Soviet Union in 1941 and 1942, and recalling that this still did not prevent her from eventually defeating the German armies and driving them from her territories. A huge number of atomic bombs would have been necessary to inflict on Russia as much damage as she actually suffered by the German invasion.

It is interesting to estimate the number of atomic bombs of existing types that would have been required to do the same damage to Germany as was actually done by the Allied bombing offensive, assuming the same average accuracy of attack and the same distribution in time. Over a million and a third tons of bombs were dropped on Germany during the war; and since, as we have seen from official American data, one improved atomic bomb can be considered as the equivalent of about 3,000 tons of ordinary bombs, we see that the dispatch of some 400 atomic bombs would have been required.

Moreover we have seen that this bombing campaign played by no means the decisive role in the defeat of Germany, which was in fact brought about mainly through the land war. The figures of German production shown in Appendix I and *Chart 2* prove this conclusively. German war production doubled between the end of 1942 and the summer of 1944, in spite of the dropping of some half-million tons of bombs during the period—the equivalent of some 200 atomic bombs—and the huge man-power losses suffered by the German armies in the land war, in which up to 400 Allied divisions were engaged. In 1944-1945, the rate rose to a peak of 150,000 tons a month; the equivalent rate of dropping atomic bombs would be about fifty a month.

It might be argued that such a calculation of the number of atomic bombs, which are to be taken as equivalent to a given weight of ordinary bombs, is inadequate, on the grounds that it does not take into account the special properties of the atomic bomb. For instance, it has often been argued that the time factor is of great importance: the argument is that atomic bombs could be dropped, say, on all the major cities of an enemy country within a few hours, and that such an attack would have an altogether greater effect than if an equivalent weight of ordinary bombing were spread out over many months.

Though it is impossible to be quite sure of the effect of such an intense but short attack, the following considerations are relevant. Firstly, it is most improbable that such a widespread attack could be launched within a few hours against a well-defended country owing to the huge air effort involved. For it has already been pointed out that each atomic bomber would have to be accompanied by many other bombers, in order to have a good chance of reaching a distant target against heavy opposition.

Then again, it is not certain that it would be a sound policy to concentrate the atomic bombs in time, even if it was possible. For the disadvantage to the enemy of having a large number of attacks to compete with at once would be partially, at any rate, offset by the shortening of the time during which defense measures, civilian evacuation, etc., would have to be maintained. In fact, one can see strong arguments for a deliberate policy of spreading the attacks over a considerable period of time, in order to tire out the defense and weary the population. Only if large armies were ready for an immediate invasion would a very short duration attack be advisable.

The other common criticism of such numerical comparisons is that they neglect the psychological factor; this presumably means that the "horror" of the atomic bomb is so great that a nation's will to resist will be rapidly sapped. To this one can reply that, from the point of view of most of the individual victims, there is not much to choose between the experience of heavy ordinary bombing and atomic bombing. Selected survivors of Hamburg, Dresden or Tokyo could have provided equally poignant material for the pen of a John Hersey as the survivors of Hiroshima. Those who remember the exaggerated expectations of the effect of the British bombing offensive on German morale current in the early days of the war will be skeptical of many of the easy predictions about the effect on morale of atomic bombs. The power of human beings to "take it" is immense; a determined people will learn to stand atomic bombardment, if that is their fate, just as Germans learned to stand ordinary bombing on a scale up to fifty times larger than that which the enthusiasts for strategic bombing thought would bring about the collapse of their war effort.

It is, therefore, certainly a legitimate conclusion that a long-range atomic bombing offensive against a large continental Power is not likely to be by itself decisive within the next five years.

The views of the Navy Department, which we have quoted, have been criticized by Bernard Brodie[19] as depending too much on the assumption that atomic bombs are at present scarce and expensive, making necessary a high chance, say, 90 per cent, that each bomb dispatched will reach its target. The Navy Department implies that sustained operations would be possible only if not more

[19] *B.A.S.*, Aug., 1947.

than, say, 10 per cent of the aircraft were shot down before reaching their objective. The critics point out correctly that a time may come when atomic bombs are no longer very expensive or in short supply, and that consequently an effective atomic bomb offensive could be staged even though 90 per cent of the atomic bombs fail to reach their target, reliance being put on the huge destructive power of the 10 per cent which do. Though there is some force in this criticism, it is itself open to the charge of undue simplification. The first criticism relates to the time when this situation may arise. Taking a guess at the possible rate of production of atomic bombs by the major Powers, it seems likely to be quite a long time before so many will be in existence that the military staffs would consider it worthwhile to throw away nine in order to land one on an enemy city. For atomic bombs will be rightly considered by the military to have great value also as tactical weapons, e.g. for attack on large enemy ships, airfields, troop concentrations, landing operations, etc.

The second criticism of Brodie's viewpoint is one that can often be made against the military enthusiast for some new weapon; the error is to neglect the enemy reaction to the proposed operation. Dr. Brodie assumes, one supposes correctly, that it is likely to be possible (for instance in his own country) to find enough young men who would be prepared to undertake the operations of destroying hundreds of thousands of the population of enemy cities even though their own chances of survival were only 10 per cent. But if this is correct, how much more certain is it that the country attacked would find it possible to create, if technically advantageous, a fighter defense force based, say, on ramming and near-suicide tactics. By adoption of such tactics it would seem likely that the efficacy of fighter attacks on bombers might be substantially increased just as the adoption by the Japanese of suicide tactics in their attacks on ships substantially raised their effectiveness. Whether or not such suicide defense tactics would be economic depends on the balance of advantages between gain of lethality and loss of trained personnel, and would depend on the circumstances of the time.[20]

[20] One can see the possibility that close formations of day bombers, as were used in the last war, would have to be abandoned, since all the aircraft might be destroyed by a single enemy suicide fighter armed with an atomic bomb.

Those strategists who lightheartedly suggest such operations as atomic bomb raids suffering a 90 per cent loss rate are apt not to think the operation through to its logical conclusions. Dr. Brodie does not, for instance, discuss what is to happen to the 90 per cent of aircraft and bombs which do not find their target. For instance, there must always be a chance that pilots may prefer to save their lives by landing and surrendering to the enemy rather than going to certain death. Of course, special devices can be fitted to the bombs to prevent them falling intact into enemy hands, but no such devices are ever quite foolproof. Then there is the problem for the attackers of what to do about those aircraft and bombs which can be expected to be shot down over enemy territory. If the bombs are set to explode, say, as soon as the craft gets out of control, then the pilot and crew will be destroyed; in these circumstances the crew will have again a strong motive to land or bail out beforehand. Alternatively, the bombs could be set to explode only on contact of the aircraft with the ground. This, however, would give the crew a strong motive to bail out as early as possible, so as to insure that the aircraft flies several miles farther on before it crashes. This situation will clearly not conduce to pressing home the attack, against heavy opposition, to the assigned target. Following Japanese practice, the crew might be chained to the aircraft. But it is doubtful if such a practice, even if acceptable to American public opinion, would be very conducive to the efficient carrying out of the highly intricate and skilled operations of navigation, bomb-aiming and defense against fighters, that are essential to a successful mission!

Considering all these eventualities, it is reasonable to doubt whether a High Command would find it often advisable to launch an attack expecting a 90 per cent loss rate with large numbers of atomic bombers, in view of the chance that an appreciable fraction might fall into enemy hands and be used against the attacking power. This would have special force in the case a country with atomic bombs waging war against another country believed not to have any—for instance, in a war between America and Russia in the next five years.

But leaving near-suicide atomic bombing aside, it is true that the greater effectiveness of the atomic bomb, and so the fewer sorties required, might make it possible to carry on repeated operations at a loss rate of, say, 30 per cent, compared with the figure of under 10 per cent which was found prohibitive for ordinary bombing.

The foregoing analysis gives little ground for taking too literally the thesis that there is no defense possible against atomic bombs, at any rate in wars between major continental Powers. The original meaning of the thesis appears to have been that there is no specific defense—for instance, atomic bombs cannot be pre-detonated in the air or otherwise rendered harmless by some scientific counter-measure. In this technical sense the thesis is true. But when later it began to be used in a wider strategic sense, it became false.

It is hardly necessary to refute in detail such statements as that of Brodie,[21] who concludes from the performance of the B29 and other bombers under development, that "any world power is able from bases within its own territories to destroy most of the cities of any other power." Dr. Brodie explicitly rejects the considered views of the military as to the range of effective operations. He writes: "It is not necessary, despite the assertions to the contrary of various naval and military leaders, including President Truman, to seize advanced bases close to enemy territory as prerequisite to effective use of the bomb." The same theme is taken up by A. J. Coale:[22]

It has been demonstrated that a B29 can transport an atomic bomb over a range of more than 1,500 miles and return to its base. Now that there have been bomber flights of more than 10,000 miles—to be sure, one-way flights not under combat conditions—it seems inescapable that combat ranges of at least 5,000 miles will soon be feasible. The strategic significance of these facts is at once evident when one draws the radii on a map. It means that, with relatively unimportant exceptions, all the centers of civilization in the northern hemisphere are within reach of destruction at the hands of any major nation in that hemisphere. . . .

The large body of experience with air attacks indicates that the interception of the majority of the participants in an air raid is difficult even when the defender has a strong advantage in air strength. Suppose now that 1,000 aircraft are dispatched against this country—heavy bombers, jet-propelled craft, or rockets, with

---

[21] Brodie in *The Absolute Weapon*, p. 39.
[22] Coale, *The Problem of Reducing Vulnerability to Atomic Bombs*, p. 80.

five assigned to each of the 200 highest priority targets, mostly big cities. Radar warning nets, A.A. fire, interception by fighter planes, and perhaps target-seeking missiles might cause the destruction of 60 per cent before they reached their targets—an unprecedented success for the first use of a defense system. Each target would then receive an average of two atomic bombs. Some would be hit by more. Those that escaped would be the target for the next raid.

It is typical of such statements that the overall military and political situation in which such devastating atomic attacks are to be carried out is left quite vague. There is no mention of the bases from which they are to be launched against America; nor any note that informed American military opinion gives the range of rockets with atomic war-heads as only a very few hundred miles. What the attacking country intends to do afterwards is conveniently overlooked.

These extravagances of opinion are not without obvious causation—though some detailed analysis is needed to bring their origin to light. More will be said of this in a later chapter. But the resemblance of these views to the exploded fallacies of the Douhet school in the 1920's is clear. Pearl Harbor and Hiroshima have been only too well remembered; but they have not been understood.

The divergence of view as to the military effect of atomic bombs is well brought out by two quotations from different authors in the same book, *The Absolute Weapon*. The first[23] is: "A world accustomed to thinking it horrible that war should last four or five years is now appalled at the prospect that future wars may last only a few days." The second[24] is: "Even atomic bombardment could hardly exceed very much the damage which the Germans inflicted on the Western and Southern parts of the Soviet Union; yet the Russians fought on."

So much has been heard of the potentialities of atomic bombs for the mass attack on cities, that it seems often forgotten—though not in professional military circles—what a valuable tactical weapon they may prove to be. Probably their direct effect on land operations in open country would not be of outstanding importance, as an adequate degree of dispersal is likely in general

[23] Brodie in *The Absolute Weapon*, p. 71.
[24] Arnold Wolfers in *The Absolute Weapon*, p. 141.

to be possible. Certainly land war tactics may have to be changed somewhat, but probably not in any striking degree, since land forces are already normally well dispersed.[25] Attacks on landing operations such as the invasion of Normandy would, however, be very profitable.

Armored vehicles would be little affected, except close to the explosion, and troops would find a considerable degree of protection in deep and narrow trenches. Of course, the existence of atomic bombs would clearly lead to the avoidance of undue concentration of troops. Very dense concentrations such as were employed preparatory to some of the later Allied offensives in France would have to be avoided, but much the same precautions would be needed against the threat of heavy normal bombing. It was only because the Allies had complete air superiority that the dense concentrations of troops in France could be safely employed.

Similar arguments apply to naval warfare. In the article by Bernard Brodie, summarizing the U.S. Navy Department's thinking on the atomic bomb,[26] the importance and possibility of tactical dispersion is strongly emphasized. Much prominence is given to the efficiency reached by anti-aircraft and fighter defense. "The active defenses of the United States fleet reached an extraordinary stage of efficiency during the latter stages of the Pacific war, permitting American task forces to operate for long periods off islands containing substantial enemy land-based air forces." It must be pointed out that this defense was not sufficient to prevent serious damage to the fleets when the Japanese adopted suicide tactics with numbers of small and maneuverable planes. So it is possible that the American naval view, in so far as it is correctly interpreted by Dr. Brodie, may appreciably overestimate the efficiency of the air defense of naval units.

The article continues: "It should be remembered that the atomic bomb seems destined to require for a long time to come a rather

---

[25] This view is confirmed by the relative lack of success of the Anglo-American heavy bomber force when used in a tactical role in the battles in France and Germany. In spite of certain successes, such as at St. Lô, few suitable targets evidently presented themselves. An atomic bomb detonated high up would have one advantage over normal high explosive bombs in that it does not crater the ground and so impede subsequent land operations. An atomic bomb exploded low down, on the other hand, would sterilize an area by the radioactivity produced—and few army commanders take kindly to sterilizing areas over which they hope to advance.

[26] *B.A.S.*, July, 1947.

large plane to carry it, and large planes lack the maneuverability so essential to pressing home an attack against well-armed naval forces." This statement confirms the view that the bomb must be of very considerable weight and size.

One clear conclusion can be made as regards naval weapons; this is that very large ships will be at a serious disadvantage, and that, wherever possible, it will be advantageous to use as small ships as can fulfill the necessary function. Atomic bomb attacks on port facilities should be very profitable, and the effect of the radioactivity produced might keep the port out of action for a very long time, as shown at Bikini.

It does not seem to have been sufficiently noticed that the airfields which are needed for the operation of a large force of long-range bombers can provide a rather vulnerable target to atomic bombs. This will not be the case where the offensive can be staged from a large number of heavily defended airfields constructed before the outbreak of war in friendly territory. However, where *advanced* air bases have to be constructed after the outbreak of hostilities in previously neutral or enemy territory, the great cost in engineering effort involved in the construction of runways and parking space for aircraft of B29 or B36 type, implies that a large number of aircraft may have to use a very limited number of airfields. In these circumstances, the closely parked aircraft and the necessary ground facilities for their fueling and maintenance would be definitely vulnerable to atomic attack. Enough details have been published of the congestion of aircraft at the American advanced bases in the Marianas, Saipan, Formosa, etc., to prove how devastating would have been an attack by atomic bombs. In one published photograph[27] there are stated to be 100 B29 aircraft lined up on one airfield at Saipan. It was only the overwhelming American air superiority over the Japanese in the later stages of the Pacific War, that made it safe to take the risks of providing such ideal targets even to ordinary bombs. Even so, quite a number of B29 aircraft were destroyed by Japanese aircraft on various airfields.

It can be seen, therefore, that any country possessing only a few

[27] In General H. H. Arnold, *Second Report to Secretary of War*, p. 67 (London, 1945).

atomic bombs, but which was threatened by attack by another country with more bombs, would certainly be well advised to employ them in a strategically defensive role by staging a tactical counter-offensive against the advanced air bases of the enemy, rather than to attempt to use them for what must be indecisive attacks on the enemy cities.

In connection with the possibility of ensuring a reasonable degree of protection to the individual life of a country, the American War Department document already quoted[28] reads as follows:

> That success in this respect is not hopeless may be indicated by the historical example of industry's ability to survive, demonstrated by German industry in World War II, which not only survived but increased its production up till 1944; and the Russian industrial effort, which survived the great German territorial advances which overran or destroyed industrial capacity representing equivalent results of an enormous amount of strategic bombing. Complete dispersion of our cities over 30,000 population which number some 200 and total fifty million inhabitants, appears beyond our capabilities—not because of the requirements of money or engineering effort, staggering as they are, but because of the political resistance of our people against being regimented, uprooted, and forcibly moved.

A detailed discussion of the technical problems involved in a policy of dispersal and protection of industries has been given by Marshak, Teller and Klein.[29] Their conclusion is that it would be economically possible to "relocate all urban dwellings, plants and non-movable equipment" in the United States in fifteen years at a cost of about a quarter of the national income. It is quite clear that any such program could not be carried out in the United States of America without revolutionary economic changes. Yet, leaving aside as quite impossible such a relocation of population and industry as is envisaged by authors quoted above, a not at all negligible degree of protection to essential installations could clearly be attained by a more modest program. Different countries would fare very differently. Those of large size, such as America and Russia, could much more easily achieve some degree of protection than small and congested countries like the United King-

[28] "The Effect of the Atomic Bomb on National Security"—*B.A.S.*, June, 1947.
[29] *B.A.S.*, 1947.

dom, which can be considered as indefensible against an atomic bomb attack from bases in North Europe. Space is of the greatest value for two reasons. It gives the possibility of wide dispersal, and so makes targets difficult to find; and it provides great depth of defense against the aircraft carrying the bombs.

The experience of the last war proved beyond all question the extreme importance of depth for successful air defense. Every hundred miles of additional distance which the enemy bombers have to fly over friendly territory greatly increases the chance of successful interception and destruction of the attackers. The faster the attacking aircraft, the greater the depth of defense necessary. However, the larger a country, the longer the perimeter to be defended, and so the thinner the spread of its peripheral defenses. This offsets to some extent the defensive value of size. But in the long run a large country gains, as the depth of defense and power of dispersion surely will outweigh the thinness of the spread. Great Britain loses both ways, as her size and shape combine to give a large periphery but little depth or dispersive possibilities.

It remains to consider biological weapons and radioactive poisons, both as yet untried. An official report on biological warfare by G. W. Merck, Chairman of the United States Biological Warfare Committee has been published,[30] in which some general principles have been elaborated, but without giving much specific information. "Biological warfare may be defined as the use of bacteria, fungi, viruses, rickettsias and toxic agents from living organisms (as distinguished from synthetic chemicals used as gases or poisons) to produce death or disease in men, animals or plants." Of importance in connection with the problem of control of weapons of mass destruction is the paragraph which reads: "It is important to note that, unlike the development of the atomic bomb, and other secret weapons during the war, the development of agents for biological warfare is possible in many countries, large and small, without vast expenditure of money or the construction of huge production facilities. It is clear that the development of biological warfare could very well proceed in many countries, perhaps under the guise of legitimate medical or bacteriological research. In whatever deliberations take place concerning the

[30] *B.A.S.*, Oct., 1946.

implementation of a lasting peace in the world, the potentialities of biological warfare cannot safely be ignored."

Further information is contained in an article by Professor K. V. Thimann.[31] "Pathogenic bacteria could be sprayed on the enemy in various ways, in missiles or from the air. Cholera, dysentery and bubonic plague would be obvious choices for such a campaign. . . . The paramount requirement in such an event would be to prepare for the disease to spread back into our own ranks. For this purpose, rapid diagnosis is essential, and the preparation of protective agents such as vaccines or antitoxins on a really large scale would require development."

The lethal dose of diphtheria toxin is given as 0.03 milligrams, giving thirteen million lethal doses from a pound of toxin. This implies individual injection, and the actual effectiveness when used as a mist would be far lower, but how much lower is not suggested. The toxin of botulism is stated to be higher than that of diphtheria. Thimann also discusses the possibility of attack on growing crops by means of new types of chemical compounds, and by the spreading of natural diseases such as wheat rust.

Some further details and a bibliography of relevant published papers are given in a report to the United Nations by the American Association of Scientific Workers,[32] from which the following extracts are taken:

A routine unpurified preparation of psittacosis virus, a representative member of the group of highly infective disease agents characteristic of bacterial warfare, has been reported to contain per cubic centimeter approximately twenty million respiratory doses for man. No published data are available on the dispersion efficiency of bacterial warfare munitions, but even if the efficiency were as low as 0.01 per cent, the potency of this material would be still extraordinarily high. Such preparations of psittacosis virus could easily be produced in liter amounts in a single small laboratory, with only such equipment and materials as are common to virus laboratories throughout the world. The pay-load in a psittacosis "bomb" and therefore probably the whole munition, could be small, cheap and easily turned out in quantity. . . . Bacterial warfare production could proceed in any civilized country irrespective of its size or relative wealth.

[31] B.A.S., Aug., 1947.
[32] Reprinted in B.A.S., Dec., 1947.

No very concrete picture of the real possibilities of biological weapons in major wars emerges from these published accounts, but it is clear that the various authors considered them of comparable danger to atomic bombs.

In the *Finletter Report*, which is discussed more fully in Appendix V, appears the following paragraph:[33]

> Atomic weapons will not long remain our monopoly. And there are other weapons of comparable destructiveness. Mankind has not indulged in biological warfare on a large scale so far; but the biological sciences are evolving so rapidly that it is impossible to predict the future. The nations might be foolish enough to try it out. Biological warfare might become a serious factor in another war and we must be alert to every aspect of defense against this kind of attack. And sabotage—heretofore a relatively unimportant means of warfare—is in the process of becoming a serious menace. The preplacement of atomic and biological weapons may soon become a major military problem.

It will be noticed that this supposedly authoritative report brackets biological and atomic weapons together as comparable dangers.

The use of radioactive poisons has been discussed in various articles, but again without much detail. There appear to be two main forms in which they can be used. In the first, the poisons occur as an aftereffect of the explosion of an atomic bomb, due to the production during the explosion of large quantities of radioactive materials with a lifetime ranging from minutes to years. At Hiroshima and Nagasaki, where the bombs were exploded well up in the air, it has been stated that very little radioactivity remained on the ground. On the other hand, after the underwater test explosion at Bikini,[34] intense radioactivity remained for several months in the water and on the ships which had been deluged with active water, and would have killed all living things remaining there for any length of time. The intensity of the radiation is given as the equivalent of many hundreds of tons of radium.

Of more importance, perhaps, as a weapon, is the possibility of spreading over enemy country the radioactive materials (fission products) which are a by-product of the manufacture of plutonium

---

[33] President's Air Policy Committee, *Survival in the Air Age*, p. 12.
[34] *B.A.S.*, Aug., 1947, p. 26.

in a pile. For every pound of plutonium produced, about a pound of fissile products are also produced with lifetimes ranging from minutes to years.[35] If these fission products could be spread by spraying or in some other way over cities or the countryside, all personnel remaining there for a considerable time would be killed. No statement seems to have been published indicating the area which could be made lethal in this way by a pound of fissile material, but a comparison of the known intensity of radiation from the fission products with the maximum safe dosage of radium rays allowed in medicine shows that the area must be extremely large.

A recent statement by political scientist Ernest Oppenheimer[36] suggests that the efficacy of radioactive poisons may be rated very high in America. Under the title "The Fallacy of Preventive War," Mr. Oppenheimer suggests that U.S. air squadrons could "eradicate more than forty million people" by an attack on the U.S.S.R. Now it hardly seems likely that this could be done with plutonium bombs, for the number required would be vast. Taking the *average* expected casualties as equal to those at Nagasaki, that is, 40,000 killed per bomb, one would need 1,000 bombs delivered at their targets. Allowing for the reduction in casualties due to the use of shelters, evacuation, etc., and for the number of bombs which would inevitably fail to find their target at all, and remembering that many of the targets would be quite small cities with many less than 40,000 people in them, the number of bombs which would have to be dispatched to kill forty million people surely exceeds by a wide margin the actual number which America could have available for many years. Mr. Oppenheimer is, however, discussing an imaginary preventive war within a few years, so it seems that he must be assuming some other atomic weapon than actual plutonium bombs. And this could hardly be other than the use of radioactive poisons.

This interpretation is confirmed by a later passage in which he imagines that Russia might reply to such an atomic attack by launching a bacterial attack on the U.S.A. Referring to both attacks he writes: "Consequently, Americans may die of plague while Russians die from radioactivity"—not, one notices, "from atomic

[35] See, for instance, J. R. Menke, "Nuclear Fission as a Source of Power," *Econometrica 15*, 1947, p. 314. Reprinted in *B.A.S.*, April, 1948.
[36] Ernest Oppenheimer, *B.A.S.*, Dec., 1947.

bombs." This seems clear evidence that what Mr. Oppenheimer had in mind was not an atomic bomb attack on the U.S.S.R., but an attack with radioactive poisons. If this is the correct interpretation, it is necessary to suppose that radioactive poisons must be credited in America with many times the specific lethality of atomic bombs.

All these considerations are, of course, still very speculative, as difficult technical problems have clearly to be solved before such a weapon can be used operationally. The two main problems would appear to be the handling and carrying in a piloted aircraft of such intense sources of radiation—the actual material would clearly have to be screened by heavy absorbers from the crew—and the dissemination of the material in a suitable way over the target area. Assuming, however, that these technical problems will be solved, we must envisage the possibility that America might soon possess a weapon very many times more lethal than the present atomic bombs. Some of the problems involved in its use are discussed in later chapters.

6. STRATEGIC CONSEQUENCES OF THE ATOMIC BOMB

THE analysis of the previous chapters, incomplete and tentative in some respects though it has been, has given us a basis for the discussion of the real strategic situation in the world today, and of the effect on it of the possession by one or more major powers of large numbers of atomic bombs. In any such further analysis, it is essential to take into account all the relevant military, political and social factors as accurately as possible.

We can start, as we did in the last chapter, with the almost unchallengeable thesis that the only war in which there is the least likelihood of atomic bombs being used as weapons of mass destruction within the next ten years is one in which the Soviet Union and the United States of America are the main contestants. For in no war between two smaller Powers would atomic bombs be used, for fear of the reaction of one or the other of these two giant Powers. And in a war between a giant Power and a smaller Power, clearly atomic bombs would not generally be used, at any rate as weapons of mass destruction, since the giant Power would prefer to take over a relatively undamaged country. So it will be well to begin our analysis with a discussion of the possibilities of an atomic bomb attack by the Soviet Union on America, or by America on the Soviet Union.

From the figures already given, it is clear that, even if Russia thought it a sound policy to drop bombs on America, she would certainly consider that it would be essential to accumulate a minimum stock pile of a few thousand before starting. Now the magnitude of the technical and industrial problems of producing bombs makes it likely that it will be many years before the Soviet Union will possess a large enough stock pile of atomic bombs to be useful against American cities. So, on this ground alone, an atomic attack on the U.S.A. by the U.S.S.R. is in the highest degree unlikely for very many years. The next question to be answered is how the U.S.S.R. would deliver them. In the heated imagination of the enthusiasts for atomic warfare, it would only be necessary for thousands of long-range atomic bombers to take off secretly from airfields within the Soviet Union to destroy the main cities of America within a few hours. We know now that the facts are different. Even if Russia at an early stage of such an imagined war had occupied the countries of Western Europe—a far from unlikely contingency if they were allies of America—she would still have no bases from which to launch effectively such an attack. Till 1960 or so, we can exclude the technical possibility of an effective and sustained Russian atomic bomb attack across the Atlantic or across the North Pole. The possibility of an attack across the Pacific from the Soviet Far Eastern Territories is equally unfeasible. Though the distance to the western seaboard is smaller, the Soviet advanced air bases would be extremely vulnerable to American counter-attack with atomic bombs.

These technical considerations do not rule out the possibility of occasional sneak raids on American cities, particularly on the coast, by one-way "suicide bombers"; but such operations would be unlikely to have any decisive military importance. Another technical possibility is that special submarines might be built to carry, say, a weapon of the VI type with an atomic war-head. In theory, such a submarine could proceed largely submerged, through the use of hydrogen peroxide fuel, to a suitable distance from the American coast, where it would surface and launch its weapon against a large city near the coast. But this again could hardly be considered a decisive method of waging war, except perhaps as a prelude for invasion.

One must now inquire what reasons the Soviet Government would have for launching an atomic attack on America. One can find none. In the first place, we have seen in Chapter 2 that the Soviet military authorities have neither in theory nor practice espoused the use of weapons of mass destruction against civilian populations as a method of waging war. Their military theory, as will be shown by further quotations in Chapter 12, explicitly repudiates the notion that wars can be won by the use of single weapons; it holds that they must be fought out by the coordinated use of all arms. Their military and political spokesmen are never tired of pointing out that it was Hitler's conception that major wars can be won by blitzkrieg methods that brought about his downfall. Therefore it seems improbable that Russia would plan an attack on America, except as part of a coordinated offensive with all arms, which must necessarily include invasion. Since a Soviet invasion of America is militarily impossible, an atomic bomb attack is very unlikely.

Even if Russia controlled the whole of Europe including Great Britain, the invasion of America across the Atlantic would require an enormous amount of shipping to carry the millions-strong invasion force required, and further would be extremely easy to repulse since complete air superiority would rest with the defenders.

If the Russian leaders believed that all Americans were politically beyond redemption—and their politico-military thesis involves the hope of winning at least a section of the industrial workers to their side—the purely military arguments against the attack on American civilian populations with atomic bombs would still be overwhelming. For, if used by Russia against America, they must be indecisive. Even if the technical possibility of destroying American cities from European bases is much higher than we have here estimated, such destruction, not followed up by invasion and occupation, would leave America time to recuperate and rearm, bitterly determined to take eventual revenge. Further, such action would alienate world opinion and tend to solidify a grand alliance against Russia. The first Russian atomic bomb that fell on an American city would be a decisive political success for the enemies of Russia all over the world. The lesson of Pearl Harbor is clear. To strike a heavy but indecisive blow at a powerful enemy, without possessing the resources to follow it up by invasion and occupation of the homeland, is to court ultimate disaster.

In the later stages of a long and bitterly fought war between America and Russia, it is not possible to predict whether or not Russia might use bombs against American cities, provided that the technical means of landing them there were available; but, even in this case, the arguments given above make it more likely that the targets would be specific military and industrial establishments, rather than built-up urban areas.

It must, of course, be remembered that atomic bombs are not at all suitable for many actual targets owing to their large area of destruction. For instance, the 600,000 tons of ordinary bombs dropped on France by Anglo-American aircraft, could in very few cases have been replaced by atomic bombs, since the targets, factories, transportation targets, etc., were far too near built-up areas. Atomic bombs would have killed far too many of our allies to have been usable. The same situation will inevitably recur in future wars, and sets a severe limitation on their use.

Even if our analysis is at fault, and atomic bomb attacks against cities are a cheaper way of winning a war against a continental Power than we have held probable, there is still the consideration of the subsequent burden on the occupying Power of the destruction of enemy cities and industry, as we are finding today in Germany. If to the cost of defeating a major Power is added the cost of the subsequent occupation, weapons of mass destruction may appear less cheap than is often held.

No sober appraisal can, however, rule out the use by the Americans of atomic bombs against Russian towns in the initial stages of a war. Apart from loose talk in America about "preventive war," there are substantial reasons which have to be weighed. The first lies in the fact that America has already access to bases from which certain parts of Russia could perhaps be effectively attacked—the Donetz Basin and Baku, from Turkey or North Africa; Vladivostok from Japan; Leningrad from Western Germany, Iceland or Greenland. Rockets would be of little use, owing to their short range; but the relevant distances are not perhaps beyond effective bomber range with large numbers of aircraft, even against heavy defenses. Thus the technical possibilities of an atomic bomb attack by America on Russia are considerably greater than the converse operation.

The second reason is that American opinion, both military and civilian, in marked contrast with Russian, seems to have accepted the use of tactics of mass destruction as a normal operation of war.

That such attacks are envisaged by the American Army is implicit in very many statements, and is made particularly clear in the following passage from the War Department document already mentioned:

> Our present strategy recognizes the overriding importance of strategic bombing. . . . It is our belief now that strategic bombardment either by piloted aircraft or by guided missiles of one form or another provides the single most important element of our military capabilities . . . (B.A.S., June, 1947)

Since guided missiles at ranges which can be called strategic have certainly not the precision to successfully attack small targets, the implication that the intended targets are the civilian population of cities is clear.

Of primary importance in this connection is the constant concern shown by thoughtful Americans over the problem of how their country can shoulder the responsibilities and reap the advantage of a Great Power without being prepared to fight overseas with major land forces. This, for instance, is well brought out by Brodie,[1] in his discussion of the type of armed forces required by a Great Power possessing atomic bombs.

> It is obvious that the force set apart for invasion or counter-invasion purposes will be relatively small, completely professional,

and trained to the uttermost. But there must also be a very large force ready to resist and defeat invasion by the enemy. Here is the place for the citizen army, though it too must be comprised of trained men.

Dr. Brodie apparently believes that a major Power such as Russia would be so devastated by an attack of atomic bombs, launched, say, by America, that a small invasion force would be all that was required for the subsequent occupation. Mr. Bullitt, formerly U.S. Ambassador at Moscow, is even more explicit.[2] "Thanks to the possession of the atomic bomb and an air force of overwhelming strength, we are today far stronger than the Soviet Union and could destroy it."

The constant preoccupation, noticeable in America, with the problem of how to minimize American casualties in any future war, leads naturally to the conception of mechanized war with a small number of highly trained troops using the maximum equipment in arms and machines. This conception fits in with the mechanical genius of the American nation, which has already, in the industrial field, achieved such great success by the replacement of human labor by power-driven machines. And great military successes were undoubtedly achieved during the war by a high degree of mechanization of warfare.

The sensitivity of American opinion to war casualties is revealed by the remark in General Marshall's report on the war:[3] "Staggering as our casualties have been, the enemy forces opposing us suffered many times as heavily." In fact, American casualties were very light. The total American battle deaths in the second World War were only about three times the road deaths in America during the same period, and, expressed as a fraction of the population, only a third of the deaths in the Civil War.

The atomic bomb appears to be the climax of this evolution toward "push-button war." Though many authoritative statements have been made discounting the possibility of "push-button war," clearly the possibility exercises a great fascination for many Americans. To be more concrete, the atomic bomb is seen in many British

---

[1] Brodie in *The Absolute Weapon*, p. 94.
[2] William C. Bullitt, *The Great Globe Itself* (New York, 1946).
[3] General George C. Marshall, *The Winning of the War in Europe and the Pacific*, p. 128 (New York, 1945).

and American circles as the answer to the power of the Soviet armies, and the only answer that does not seem to involve large overseas military commitments. If not the atomic bomb, then "What else?" These arguments are reminiscent of those used in England in the dark days of 1940 to justify the launching of the strategic bombing offensive in Germany. Fear of heavy losses in a land campaign in Europe—Passchendaele was still a bitter memory—was one of the main driving forces behind the Bomber Offensive. With the German Colossus bestriding Europe, it was difficult to find another answer to the question: "What else?"

Whatever its origin, there is no doubt that there is a large body of opinion in America which assumes that weapons of mass destruction have become the natural weapons of war. Combining the existence of this belief with the technical possibility of launching such an attack on the U.S.S.R. from bases in Turkey, Japan or Western Europe, it is necessary to consider the possibility that in the event of war breaking out, America might begin her offensive with an atomic bomb attack on Russian cities.

Though, judging by the press, such a move would be widely accepted in many American circles as a natural one, it might well be opposed by the armed services for very strong military reasons. For the military, who after all have the responsibility of carrying through such a war to a successful conclusion, cannot fail to ask: "What happens next?" They have to think calmly and objectively of what the Soviet armies would do, and with what speed and in what strength and in which direction they would move. The American Chiefs of Staff would be studying the problem of how to meet such moves, and with what troops. Some armchair strategists (including some atomic scientists) tend to ignore the inevitable counter-moves of the enemy. More chess-playing and less nuclear physics might have instilled a greater sense of the realities.

It is clear that to any sustained atomic bomb attack on Russia within the next decade, there are possible Russian counter-measures, mainly with land forces, which would have the object of capturing the bases from which the atomic bombers were operating, or if this were not possible, of neutralizing them as far as possible by pushing forward her air-defense zone.

79

If the country in which the bomb bases were situated was close to or bordering on Russia, for instance Sweden or Persia, then it would expect immediate armed attack by land forces. If, however, the bases were far from Russia, with perhaps a neutral country in between, the outcome is difficult to estimate in general terms. If Russian air defense within her own territory were very efficient, and if the intervening country asserted her intention to remain strictly neutral in the conflict, then it is quite possible that it would be to Russia's advantage to respect her neutrality, as both contestants did that of Sweden and Switzerland in the last two World Wars. In so far, however, as the determination and ability of the intervening nation to prevent her country from being used as an atomic bomb base were in doubt, so would an attack by Russia become more probable. In certain circumstances, Russia might demand only air-defense facilities, such as the setting up of radar stations and fighter airfields in the intervening country; such a demand would be analogous to the Allied use of Persia and Egypt in the last war. If Russia possessed atomic bombs at the time, they would surely be used in the first instance to attack such targets as air bases and other military objectives rather than to attack American cities, even if this were feasible.

The American Chiefs of Staff would be concerned with the problems: (a) how to get the requisite American military strength to the spots likely to be threatened by a Russian counter-stroke, and (b) how to insure the greatest possible assistance from the military forces of the countries which must provide the bases. These preparations must clearly be made before the atom bombs are launched, if they are to have a reasonable chance of being successful. For Russia, in this situation, possesses the interior, and so shorter, lines of communication. Now no one, least of all the British and American military authorities, and in particular Secretary of State Marshall, with their vivid memories of the logistic problems behind the invasion of North Africa in 1942, of Normandy in 1944, and the plan for the invasion of Japan in 1945, can have any illusion that the preparation to throw major Anglo-American units into, say, Scandinavia, Western Europe or the Middle East, would be anything but a vast task and one that would be almost impossible to conceal in peace time. Once such preparations were detected by the U.S.S.R. one might expect counter-moves, perhaps overt, perhaps with tactics difficult to counter without precipitating prematurely the final clash.

It is not necessary to pursue this analysis further. Enough has been said to show convincingly the very obvious truth—though a truth somewhat obscured by a wave of inaccurate and superficial reasoning based on the destructive power of the atomic bomb—that a war between America and Russia would be of world-wide extent and would be a war of all arms, and probably of very long duration. The first World War lasted four years; the second, in spite of the technical advances—or perhaps *because* of them—lasted nearly six years.

The obvious and inevitable Soviet answer to the clearly expounded views of the American fighting services on the value of strategic bombing is to ensure by all possible means that her effective military frontiers are pushed as far away from the Russian homeland as possible. There is no need to seek ideological motives, however much these may or may not have been present, to explain recent events in the Eastern European countries bordering on Russia. The possession of atomic bombs by America, and the implicit threat of their use against the U.S.S.R., provided sufficient, even though not the only motive, for the consolidation of Poland, Czechoslovakia, Hungary, Rumania, Bulgaria and Yugoslavia within the Russian sphere of interest, and for the Soviet's apparent determination to maintain her influence in Austria and Eastern Germany.

Far apart as they are politically, Henry Wallace and Walter Lippmann have expressed similar views on this question. The former wrote, in his "Letter to the President," in 1946:

> There is a school of military thinking which recognizes these facts, recognizes that when several nations have atomic bombs, a war which will destroy modern civilization will result and that no nation can win such a war. This school of thought therefore advocates a "preventive war," an attack on Russia now before Russia has atomic bombs. This scheme is not only immoral but stupid. If we should attempt to destroy all the principal Russian cities and her heavy industry, we might well succeed. But the immediate countermeasure which such an attack would call for is the prompt occupation of all

continental Europe by the Red Army. Would we be prepared to destroy the cities of all Europe in trying to finish what we started? This idea is so contrary to all the basic instincts and principles of the American people that any such action would be possible only under a dictatorship at home.

Walter Lippmann wrote in the same year:

> No atomic bombardment could destroy the Red Army; it could destroy only the industrial means of supplying it. The Russian defense to atomic attack is, therefore, self-evident; it is to over-run continental Europe with infantry, and defy us to drop atomic bombs on Poland, Czechoslovakia, Austria, Switzerland, France, Belgium, the Netherlands and Sweden. The more we threaten to demolish Russian cities, the more obvious it is that the Russian defense would be to ensconce themselves in European cities which we could not demolish without massacring hundreds of thousands of our own friends.

Though these two statements bring out clearly one aspect of the dilemma facing American military policy, it is by no means certain that the American General Staff would share the scruples of Mr. Wallace and Mr. Lippmann about bombing the cities of her "friends." On the contrary, what seems quite likely is that any nation accessible to Russian attack which offered base facilities to American atomic bombers would first be overrun by the Russian armies and then would have her cities attacked by American atomic bombs.

One could criticize also the assumption of both statements that Russia would immediately occupy all neutral European countries, even if this was militarily possible. For the occupation of a country would bring a big drain on Russian manpower and so would do serious harm to her economy. It would therefore only be done if it was militarily essential, that is, to prevent the country from being used as a base, or in certain circumstances to advance her fighter defense zone.

Returning to the question of the possible effects of an American atomic attack on Russia, we note that even the destruction of all the major cities of Russia would not impair the striking power of the Soviet armies until many months had elapsed. For even at the height of a major war, and still more so in a well-prepared country at the outset of a war, the time that elapses between the manufacture of arms and their delivery to the fighting troops, amounts to many months. That the destruction of cities would not necessarily interrupt for long their use as railway centers is clear from what happened in Hiroshima. "The railroads running through the city were repaired for the resumption of traffic on August 8, two days after the attack."[4] That military staffs and essential government facilities and personnel would not be evacuated from large cities before such an attack took place, is not to be credited.

One further possibility must be mentioned. America might attempt an atomic bomb attack on Russia from aircraft carriers in the North Sea, Arctic Sea and Mediterranean. However, the figures we have given for the number of atomic bombs required to have an important effect in a major war combined with the relatively small numbers of sorties that could be made from carriers by aircraft large enough to carry atomic bombs the requisite distance, show that such operations could not possibly be of much strategic significance.

The general conclusions of this section will be seen later to have great importance in connection with the operation of sanctions against possible violations of an atomic energy control system.

In the military thinking of the United States, the acquisition of adequate far-flung bases is continually being stressed, and from a military point of view, correctly so. For instance, we read that the Navy Department's view, in relation to the possible use of V2 types of weapons, is:[5]

> What is necessary to reach the target is a launching base relatively near the target—to put it literally, within five hundred miles. . . . Under the conditions of war in which atomic bombs are available to a possible enemy, the importance of depriving the enemy of bases near one's own shore and preferably of acquiring and maintaining bases close to his territory remains as great as before. The logic supporting this proposition derives from the characteristics of atomic bomb carriers presently known or conceivable. . . . The outlying base, if properly placed, is also a tremendous advantage to the defense as a further measure of protection against long-range bombing aircraft. For such bases provide means of advance protection and interception which greatly augments the obstacles to penetration of vital territories by attacking bombers. These bases may themselves be

[4] *U.S.S.B.S.* *4*, p. 24.
[5] "Navy Department Thinking on the Atomic Bomb," *B.A.S.*, July, 1947.

vulnerable to atomic bomb attack, but so long as they are there, they are not likely to be by-passed. In this respect the advanced base may be likened to the pawns in front of the king on a chess-board; meager though their power may be individually, so long as they exist and the king stays severely behind them, he is safe.

This is impeccable American military logic. But Britain, France and Scandinavia may object to being "pawns" on the American chessboard.

Where the Navy thinking needs amplification, the Army thinking provides it:[6]

> From a political point of view then, of vital importance to counteract our loss of the cushion of time is a need for allies. We cannot stand alone in the world today, if for no other reason, for lack of strength to do so. . . . The shock of a powerful aggressor, with modern weapons, including the atomic bomb, can better be absorbed by a number of nations than by a single nation. The ability to retaliate promptly, and eventually to overcome the aggressor, likewise, is dependent, if success is to be reasonably certain, on bases, resources, and forces dispersed in more than one nation.

No easy criticism can be levelled at this clear statement of a military truism. Britain clearly is in a fix, destined by American military thought to provide the essential "cushion in time" by absorbing the atomic bombs.

It is immediately clear that if England were an ally of America in a war with Russia, and if Russian forces held the Channel coast, then the technical possibility would exist for Russia to destroy London and the southern cities of England with rockets even carrying only ordinary explosives, though we have given reasons for believing that it is not very likely that Russia would in fact do so. Even a heavy attack on Russian cities by American atomic bombers would not by itself serve to prevent such an attack; the only adequate defense would be, as in 1944, an invasion of the Continent and the capture of the launching sites.

On the other hand, if Great Britain adopted a policy of armed neutrality and was prepared to oppose by force the attempts of either major contestant to occupy the country and use it as a base against the other, then it is very probable that she would be success-

[6] "The Effect of the Atomic Bomb on National Security," *B.A.S.*, June, 1947.

ful. For the occupation of Great Britain would not be a major objective to either side, but only a subsidiary operation preliminary to the waging of a further campaign against the other. Though America might rate very highly the value of atomic bomb bases in England, the invasion of England by American forces is improbable on many grounds. Equally a Russian invasion from Europe would be a highly formidable task against a determined defense and the complete command of the air over the coast line which would almost certainly be held by the R.A.F. Moreover, Russia would gain very little, if any, strategic advantage by occupying England, if she were already in control of most of Western Europe.

It is necessary to discuss in a little more detail the probable nature of a war in which America and Western Europe together fought Russia and Eastern Europe. If one discounts the possibility—and all our calculations have shown that we must discount it—that an initial atomic bomb attack would cause Russia to capitulate, then it is certain that such a war would be fought out in Europe on land, as were the last two World Wars. Clearly the French military staff must attempt to obtain a hard-and-fast guarantee of military aid in the form of so many divisions of American and British troops within so many days of the outbreak of war. If they did not do this, they would have to stand nearly alone, as in 1914 and 1940, against the assault of a much stronger land power. Clearly, therefore, preparation for *land* warfare would have to dominate the military programs of France and England, even if not of America. In such a war America would, presumably, use her stock of atomic bombs against Russia from bases in France and England, leaving the first months of the land battle to be fought by European troops. If such a war occurred after Russia had acquired a stock pile of atomic bombs, these would be used, presumably, in the first instance against air bases and military establishments in France and England, and only in certain special circumstances against cities as such. But at any rate it is clear that at the outset of such a war, France and England would both have to do the major part of the land fighting and become the target for atomic bombs, while America prepared to throw major forces into Europe.

This unpleasant prospect for France and Britain would be altered if America, in peacetime, installed many tens of divisions in

Europe, so as to be on the spot if war did break out. But this policy raises such exceedingly difficult political problems both in Europe and America that it is rather unlikely to be followed.

If a war of this type did occur, acute controversy would be certain to arise between the military staff of America, on the one hand, and France and England on the other, as to the advisability of the use of Anglo-French bases for attacks on Russian cities by American atomic bombers. For, if that happened, England and France would expect to get atom-bombed—not America. And the military staffs of both European countries would certainly be made aware by their political colleagues of the difficulty of convincing the public of each country that such a role was a reasonable one for their countries to undertake.

We have expressed the view that, both for military and political reasons, the U.S.S.R. is much less likely to initiate an atomic attack upon European and American cities than the U.S.A. is likely to use them against Russian cities. There are, however, clearly circumstances in which it might prove so advantageous militarily to the Soviet High Command to use atomic bombs against British cities that they would probably do so in spite of their general repudiation of weapons of mass destruction. If the United Kingdom was providing the base for an atomic bomb attack on Russian cities, and if the Soviet forces were not in a position to stop this by a quick and successful invasion of England, the Soviet High Command would have to consider what other means existed of stopping the Allied atomic bomb offensive. No doubt the first attacks would be on port facilities, airbases, etc.; but, if these failed, mass attacks on cities might follow. But this imaginary situation brings into vivid relief the limitation of weapons of mass destruction. For the destruction of London and other British cities would not by itself quickly stop American or British aircraft using British airfields as advanced refueling bases, though after a time it might do so owing to the interruption of the transport system, by which the bases were supplied with fuel. The only possible way by which such attacks could be stopped quickly would be for the British people themselves to take steps to stop the attacks being made from British bases. In these circumstances, it seems unlikely that Russia would, even if she could, drop atomic bombs on London.

The lesson of the bombing of North Italian cities by Allied planes in 1943 should be remembered. After the fall of Mussolini the Italian Partisans with support and encouragement of the Allies were very active in the north of Italy. When they expected more help and arms, they had their cities bombed.

Again, from the British standpoint, it is clear that atomic bombs would be most useful tactical weapons to be used against the assembly and assault of an enemy invasion force. To use atomic bombs in this way would be effective militarily and free from the disadvantage of making atomic attacks on British cities much more likely.

In general, one can consider it probable that atomic bombs would not be used in a European war against European cities by a nation with strong land forces which could expect to capture the cities intact.

Very similar arguments apply to other weapons of mass destruction, such as biological warfare and the use of radioactive poisons. These are still more indiscriminate in their effects even than atomic bombs and so would be unsuitable weapons for a strong land Power which expected to invade its enemy's territories, but might more likely be used by a weak Power as a desperate weapon against a strong Power.

The conclusions of this and previous chapters stand in striking contrast with the thesis, so energetically argued in many circles, that there is no defense against atomic bombs. Purely qualitative statements of this kind are usually misleading, and must be replaced by more quantitative statements. Of course, there are strategic situations in which atomic bombs would certainly have decisive results; but this is also true of other weapons too. It is equally certain that there are strategic situations in which atomic bombs would not be decisive, and it is undeniable that the only important war with the possibility of which the world is now faced is one of them. In anticipation of such a war, both America and Russia are now taking defense measures. On the Russian side, an important part of her defensive measure consists mainly in extending the depth of her defense system by pushing her effective military frontiers as far away from the essential area of her homeland as possible. While on the other hand, American steps include the gaining of bases as near as possible to the Russian homeland.[7] These reciprocal steps constitute the present cold war.

It may be useful, finally, to return again to the question: what is the order of magnitude of the number of atomic bombs which would be required to play a decisive part, along, of course, with other arms, in a major war between continental Powers. What we need is a way of estimating the bombing effort necessary to inflict a given amount of damage on a country of a given area and population. All will agree that to inflict on America or Russia an industrial dislocation comparable to that which was actually inflicted on Germany by the bombing offensive, would require a much greater weight of bombs. The question is: "How much greater?"

We can safely assume that the number of atomic bombs required to produce decisive military results will increase with the area and population of the country under attack. Remembering that 1.3 million tons of ordinary bombs were dropped on Germany during the second World War without decisive result, and assuming that some 400 improved atomic bombs would be required to produce the same material destruction, it is certain that the number of atomic bombs required to produce decisive results in a war between America and Russia would run into thousands.[8]

It is useful to compare the areas and population of Germany in 1939 and Russia and America in 1947 (See Table, page 89).

One important and quite certain deduction is that a small number of atomic bombs, say, a few dozen, are likely to be of little military significance if used for mass destruction in a war between two major Powers. This fact has a great significance in relation to the problems of control of atomic energy as it makes the possibility of diversion of small quantities of fissile materials from atomic energy plants of far less danger than is often imagined by those

[7] See, for instance, General Arnold's pre-atomic bomb view. "Air power must be employed from fully equipped strategically located bases. Our air forces must be able to meet and overpower the aggressor's air threat as near as possible to its source."

[8] Coale states that in the event of failure of attempts to get international control, "the United States will begin (or continue) constructing atomic bombs at the maximum rate. A reasonable conjecture is that bombs could be made at the rate of hundreds a year." Dr. Oppenheimer is quoted as saying that it would take about two years to accumulate one thousand bombs if the country knew how to make them, and started with peacetime atomic plants.

Country	Area (sq. miles)	Population (millions)
United Kingdom	94,000	48
Germany	180,000	66
U.S.A.	3,020,000	132
U.S.S.R., European	1,490,000 }	{ about
Asiatic	6,750,000 }	{ 200

who have not studied the effect of the bombing offensive on Germany.

Much of the earlier discussion of atomic bombs and their effect on warfare and of the requirements of an effective control system seems to have been vitiated by an exaggerated idea of the military results of a few bombs dropped on the civilian population of cities. Derivative from this was the consideration of the danger of "secret war," in which agents would plant atomic bombs in another country during peace time. In a memorandum written in 1945 intended for President Roosevelt, Dr. Leo Szilard[9] wrote: "Russia may [soon] have accumulated enough of some fissile elements for constructing atomic bombs. . . . Clearly, if such bombs are available, it is not necessary to bomb our cities from the air to destroy them. All that is necessary is to place a comparatively small number of such bombs in each of our ten major cities and to detonate them at some later time." In such discussions there is seldom any mention of the object behind such an action, or of what the supposed aggressor would do next. Another example[10] of such over-abstracted discussion is the following: "Would the United States concede victory to the enemy if ten of its principal cities were wiped off the map? And if not ten cities, then how many?" It is the belief of the writer that this type of thinking, so abstracted from the real world with its real wars for real ends, has done a great deal to bedevil the issue of what type of control system is required, by implying that major wars can be won by a few atomic bombs. Not only does it lead to exaggeration of the danger of "secret war," but it also leads to far too much emphasis on the danger, or efficacy, as the case may be, of very long flights by

[9] B.A.S., Dec., 1947, p. 351.
[10] Lapp, B.A.S., Feb., 1948.

small numbers of aircraft. On the other hand, too little emphasis seems to have been given to the value of atomic bombs as tactical weapons. Admittedly the occasions in which they would be useful may not arise very often, but when they do, a relatively few atomic bombs might have important effects. These considerations lead to the view that relatively few atomic bombs would bring considerable added military power to a nation which was already very strong in conventional armaments, in particular in land forces whereas a very large number of bombs would not add decisively to the military power of a nation deficient in conventional armaments and land armies, since the lack of power of follow-up drastically limits their value.

A final matter of importance that requires discussion is the effect of a threat of atomic bombing on the civilian population of a major country. At the outset of a war in which atomic bombs were likely to be used, the major cities of a country expecting attack would be largely evacuated. If the government had made no preparations, the evacuation would take on a spontaneous character. The immediate effect would be to bring industry and business in large centers to a standstill. This might have definite military value to the possessors of the bombs provided it could be maintained. But, if no bombs were dropped, the population would start to drift back and could be kept from doing so only by the actual dropping of at least a few bombs on a few cities, assuming of course that the means to do so were available. By this means, that is, by the sporadic dropping of a bomb every now and then on a city, the productive life of a nation might be considerably reduced. But this in itself is a by no means decisive result, as all the experience of the last war shows, unless the nation attacked is already fully extended militarily and productively. As a part, however, of a long-drawn-out campaign of invasion of one country by another, such a continued threat might bring some dividends in reduced production without the disadvantage of destroying all the cities which the armies expected to capture.

If the object is the killing of as many civilians as possible, as in some accounts was the case in Japan, then surprise is essential, for evacuation would reduce casualties very greatly. The continual assertion in America that surprise attacks on the U.S.A. are what is most feared, implies the assumption that the object of the attack would be to kill civilians, rather than to do physical destruction, which can equally well be done by bombing an evacuated city.

7. THE ATOMIC BOMB AND THE UNITED NATIONS ORGANIZATION

THE arguments of the last chapter allow us to approach the problem of whether the invention of atomic bombs demands a new type of United Nations Organization. One view, which has been much propagated, is that the atomic bomb has put into the hands of the United Nations a weapon of such power as to make possible the application of sanctions to a Great Power without precipitating a major war, whereas before the invention of the atomic bomb this was not so. This view was clearly derived from the belief, which gained wide currency in the months following the dropping of the two bombs, that wars against Great Powers could be won by quite small armed forces, provided these forces were provided with an adequate supply of atomic bombs.

A clear statement of this view is found in an article by Dr. Arthur H. Compton:[1]

Now for the first time also it becomes feasible for a central authority to enforce peace throughout the world. Before the second World War, many parts of the earth were difficult of access by a world police. Today this is changed. Fast airplanes, long-range rockets and atomic bombs have now solved the technical problem of bringing to bear on any area at any time, whatever destructive force may be required to quell resistance. A central authority having virtual monopoly of these major means of warfare can now be equipped to enforce international peace.

The fact is that the United States now has in its possession a sufficient monopoly of the weapons needed for such policing that it might be able to act in this capacity of world police. That Americans do not set themselves up as the world governors is simply because they do not want the job. They feel that world control is the world's business, not theirs alone.

[1] Substance of an address before the American Philosophical Society and National Academy of Science on November 11, 1945. Reprinted in *Nature*, London, Feb., 1946.

Though less is heard of this thesis now, it may be worthwhile to follow the arguments through to their conclusion.

One variant of the views of those who wish to revise the Charter is that the UN itself should possess a long-range atomic bombing force to subdue any offending member, either by threat of having its cities destroyed or, if recalcitrant, by their actual destruction. In addition, presumably the UN would also be provided with a small but highly trained army to occupy the country after its surrender.

The facts and figures given in the former chapter show the absurdity of all such views. A great nation cannot be kept in order by small armed forces even if such forces are provided with atomic bombs. For the application of sanctions on a Great Power, it would clearly be necessary for the UN to prepare for a major war of all arms, involving millions of trained men, and the industrial backing of some Great Power. Since the UN itself cannot possess such resources, these must be provided by the member nations. We are therefore back at the point where those who drafted the Charter of the United Nations in 1945 started from: that the UN itself cannot be a super-power, but must be an association of existing Powers. The atomic bomb has not altered this.

The next view to consider is that which admits that the UN itself cannot possess sufficient armed forces to apply sanctions against any Power, but that an alliance of the majority of the member States could bring an overwhelming superiority of armed might against any recalcitrant Power, so as to induce capitulation without war, or to defeat it quickly and cheaply in the case of war being necessary. It is obvious that this proposition is true in all cases where the offending Power is relatively weak and isolated; but it was also true in these circumstances before atomic bombs were invented. There never has been any difficulty, in principle, of keeping weak isolated nations in order.

The real problem arises when the offending nation is either a Great Power, or, what amounts to much the same thing, is a small Power backed by a Great Power. The answer then of course depends on the relative strength of two contesting camps. If we consider the application of sanctions as only possible when there is such overwhelming superiority on the side of the majority as to force the offending nation either to capitulate without war or to defeat her quickly if armed action is necessary, then if sanctions are applied against a major Power without these conditions being fulfilled, the effect of the attempt to inflict sanctions will be to precipitate a major war.

In the actual present world situation, the problems of the application of sanctions by the UN boils down to one problem only. Can sanctions be imposed on Russia? For no one imagines that there is at present any actual grouping of Powers which would be both able and willing to impose armed sanctions on America.

To investigate whether sanctions could be imposed on Russia, it is convenient to consider first the situation that will arise when the U.S.S.R., as well as America, has a stock of atomic bombs, even though a much smaller stock. For the purpose of our discussion we assumed this period to start in about five years. Leaving out of account the possibility of major changes in the political orientation and internal strength of the various Powers, we can be quite certain that under these circumstances sanctions could not be inflicted on Russia without precipitating a major war. In particular, the tactical value to Russia of atomic bombs or weapons for this counter-attack on the military bases from which she was being threatened, would make her defensive position very strong.

Even in the period before Russia acquires a stock pile of bombs, that is, on our assumption, till 1953, the conclusion that sanctions cannot be imposed on Russia without precipitating a major war is almost equally clear. There is room for argument as to what the final outcome of the attempt to impose them might be; but there can be none as to the conclusion that Russia would neither capitulate without fighting, nor be quickly and cheaply defeated. The detailed military consideration which we have been concerned with in the previous chapter has shown that a war in which America and many Western Powers were ranged against Russia and her Eastern allies would certainly not be a short and cheap war but, on the contrary, would be of long duration, and be extremely expensive to both sides in men and material; and this is true in spite of our assumption that Russia would have no atomic bombs. We conclude, therefore, that sanctions against Russia almost certainly could not be applied. The problem of maintaining peace in the world, though made more urgent by the invention of atomic bombs, has not essentially changed its character.

Under the Charter of the United Nations, the Security Council is charged with the responsibility of ensuring that action by way of economic or military pressure, including the actual waging of war, is taken against a nation which disturbs the peace. The relevant clauses governing the voting of such sanctions are the following:

Article 27

1. Each member of the Security Council shall have one vote.
2. Decisions of the Security Council on procedural matters shall be made by an affirmative vote of seven members.
3. Decisions of the Security Council on all other matters shall be made by an affirmative vote of seven members including the concurring votes of the permanent members.

The method of application of sanctions, for which the unanimity rule of the permanent members, as laid down in Article 27, Paragraph 3 above applies, is described in Articles 42 and 43:

Article 42

Should the Security Council consider that measures provided for in Article 41 would be inadequate or have proved to be inadequate, it may take such action by air, sea or land forces as may be necessary to maintain, or restore, international peace and security. Such action may include demonstrations, blockade and other operations by air, sea or land forces of Members of the United Nations.

Article 43

1. All Members of the United Nations, in order to contribute to the maintenance of international peace and security, undertake to make available to the Security Council, on its call and in accordance with a special agreement or agreements, armed forces, assistance and facilities, including rights of passage, necessary for the purpose of maintaining international peace and security.
2. Such agreement or agreements shall govern the numbers and types of forces, their degree of readiness and general location, and the nature of the facilities and assistance to be provided.

The British publication entitled *A Commentary on the Charter* discusses as follows the question of what would happen if the attempt were made to oppose sanctions against a Great Power:

It is also clear that no enforcement action by the Organization can be taken against a Great Power itself without a major war. If such a situation arises, the United Nations will have failed in its purpose and all members will have to act as seems best in the circumstances.

Though the subject of acute controversy at the time, the rule that the application of sanctions can only be carried out if all permanent members of the Security Council (U.S.A., U.S.S.R., United Kingdom, France and China) are unanimous, was finally incorporated as a result of the realization that the attempt to apply the sanctions against a Great Power could only lead to a major war. This unanimity rule is an essential safeguard against the possibility that the United Nations Organization will be used to "legalize" a third world war. Whether or not the UN will in the future fulfill the hopes of mankind placed in it, there can be little doubt that it would have already collapsed, had not the unanimity rule existed. For on several different occasions in the last two years a majority of the Security Council would undoubtedly have been in favor of courses of action which the Soviet Union would have considered as impinging on her vital interests. If such measures had been passed, Russia would have had no option but to leave the UN. Thus, for good or ill, the continued existence of the UN depends on the maintenance of the unanimity rule. There is also reason to doubt whether the United States itself would have signed a charter that did not include the veto—except, that is, under circumstances in which she could be almost certainly guaranteed of the support on all important measures of an adequate majority of the members of the Security Council.

Whatever criticism may be levelled at the use made of the veto rule in minor disputes, as for instance by Russia over the mining of the Albanian coast, there is no possibility of doubt that a rule demanding the unanimity of the Great Powers—at least on matters relating to the imposition of sanctions, is an essential condition for the continued existence of the United Nations Organization.

The matter has been dealt with here[2] because of the great

[2] I have discussed this question more fully in a pamphlet entitled *The Atom and the Charter,* published jointly by the Fabian Society and the Association of Scientific Workers, in 1946.

significance of the proposals by the United States to abolish the veto in important matters relating to atomic energy. This will be discussed further in Chapter 11.

It is necessary here to draw attention to a recent and very important statement[3] to the House of Representatives Foreign Affairs Committee by Secretary Marshall, in which he argues strongly against any modification of the Charter. In the main his conclusions closely parallel those already given.

"A number of projects," said Mr. Marshall, "designed to improve international conditions by new forms of international organization have been proposed. These projects envisage radical changes in the existing United Nations Charter. Some people propose the elimination of the veto on enforcement measures." He went on to explain that those who put forward this view are apt to consider that the "present unsatisfactory state of world affairs is a result of inability on the part of the United Nations to prevent aggression; that this inability arises from the exercise of the veto power in the Security Council and lack of a United Nations police force; that if the veto power on enforcement decision could be removed and the United Nations provided with armed forces, aggression could be prevented and that the principal barrier to world peace would thereby cease to exist."

> The general assumption rests, I think, on an incomplete analysis of our main problems of foreign policy at this juncture and of the part which international organization can play in solving them. Let us not, in our impatience and our fears, sacrifice the hard won gains that we now possess in the United Nations Organization.

According to *The London Times,* "Mr. Marshall, who was questioned for over an hour by members of the Committee, returned again and again to his contention that an attempt in these critical days to alter the Charter would scatter fear throughout many countries." According to the report in the *Manchester Guardian,* Mr. Marshall said that the Senate would probably not have ratified the Charter if it had not granted the United States

[3] *Manchester Guardian* and *The London Times,* etc., May 6, 1948.

veto right with respect to combating acts of aggression—thus confirming our surmise. Marshall said he was in favor of abolition of the veto in pacific settlement of disputes, but the veto was necessary where acts of aggression were concerned. "We do not want our manpower and our strength committed by a two-thirds vote." As pointed out in Chapter 1, this statement by Marshall appears to be in conflict with official American policy, which still insists on the full Baruch plan and so on the abolition of the veto on all questions involving sanctions for violations of an atomic energy agreement.

8. POWER FROM ATOMIC ENERGY

THE main non-military applications of atomic energy at present in sight are of three kinds: (*a*) to produce radioactive elements for medical curative processes; (*b*) to produce radioactive tracer elements and radiations for use in scientific research and in industrial processes; and (*c*) to produce power and heat for industrial and domestic purposes.

Now these three aspects have a very different significance to different nations at different levels of industrial and technological development. For a nation already provided with adequate supplies of power for industrial and domestic purposes from coal, oil or water power, the main value of atomic energy may lie, or perhaps may seem in the short run to lie, in the very great advances which may be expected in many branches of the sciences, particularly chemistry and bio-chemistry, from the widespread availability of radioactive tracer elements. This view is expressed clearly by the authors of the Acheson-Lilienthal plan, who quote with approval the conclusion of a report by a panel of scientists[1] that: "It is probable that the exploration of atomic energy as a tool for research

[1] This panel included Arthur H. Compton, Enrico Fermi, Ernest O. Lawrence and J. R. Oppenheimer.

will outweigh the benefits to be derived from the availability of a new source of power." Though this may possibly eventually prove true, it is primarily the already highly industrialized nations which alone possess the necessary scientific and technological background to be able to make use of these new scientific and technical methods. In any case, there is no serious clash between the use of atomic energy for power and its use for research, since the latter requires only an infinitesimal output of energy. To a relatively unindustrialized nation, however, perhaps deficient in coal, oil and water power, but possessing supplies of uranium and thorium, the long-term possibilities of augmenting its power supplies by atomic energy plants, and so raising its standard of living and its industrial strength, must appear of the highest importance.

The theme that radioactive isotopes are more important than power goes back to the *Franck Report* of June, 1945. "The amounts of ore taken out of the ground could be controlled . . . and each nation allotted only an amount which would make large-scale separation of fissionable isotopes impossible . . . Such a limitation would have the drawbacks of making impossible also the development of nuclear power for peacetime purposes. However, it need not prevent the production of radioactive elements on a scale sufficient to revolutionize the industrial, scientific and technical use of these materials, and would thus *not eliminate the main benefits which nucleonics promises to bring to mankind*"[2] (Author's italics).

It is not always recognized how very intimately a modern nation's industrial strength, and so both its standard of living and its military potential, depends on the availability of power. Nor is it always remembered what an essential part the availability of cheap energy played in the emergence of the industrial system itself.

In a well-known analysis the economist Dr. L. Rostas[3] has shown that the productivity of a large group of American industries is about twice that of the same industries in Great Britain. It has further been shown that the greater efficiency of American industry is correlated with the fact that it has nearly twice as much

[2] *B.A.S.*, p. 2, May, 1946. See also Editorial, *B.A.S.*, p. 281, Oct., 1947.
[3] Rostas, *Economic Journal*, London, April 1943.

installed horsepower per operative employed.[4] Then again, the Indian physicist Professor Megnad Saha[5] has shown that the very wide difference in the per capita wealth of such an unindustrialized country as India or China today, or western Europe in the Middle Ages, compared with a highly industrialized country such as the U.S.A. (a difference which Saha estimated as about twenty to one) is paralleled by nearly the same difference in total available supplies of energy, including human and animal power. He estimates that the per capita energy available in India, from other than human labor, is about one-sixtieth of that available in America. In India nearly 70 per cent of all energy is from human and animal exertion; in America under 4 per cent.

TABLE I

Per capita Real Income and Total Energy Consumption from coal, oil, water and gas (expressed as a percentage of the figures for the U.S.A.)

Country	Population (millions[6])	Total per capita energy[7]	Per capita wealth[8]
U.S.A.	137	100	100
U.K.	45	73	77
U.S.S.R.	162	18	35
China & India	760	2?	11
Total World	2000	16	25

In *Table 1* is given the relative total energy as measured in thermal units produced per head of the population for selected countries, together with the average per capita wealth.

[4] Philip S. Florence and W. Baldamus, *Investment, Location and Size of Plant,* (London, 1948).

[5] Saha, *Nature,* February 1945.

[6] Population figures for 1935 from *Whitaker's Almanack* (London, 1936).

[7] Total energy figures from *The World Coal Mining Industry,* I.L.O. (Geneva, 1938). The figures given are calculated from: (*a*) the coal production in 1936 of each country (pp. 35-7), together with (*b*) the fraction of the total energy supply which derives from coal. For India and China the sources of energy other than coal are roughly estimated following Saha.

[8] The figures for per capita wealth, except for the U.S.S.R., are calculated from figures given by Colin Clark, *Conditions of Economic Progress,* p. 41 (London, 1940). The figures for the U.S.S.R. are taken from Wyler, *Social Research,* Dec., 1946, and Baran, *Review of Economic Statistics,* Nov., 1947.

We notice the striking fact that the energy consumption in 1935 in the U.S.A. was about six times that in the U.S.S.R. and some sixty times that in India. We see at once the close relationship between power output per capita and standard of living. It is quite certain that any nation which intends to reach or surpass the present productivity of America—and what nation does not?—must base its plans on the provision of a power supply of at least the magnitude of that in America today. This implies, for instance, that the U.S.S.R. must increase her power supply by six times over that of 1935, and that India must increase hers by some sixty times. For the world as a whole to reach the living standards of America requires again a sixfold increase of power supply.

We see also from these figures that the output of energy per head of the population forms a broad index of industrial progress. Though cheap power may not be the major cause of progress it certainly is an indispensable element of it.

Let us consider the needs for power of the three nations, America, Russia and India—so diverse in their social organization and technical development—from the standpoint of the large-scale production of atomic power. India, as the least industrialized country, stands, in the very long run, to gain the most from any technological developments which promise additional supplies of energy. She has ample supplies of thorium and possibly also of uranium, but she is too weak in industrial and technological resources to exploit atomic energy at present unaided.

The special position of the United States as regards fuel supply is well brought out by J. R. Menke,[9] who gives the following figures for the demand for power in the United States in 1940 and in the world as a whole:

TABLE 2

	United States (million K.W.H.)	World Total (million K.W.H.)
Coal	500	2000
Petroleum Products	300	500
Natural Gas	100	100
Water Power	10	25

[9] Menke, "Nuclear Fission as a Source of Power," *B.A.S.*, April, 1948.

The United States, with 7 per cent of the world population, has now 25 per cent of coal power, 60 per cent of oil, 100 per cent of natural gas and 40 per cent of water power.

Though already an industrialized state, the U.S.S.R. has still far to go before her total productivity and so the average standard of living of her citizens can reach the level of America. The magnitude of the task of bridging this gap is constantly being stressed by the Soviet leaders, as is also the vital part that a greatly increased power supply must play if it is to be successfully achieved. An article by Professor Modest Rubinstein[10] entitled "Electrification as the Basis of Technical Reconstruction of the Soviet Union," published in 1931, gives a clear view of Soviet opinion on this question, and quotes Lenin as having stated that: "The only material basis of socialism can be the large-scale machine industry, capable of reorganizing agriculture also. . . . Large-scale industry, answering to the needs of the latest technique, and capable of reorganizing agriculture, involves the electrification of the entire country."

This early emphasis on the importance to the U.S.S.R. of an increased power supply has been maintained ever since.

Now the scientific and technological resources of Russia are certainly adequate for the rapid development of atomic power. What supplies of uranium and thorium she possesses is of course not known, but the extent of her vast territories makes it not unlikely that adequate supplies have been or will be found. Russia has also a social and industrial organization very well suited to the rapid exploitation of such new technological developments.

Irving Langmuir[11] on his return from the U.S.S.R. Academy of Science in 1945, expressed the view that the U.S.S.R. might well outdistance the U.S.A. in the production of atomic bombs, but the same arguments apply equally to atomic power. Langmuir lists the advantages possessed by the Russians in such a race. "1. They have a large population: it can be regimented and is willing to sacrifice living standards for a long-range defense program. 2. They have a remarkable system of incentives, which is rapidly increasing the efficiency of their industrial production. 3. They have no unemployment. 4. They have no strikes. 5. They have a

---

[10] Kniga, *Science at the Cross Roads,* p. 115 (London, 1931).
[11] Irving Langmuir in *One World or None.*

deep appreciation of pure and applied science, and have placed a high priority on it. 6. They have planned a far more extensive program in science than is contemplated by any other nation."

When we now turn to America we find a different situation. In the first instance, we note that before the second World War, America had already reached a very high output of energy and that the rate of increase of energy had slowed down considerably. This can be seen by the curves in *Chart 4*, giving the variation of electricity from central steam power stations between 1926 and 1936. It will be seen that during this period Russia increased her power supplies, starting from a very low level, by twenty times, England by three times and America by only 60 per cent. Incidentally, the effect of the great Depression of the 1930s can be seen clearly by the marked drop in energy production between 1931 and 1935. It is clear that the importance likely to be placed on sources of new energy in the U.S.A. may be less than in the U.S.S.R. For in America the remarkable achievements of U.S. scientists, engineers and industrialists have already exploited the coal, oil and water power resources of the country so as to give so high a per capita output of power, that a great further increase may seem redundant. The memory of the period of the great slump, when the consumption of power clearly fell markedly below the available supplies, must necessarily have led to some reluctance on the part of the owners of existing power supplies to admit the emergence of a new and powerful competitor in the form of atomic power. We do, in fact find clear evidence that some, at any rate, of the public utility interests in America are far from being enthusiastic about the development of atomic power. For instance,[12] the Association of Edison Illuminating Companies, in evidence before a Senate Committee, expressed the view that large reductions of power costs are not foreseen, and that never at any time has America suffered from a deficiency in the supply of power available, and further, that the coal and water power resources of the country are ample for centuries to come.

We see that America is in a rather different position with regard to atomic power compared with other countries of the world. On the one hand she has unrivalled technological and industrial re-

[12] *B.A.S.,* p. 12, March, 1946.

Chart 4

ELECTRICITY PRODUCTION IN U.S.A., UNITED KINGDOM AND U.S.S.R. 1926-1936

Electricity produced in Central Steam Supply Stations

[From *The World Coal Mining Industry*, I.L.O. (*Geneva, 1938*)]

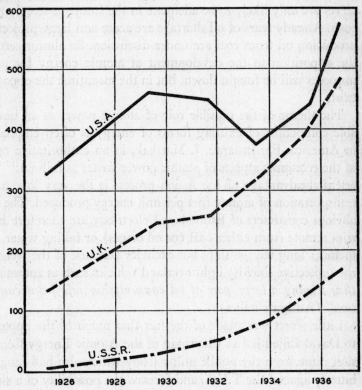

sources for the rapid exploitation of atomic power, but on the other, she has less need of the additional power owing to the very high level of her existing supplies. Further, the cost of power in America today is already so low, due to the abundance of easily mined coal and large local supplies of oil and natural gas, that atomic power may well prove uneconomic, at any rate for a long time.

Nevertheless, there are also very strong factors making for a rapid development of atomic power in the United States. In the first place, new technical discoveries stir the imagination of Americans more than most other people, and secondly, America in fact needs a great deal more power, even though she has far more already than any other country. There are many great areas of the U.S. which would greatly benefit by projects of the type of the T.V.A., but based on atomic energy. Thirdly, America's fuel reserves are only likely to be adequate in the future at steeply rising costs. Already fears of oil shortage are acute and large projects for producing oil from coal are under discussion. So almost certainly the opposition to the development of atomic energy for power purposes will be fought down. But in the meantime the opposition exists.

The theme of the possible role of atomic power as an undesirable competitor of existing forms of energy is often emphasized in America. For instance, J. Marshak, in an authoritative review of the economic aspects of atomic power writes as follows:[13] "The essential advantage of the fission process is the very low cost of transportation of atomic fuel per unit energy produced. The most obvious consumers of fission-based electricity are therefore industries remote from either coal (or oil or gas) or falling water. This includes long voyage ships but excludes (because of the weight of the protective shields) light overland vehicles such as automobiles, *thus leaving a large part of oil consumption safe from competition*" (Author's italics).

Little secret was made of the fact that much of the opposition to David Lilienthal as Chairman of the Atomic Energy Commission came from the public utility lobby which also had fought so bitterly against the T.V.A. and foresaw the possibility of a similar fight against a state-owned atomic energy power supply.

In these circumstances it is easy to understand the recurring theme in so much of American, and to a less extent in British, writing on atomic energy, that the military dangers outweigh the probable economic benefits to mankind.[14] This was certainly the view of many of the atomic scientists themselves, and of many

[13] Marshak, *B.A.S.*, Sept., 1946.
[14] Daniels and Squires, *B.A.S.*, April-May, 1947.

other writers on the subject. Two American engineers, who have clearly specialized in the study of the future development of atomic power, begin a recent article on the control of atomic energy with this paragraph: "Are the benefits of industrial atomic power worth the risk? We believe they are not. We believe that the problems of the international control of atomic energy can be reduced to manageable proportions only by an international agreement not to develop industrial atomic power for a generation. We believe that most of the foreseeable benefits of atomic power to our generation can be had without its use for industrial power plants. . . . We propose the following compromise between the Russian and American positions: Let there be a world agreement that no new industrial atomic plant shall be built anywhere in the world for a number of years."

This view is also strongly supported by David F. Cavers, Professor of Law at Harvard, in a recent article. "In this present period of tension among nations, the fact that so many people should be calmly contemplating the large-scale production of fissionable materials simply to exploit the power of using atomic energy would be astonishing to any observer who did not know the tremendous force which scientific discovery exerts on the imagination of modern man. . . . There is little evidence that the public, or indeed many of its leaders, are aware of the great gain to security which would result from forbidding the use of atomic energy until relations of greater trust and amity have been established among the nations."[15]

In the Editorial of *Bulletin of Atomic Scientists* of August 1947 (*p.* 202) we read: "If and when the Soviet Union arrives at this stage, it may begin to dawn on her why some scientists in America—without being in the service of vested coal or oil interests—have suggested the limitation of production of atomic fuels to a level excluding large-scale power production."

As will be seen later, such views are generally based explicitly on the easement of the problem of control which it is thought that such a voluntary abstinence would bring. It is pertinent, however, to suspect that the arguments might not have appeared quite so intellectually convincing if their exponents had not had the for-

[15] Cavers, *B.A.S.*, Oct., 1947.

tune to live in a country with a power supply six times as large as the world average. The shivering citizens of war-devastated Europe, the unemployed workers of its fuel-short factories, in fact all those who feel that the material conditions of American life are enviable, may well also feel that the risk of destruction by American atomic bombs is worth taking in order to have the hope of a more rapid economic advance towards American living standards.

A very clear statement of the case for the rapid development of atomic power as seen from the angle of a small nation inhabiting a large country is found in a speech by Dr. Herbert V. Evatt, Australian delegate to the United Nations, at a meeting of the Atomic Energy Commission, June 25, 1946:

> It is to be expected that countries that are relatively poor in existing power resources, and particularly those countries which also possess significant deposits of uranium ores and thorium concentrates, should be concerned with the possibility of rapid application of nuclear energy for the production of industrial power. There are nations whose industries may decline in the absence of an alternative to coal as a source of power. And to such countries, even the terrors of atomic warfare may often appear more remote than a dwindling economy or decreasing standards of living. There are other countries where the supplies of power not involving the transport of large quantities of coal or the building of long electrical transmission lines would open up new areas of agricultural or mineral development. Abundant power at reasonable cost is the life blood of modern industry. *Power from atomic energy may enable modern communities to flourish in regions remote from existing sources of power* (Author's italics). Such nations, for whom the peaceful uses of atomic energy are of more immediate importance, will be likely to demand access at the earliest possible moment to such materials and information as may be necessary for them to develop atomic energy for peaceful purposes.

The physical and geographical nature of the Australian continent have clearly had much to do with the formulation of these views, especially of that expressed in the italicized sentence.

The probable time scale for the production of atomic energy on an appreciable scale has been the subject of much discussion. It is universally agreed that the outstanding problems still to be solved are mainly technological rather than scientific. The Hanford piles are producing many hundreds of thousands of horsepower in the form of low grade heat, which even now could, in principle, be used for district heating. The main technical problem to be solved before cheap atomic power is possible is to design a pile in which the temperature of the cooling fluid or gas, whatever it may be, is raised to about 800° C. When this has been done, the heat will be in a suitable form to operate a suitable prime mover such as a steam or gas turbine. Estimates as to when this will be achieved vary, but there seems fairly general agreement that experimental piles producing useful power are likely to be in operation in the United States within a year or two, but that it will be nearer five to ten years before large-scale power production will begin, and between twenty to thirty years before an appreciable contribution will be made to *world* power resources.

The view of the panel of scientists quoted in the Lilienthal report on this subject is as follows: ". . . . we believe that the development of rather large power units for heat and conversion to electrical energy is a program for the near future; that operating units which will serve to demonstrate the usefulness and limitation of atomic power can be in existence within a few years, and that only the gradual incorporation and adaptation of such units to the specific demands of contemporary economy will involve a protracted development."

Dr. Philip Morrison, in an article in the *New Republic* of March 24, 1947, expressed the view that the scientists at the Oak Ridge Laboratory, now operated by the Monsanto Chemical Company, might have built by the end of 1948, a power reactor with helium as cooling material which could drive a turbine, and that by 1950, a high power nuclear reactor might be working. On the other hand, Dr. Oppenheimer, in evidence to the Atomic Energy Commission of the UN, held that within five years or possibly sooner, there would be a demonstration of usable electric energy; within ten to twenty years useful application to specific needs, but thirty to fifty years before much increase could be effected in the general power resources of the world.

The American Atomic Energy Commission, in its report to Congress on January 31, 1948, said: "Assuming even a most favorable technical development, we do not see how it would be possible to have any considerable portion of the present power supply of the world derived from nuclear fuels before the end of the expiration of twenty years."[16]

Many studies have been made of the probable cost of atomic power. One of the most recent and authoritative is that by Sam H. Schurr,[17] from which the following views and extracts are taken.

Mr. Schurr holds that it is not generally considered in America as economic to transmit electric power beyond a radius of about 300 miles. The cost of transport of coal from a mine in the United States to a power station 400 miles away is stated to add 0.2¢ per KWH (kilowatt hour), that is, 30 per cent to the cost of the power. Since the cost of transport of atomic fuels is very small compared with that of coal, atomic energy power plants will be particularly useful mainly, in the first instance, in areas more than a few hundred miles from coal mines or from water power. *Table 3* gives a summary of the figures given by Schurr for the relative cost of electricity in selected countries, together with the estimation of the probable cost of atomic power made by a group at Oak Ridge under Dr. C. A. Thomas, Vice-President of the Monsanto Chemical Company, and by a group under Professor Condliffe at the University of California.

TABLE 3

Estimated Cost of Electricity from Atomic Energy (after Schurr)

Thomas Report[18]	0.8—1¢ per KWH
California Report[19]	0.4¢

Actual Average Cost of Electricity in 1947

Argentina (coastal region)	1.6¢ per KWH
(inland)	1.8¢
Great Britain	1¢
United States (at mines)	0.6¢
(far from mines)	1¢

It will be noticed that the most optimistic estimate of atomic power costs is well below all existing costs of coal generated elec-

[16] *B.A.S.*, p. 91, March, 1948.
[17] Schurr, "Economic Aspects of Atomic Energy as a Source of Power," *B.A.S.*, April-May, 1947. (The article is based on a speech to the American Economics Association.)
[18] Estimated for 75,000 kw. plant at 100 per cent and 50 per cent load factor respectively.
[19] Estimated for 500,000 kw. at 45 per cent load.

tricity, while the most pessimistic estimate, though the same as the cost of coal power in Great Britain, is a long way below the costs in Argentina. Now Argentina is typical of the many countries without present adequate supplies of cheap coal. It is clear, therefore, that Schurr's figures show that the development of atomic power is likely to prove extremely important, particularly for the progress of the relatively under-industrialized countries and those without adequate or suitable located supplies of coal and water power. Clearly Mr. Schurr had the U.S.A. mainly in view when he wrote in his concluding paragraph as follows: "Measured purely in terms of the savings involved in substituting atomic fuels in the generation of electricity, the economic importance of atomic energy does not appear to be great. However, this calculation neglects the factor that historically the cheapening of power has been of major importance in economic growth, a factor which transcends in importance the savings involved in the substitution of one fuel for another. In this connection, it was noted that the unique mobility of atomic fuel renders it ideal for the purpose of providing cheap power in regions remote from other energy resources. Finally, it was stressed that even in regions with abundant fuel resources, atomic energy might have important implications for the major energy consuming industries."

These conclusions reached by Schurr reinforce very strongly the view that atomic power is likely to be of a special importance in the development of the U.S.S.R. The relative low level of present power supplies, the large distances, the relatively sparse railway system, the clear appreciation in Soviet thought of the vital dependence of living standards on energy supply; all these factors combine to make it certain that the Soviet Government must consider the most rapid possible development of atomic power of the greatest importance.

Even if atomic power proves no cheaper in money costs than coal-produced power, it may prove appreciably cheaper in manpower. For atomic power will bring a large expansion of the highly skilled engineering and chemical engineering trade, whereas coal power demands a very large population of miners and heavy-transport workers. Such a shift in the demand for labor could only benefit the general economy of a country.

It is interesting to note that the U.S.S.R. would have to raise its coal production from the figure of 120 million tons in 1935 to some 650 million tons to equal the present level of per capita coal production in Britain today, and that a goal of this order and magnitude has been explicitly set by the Soviet Government.[20] This would mean an additional two million miners, together with a substantial augmentation of her transport system. Clearly the possibility of easing their task by substituting atomic power for some of the coal power must appear very attractive to the Soviet planning authorities.

It is true that the development of atomic power may prove a long project. But the Soviet Government is in the habit of taking long views. On any hypothesis, the bridging of the gap between the power resources, and so the standard of living of the U.S.S.R. and America, as shown in *Table 1* and *Chart 4* must take a long time. Any conceivable way of shortening this time is likely to be seized upon with avidity.

Even if the hypothetical time scales of development given by various technicians turn out to be too optimistic, the arguments for the most rapid possible advance in research and development not only remain but are strengthened; for the longer the road, the more time that is saved by going fast.

The different needs of different countries for additional power has been noted by Daniels and Squires in the article already mentioned.[21] "England, France and Russia all stand in greater need of an increased power supply than the United States; a given expenditure of technical and industrial effort directed towards the generation of electricity from nuclear fuels will produce results of far less economic importance for these countries, in our opinion, than an equivalent effort directed towards improved mining and gasification of coal and the manufacture of B.T.U. gas and liquid fuels." Messrs. Daniels and Squires may possibly prove to be right—only the future can tell—but clearly this is a matter on which each major country will want to decide for itself on the advice of its own experts, and in the light of its own local conditions.

[20] In the UN report, *A Survey of the Economic Situation and Prospects of Europe* (Geneva, 1948), Stalin is quoted as laying down a goal of 500 million tons of coal by 1961.
[21] *B.A.S.*, April-May, 1947.

It is not unlikely that Daniels and Squires' view may be correct for the United Kingdom; that is, that the development of atomic energy offers less in the next two decades or so than a rationalization of our present energy system. Even if this proves to be the case for this country, which is, however, by no means certain, the conditions in other countries may be quite different. It is essential not to lay down rules for all countries on the basis of the interests of one alone.

Daniels and Squires write: "If nuclear fuels were free and were capable of replacing coal in all its uses, the saving (*i.e., to the U.S.A.*) would be 2 per cent of the national income." The fact that this figure is small has led many[22] to conclude that the possible gain to the world of the successful development of atomic energy is also quite small. These writers, however, themselves point out "that no one can predict what new industrial combinations would arise from the widespread use of atomic power. Like the automobile, which did not just replace carriages, atomic power might have far-reaching and unpredicted effects upon our entire technology." This is well said and provides another argument for expecting that no major country will be willing to submit its peacetime atomic power projects to American theories of control.

Actually for Great Britain, the total cost of the mining and transport of coal is a considerably larger fraction of the national income than in America. For instance, the present output is around 200 million tons a year, and this at $12 a ton for mining and transport, gives a total equivalent cost of almost 2½ billion dollars a year, which is 6.6 per cent of the equivalent national income of 36 billion a year—compared with about 2 per cent for the U.S.A.

There is, however, an obvious fallacy in equating the possible gain to any country from the development of atomic power with the cost of its *existing* power supplies. For this would imply that the less power a country now has the less it stands to gain by the

[22] For instance, Lord Cherwell (Debate in House of Lords, April 30, 1947): "In the American Atomic Scientists' Bulletin—and American atomic scientists are not prone to underestimate the importance and possibilities of their subject—it is stated that the use of atomic energy for peaceful purposes might make a difference of between 1½ per cent and 2½ per cent to the nation's standard of life. Against this not very glittering prospect we must set the threat to civilization implied in the staggering possibilities of destruction."

development of additional power. On this basis, Russia has less to gain than America, and India less than Russia. Of course in the long run the opposite is true.

Applied to food, the argument that the importance of a commodity in any community is given by the cost of the existing supplies of that commodity, would imply that additional food supplies were more valuable to the well-fed than to the starving.

The sounder way of estimating the potential gain to any country from increased power supplies is to calculate the total social cost, not of replacing its existing power supplies by atomic power, but of raising them to the level found necessary for the attainment of an adequate living standard; that is, the cost of raising power supplies up to the level, say, of America today. Enough has already been said to show the magnitude of the social cost that must be incurred by a relatively unindustrialized country to reach this goal, and therefore the magnitude of the potential saving by the successful development of a new and possibly cheaper source of power.

It may be objected that Britain might lose by the general adoption of atomic energy over the world, by the resulting cessation of British coal exports on which it may have to rely to buy its food. In the very long run this might happen, but in the shorter run, Britain can only gain by being near the forefront of this development. For, firstly, the early use of atomic energy in the United Kingdom would make available for export large additional supplies of coal, and, secondly, would insure a market lasting many decades for the export of atomic energy plants to the under-industrialized countries possessing uranium or thorium supplies.

One more question remains to be discussed—the adequacy of the supplies of uranium and thorium. This is partly a complicated technical problem, about which not very much has been published. The present method, as used in the Hanford piles, appears to utilize effectively the energy of only a fraction of the rarer isotope Uranium 235, which itself amounts to less than 1 per cent of natural uranium (238). It is generally believed by scientists that methods will be devised by which a large part of the remaining 99 per cent of Uranium 238 can also be used. When this is achieved the amount of natural uranium required for a given amount of power may be reduced by over a hundredfold. Further, essentially the same type of process should allow the extraction of energy from thorium, provided a certain minimum amount of uranium is available. Now thorium is in fairly abundant supply, particularly in the form of monazite sand in India, South America, etc.

The present known (or at least published) resources of uranium would not be sufficient to make an important contribution to *world* power resources if only the Uranium 235 is utilized. But there is every reason to believe that now the intensive search has started, additional supplies will be forthcoming, though possibly much of it will be relatively low grade and require a large mining and refining effort. But as soon as the scientific problems of burning up Uranium 238 and thorium are solved, the present known supplies will be adequate to furnish an important contribution to world power supplies.

Let us consider the needs of such a country as Russia. How much uranium would be required to supply an additional amount of power equal to that actually generated by steam power stations in 1936, that is, 2.4×10^{10} KWH? The complete fission of 1 kilogram of Uranium 235 or plutonium gives 1.1×10^7 KWH of power. Let us assume that the plant works at an overall thermal efficiency of 25 per cent. Then one requires $2.4 \times 10^{10} \div (1.1 \times 10^7 \times 0.25 = 8,800$ kilograms $= 8.8$ metric tons a year. Since Uranium 235 amounts to only 1/140 of natural uranium, the amount of the latter required will be $8.8 \times 140 = 1,240$ tons per year. This assumes that all the Uranium 235 can be burnt up, which may not be achieved. Supposing one-third only of the Uranium 235 were burnt up, some 4,000 tons of uranium a year would be needed. If, on the other hand, as has already been mentioned, it is likely to prove possible to burn up one-third of the Uranium 238 as well, the amount required would fall to some forty tons a year.

No authoritative figures have been published of the world production of uranium, but it is generally believed that the Belgian Congo mines are the richest in the world and have an output of at least a few thousand tons of uranium a year.[23] If this is the case,

[23] In the issue of *B.A.S.,* for March, 1948, appeared the following paragraph (p. 76): "A newspaper report from Brussels on January 3 announced that the U.S. had purchased 3,650 tons of uranium ore from the Belgian Congo in 1946 at a cost of $5,332,000. Britain purchased 2,600 tons for an equivalent of $4,250,000."

then the figures quoted above show that, if Russia should find within her territories a supply of uranium of richness comparable with the Congo mines, she would have at her disposal enough raw material to allow atomic power production to play a vital role in her national economy.

9. THE FIRST STEPS TOWARD CONTROL

1. The James Franck Report: June, 1945

WELL before the first atomic bombs were exploded, American atomic scientists had been concerning themselves actively with the social and military consequences of atomic energy. In June, 1945, over a month before the first experimental bomb was exploded in New Mexico, a "Committee on Social and Political Implications," appointed by the Metallurgical Laboratory in Chicago, presented a report to the Secretary of War. The Chairman of this committee of seven scientists was Professor James Franck, but the names of the other members do not appear to have been published. The text of the *Report* was later released by the War Department and published.[1]

In this article, many cogent arguments, with which the world has now become familiar, were set out clearly and for the first time. In particular, these scientists stressed the impossibility of the United States' maintaining a monopoly. They wrote: "Thus we cannot hope to avoid a nuclear armament race, either by keeping secret from competing nations the basic scientific facts of nuclear power, or by cornering the raw materials required for such a race." The defensive importance of dispersion over large territories was emphasized. The *Report* expressed the view that "Russia and China are the only great nations at present which could survive a nuclear attack."

The outlines of the proposals elaborated later into the "Lilienthal Plan" are to be found in this able document. Methods of in-

[1] *B.A.S.*, May, 1946.

ternational control and inspection were discussed, and the rationing of raw materials was recommended as a first step. Of great significance, and subsequent importance, is the admission that the proposed control system would explicitly prevent the development of atomic energy for power production:

> The amounts of ore taken out of the ground at different locations could be controlled by resident agents of the International Control Board, and each nation could be allotted only an amount which would make large-scale separation of fissionable isotopes impossible. Such a limitation would then have the drawback of making impossible the development of nuclear power for peacetime purposes.

The significance of the fact that such a proposal should originate in the country which has the highest per capita production of power in the world has already been stressed in Chapter 8. Clearly the authors of this report had not in mind the vital part that atomic power might play in the development of the under-industrialized and under-powered countries of the world.

Emphasis has been given to this part of the *Franck Report* because the same theme runs through nearly all American proposals for control of atomic energy, and has certainly been one of the causes of the present impasse. Under one guise or another, most American statements express the viewpoint that the military danger of atomic bombs is so great that either atomic power development in other countries must be sacrificed at the outset, or, if allowed, must be subject to control by an international organization on which the United States is reasonably assured of a permanent majority.

Actually the main object of the *Franck Report* was to advise against the use of the bomb against Japan. The arguments were presented clearly and forcibly:

> Russia and even allied countries which bear less mistrust of our ways and intentions, as well as neutral countries, may be deeply shocked by this step. It may be very difficult to persuade the world that a nation which was capable of secretly preparing and suddenly releasing a new weapon as indiscriminate as the rocket bomb and a thousand times more destructive, is to be trusted in its proclaimed desire of having such weapons abolished by international agreement. . . . The military advantages and the saving of American lives achieved by the sudden use of atomic bombs against Japan may

be outweighed by a wave of horror and repulsion sweeping over the rest of the world. . . . From this point of view, a demonstration of the new weapon might be made, before the eyes of all the United Nations on the desert or a barren island. . . . After such a demonstration the weapon might perhaps be used against Japan if the sanction of the United Nations (and public opinion at home) was obtained after a preliminary ultimatum to Japan to surrender. . . . We believe that these considerations make the use of nuclear bombs for an early attack against Japan inadvisable. If the United States were to be the first to release this new means of indiscriminate destruction of mankind, she would sacrifice public support throughout the world, precipitate the race for armaments, and prejudice the possibility of reaching an international agreement on the future control of such weapons.

To reinforce the effect of the Committee's report, a petition on similar lines signed by sixty-four scientists associated with the Metallurgical Project was sent direct to President Truman. However, the advice and warning of Professor Franck's Committee were not heeded, and the bombs were dropped on Hiroshima and Nagasaki without warning. A generalized threat had previously been issued to Japan, and thirty-five towns were specifically warned that they were open to attack. Hiroshima and Nagasaki, chosen among other things for their dense population, were not among them. Much has been written justifying this action. A critical discussion of some aspects of this decision is given in the next chapter.

2. *The Atomic Energy Commission*

After the dropping of the bomb an immense spate of articles and announcements representing a wide variety of viewpoints filled the newspapers and periodicals of the world. Many of the scientific and technical aspects of atomic energy were released to the world in the official American report, usually called the *Smyth Report*, and the shorter British Report, both of which were published in August, 1945. On October 3, 1945, President Truman in his statement to Congress said:

> In international relations, as in domestic affairs, the release of atomic energy constitutes a new force too revolutionary to consider in the framework of old ideas. We can no longer rely on the slow progress of time to develop a program of control among nations. Civilization demands that we shall reach at the earliest

possible date a satisfactory arrangement for the control of this discovery in order that it may become a powerful and forceful influence toward the maintenance of world peace instead of an instrument of destruction. Scientific opinion appears to be practically unanimous that the essential theoretical knowledge upon which the discovery is based is already widely known. There is also substantial agreement that foreign research can come abreast of our present theoretical knowledge in time. The hope of civilization lies in international arrangements looking, if possible, to the renunciation of the use and development of the atomic bomb, and directing and encouraging the use of atomic energy and all future scientific information toward peaceful and humanitarian ends. The difficulties in working out such arrangements are great. The alternative to overcoming these difficulties, however, may be a desperate armament race which might well end in disaster. Discussion of the international problem cannot be safely delayed until the United Nations Organization is functioning and in a position adequately to deal with it.

On November 15, 1945, a statement issued at Washington by President Truman, Mr. Attlee, and Mackenzie King laid the basis for the subsequent resolution at the first meeting of the UN. A few weeks later the Foreign Ministers of the U.S.A., U.S.S.R. and U.K. signed an agreement at Moscow stating that the three nations would sponsor at the first meeting of the UN a resolution to set up an Atomic Energy Commission. Finally, we have the resolution of the Assembly on January 24, 1946, setting up the Atomic Energy Commission in words which follow closely the Attlee-Truman-King Declaration. The most important passages in this resolution are as follows:

The Commission shall proceed with the utmost dispatch and inquire into all phases of the problem, and make such recommendations from time to time with respect to them as it finds possible. In particular, the Commission shall make specific proposals:

A. For extending between all nations the exchange of basic scientific information for peaceful ends.

B. For control of atomic energy to the extent necessary to insure its use only for peaceful purposes.

C. For the elimination from national armaments of atomic weapons and all other major weapons adaptable to mass destruction.

D. For effective safeguards by way of inspection and other means to protect complying States against the hazards of violation and evasion.

The work of the Commission shall proceed by separate stages, the successful completion of each of which will develop the necessary confidence of the world before the next stage is undertaken.

An important feature of these developments was the coupling of the problem of controlling atomic energy with that of controlling "all other major weapons adaptable to mass destruction." This was of special significance for two reasons. Some publicity had been given to the possibilities of biological warfare becoming as dangerous as atomic weapons. Further, after the first wave of horrified awe which followed the dropping of the atomic bombs had passed, a mood of calmer reflection arose in which the very considerable destructive power of ordinary bombs was remembered. The phase in which the atomic bomb could be considered as the unique, all-powerful and yet cheap weapon, capable of destroying civilization, or, on the other hand, of being used to usher in utopia via immediate world government based on international control of atomic energy, gave place in many, but not all, quarters to a more sober estimate of the power of atomic bombs and of the consequent necessity of tackling the problem of other weapons of mass destruction and of conventional armaments. These events provided an encouraging start to the deliberations of the United Nations Atomic Energy Commission.

3. The Acheson-Lilienthal Report

In March, 1946 the State Department issued the report of a committee appointed to advise on the problem of the control of atomic energy.[2]

This brilliantly written document is so well known that no more than a brief comment on some of its more significant recom-

[2] United States State Department, *A Report on the International Control of Atomic Energy* (Washington, 1946).

The Report was written by a Board of Consultants consisting of:

Mr. David E. Lilienthal, Chairman of the Tennessee Valley Authority, who acted as Chairman of the Consulting Board; Mr. Chester I. Barnard, President of the New Jersey Bell Telephone Company; Dr. J. Robert Oppenheimer, of the California Institute of Technology and the University of California; Dr. Charles Allen Thomas, Vice-President and Technical Director, Monsanto Chemical Company; Mr. Harry A. Winne, Vice-President in Charge of Engineering Policy, General Electric Company.

The Report was transmitted to the Secretary of State, James F. Byrnes, by a Committee consisting of:

Dean Acheson, Under Secretary of State, Chairman; Vannevar Bush, Director of the Office of Scientific Research and Development; James B. Conant, President of Harvard University; Leslie R. Groves, Major-General U.S.A.; John J. McCloy.

mendations will be given here. The Plan was modestly put forward not as a final plan, but as "a place to begin, a foundation on which to build"; and the spirit in which the Committee approached their task is shown in the following sentence. "Therefore the Plan must be one that will tend to develop the beneficial possibilities of atomic energy and encourage the growth of fundamental knowledge, stirring the constructive and imaginative impulses of men rather than merely concentrating on the defensive and negative. It should, in short, be a plan that looks to the promise of man's future well-being as well as to his security."

Its initial assumptions, that there can be no monopoly by one nation on the atomic bomb, and that there can be no effective direct military defense, follow closely those of the earlier *Franck Report*. It is emphasized that developments of atomic energy for peaceful and military purposes run parallel for a long way, so making difficult the control of the one without stopping the other. What was new and striking was the suggestion that, instead of a system of international inspection of national plants, there should be substituted international *ownership* of all mines and key plants concerned with atomic energy. The proposed Atomic Development Authority (A.D.A.) would own and operate all key atomic plants (that is, plants characterized as *dangerous* in that they could be easily diverted to bomb production); these would include all major power-producing units. National governments and private enterprise would be allowed to operate only *safe* plants (that is, those that could not be diverted to bomb production). The A.D.A. would also engage in research on a major scale and would have the right to carry out geological surveys all over the world.

The Report starts by emphasizing the economic as well as the military importance of atomic energy. "It is further recognized that atomic energy plays such a vital part in contributing to the military power and no doubt to the security of the nation, and in providing economic welfare, that the incentive to other nations to press their own developments is overwhelming." Much stress is laid on the expectation that the present monopoly position of the U.S. will not last, and that in a world where atomic armaments were general, the U.S. would be at a disadvantage.

119

The main burden of the case for international ownership, rather than international inspection of nationally-owned plants, is contained in a number of arguments which purport to show that the latter system would not work in practice, but that the former would. The difficulties of international inspection of national plants, the number of inspectors required, the unattractiveness of such police-type work to the right type of people, the social frictions involved in their operations, are all eloquently emphasized.

The plan envisages that the plants owned by the A.D.A. would be located in the various countries, so as to attain a strategic balance between nations, and that it would probably be essential to write into the proposed Charter itself a systematic plan to this effect. It was clearly in the minds of the authors that the location of plants owned by A.D.A. in different countries would provide a method of avoiding the restriction on the use of atomic energy for industrial purposes that had clearly been envisaged in the original *Franck Report* and yet would retain security against the illicit production of bombs.

A valuable feature of the Report was that it showed that the control of atomic energy was *technically* possible. The system of control proposed was based on two special properties of the present methods of exploitation of atomic energy. The essential raw material, uranium, is only found in a limited number of regions of the earth, and the plants necessary to produce atomic explosives or industrial power are very large and difficult to conceal. The authors of the Plan were quite clear that the proposed control scheme depended essentially on these two facts and would not work if, for instance, atomic explosives could be made from common materials, or in small and easily concealed plants. In that case, no such scheme would be suitable for the control of biological weapons.

The publication of the Lilienthal Plan was received with enthusiasm in most of the Western world. In particular it was acclaimed in the liberal press of America and England as a document of great vision and profound statesmanship. It was supported enthusiastically both by individual scientists and by all the main bodies of organized atomic scientists, such as the American Federation of Atomic Scientists, and the British Association of Atomic Scientists. However, the plan was vociferously attacked by certain conservative and isolationist circles in America as being: (*a*) ideal-istic and (*b*) giving away vital American secrets and so throwing away the American monopoly of atomic energy.

This wide acclamation with which the Lilienthal Plan was received in liberal circles in America and Western Europe was a result not only of the brilliant presentation of the Report, its verbal felicity, its logical method of analysis and its conclusions that control was technically possible, but also because it successfully appealed to the deeply felt internationalist longings which are always to the fore after a destructive war. Furthermore, there was a very concrete basis for the support which was so widely given to the Plan: this was concerned with an internal political struggle in America over the question of military or civilian control of atomic energy.

At the time of the appearance of the Lilienthal Plan a bitter political fight was being waged over the question whether atomic energy in the United States should be controlled primarily by the military or by civilians. Supporting military control (the May-Johnson Bill) were lined up, by and large, the main conservative and isolationist groups, while supporting civilian control (the McMahon Bill) were the ex-New Dealers and other liberal groups. Remembering the power and prestige that the military inevitably wield at the end of a long and victorious war, the fight was one of real substance; and the successful outcome—the rejection of the May-Johnson Bill and the passing of the McMahon Bill—was a real tactical triumph for the progressive forces. A very important part in this fight was taken by American scientists themselves, organized initially into local atomic scientists' committees, and later, on a national scale, into the Federation of American Atomic Scientists. American scientists, who in general had previously taken little part in politics, found themselves impelled by an intense feeling of responsibility for the horrifying results of their scientific achievements to take a very effective part in an energetic and bitterly fought political campaign. In this campaign,[3] support

[3] A vivid account of this campaign has recently been given by James R. Newman and Byron S. Miller in their book *The Control of Atomic Energy* (New York, 1948): "In the struggle over military representation on the Atomic Energy Commission, the contestants all claimed to seek the same objects—civilian control of atomic energy and national security. The partisans of the May-Johnson philosophy, however, charged that their opponents were radicals who, either because of irresponsibility or subversion, were

for the McMahon Bill nationally, and the Lilienthal Plan internationally, came on the whole from the same politically progressive groups; and support for the May-Johnson Bill and opposition to the Lilienthal Plan from the conservative and isolationist groups.

A recurring theme in the Report is that success in achieving international cooperation in the field of atomic energy may form a useful precedent for success in other fields also. Atomic energy was seen as a suitable medium in which to attempt to create a closer pattern of international cooperation than had been achieved in the world before. Closely connected with this is the view that the atomic scientists themselves must take the initiative in guiding these vital steps. The deeper insight into these matters possessed by the scientist, compared with that of the politician, is constantly expressed in the literature on atomic energy. For instance we read: "For the scientists who have grappled with this problem for two or three years, the proposition that its solution cannot be achieved except by a bold departure in international affairs has become trivial; but the same cannot be expected of laymen—be they politicians, lawyers or bankers."

Clearly the authors of the Lilienthal Plan envisaged A.D.A. as controlled by internationally-minded administrators and scientists free from the direct control of their governments. In fact, of course, the members of A.D.A. would be fully briefed representatives of the individual nations, and would be the instruments of the economic and political policies of their governments. Some misunderstanding of the possibilities in this respect may have arisen from

willing to jeopardize the welfare of the country. They, in their turn, were accused of seeking to establish a system that would be authoritarian, repressive, militaristic, and xenophobic. These were the symbols about which the battle was fought—little wonder that it was fierce . . .

"The alignment of forces lacked crispness of definition, and no doubt the differences between the two sides were considerably less than the extremists of either persuasion were prepared to admit, but it appears clear in retrospect that there was a fundamental difference of emphasis and intent. On the side of the May-Johnson bill were those who were skeptical of internationalism, willing that the services should continue in the dominant position they had occupied during the war, distrustful of generalities such as 'scientific freedom,' and sympathetic with the principle of authority. Those in opposition believed with varying intensities of conviction in the cause of international understanding, in the principle of freedom, in the relegation of the military services to a subsidiary position in our society. These differences, it seems fair to say, signified a divergency of fundamental importance in the manner in which Americans face the post-war world."

the fact that such an outstanding scientist as Sir John Boyd Orr was appointed director-general of the Food and Agricultural Organization of the UN, and was certainly not acting as a delegate of any Power. The analogy, however, of F.A.O. with the projected A.D.A. is not at all close, since the former is a purely advisory body whose recommendations can be, and often are, ignored by governments, while A.D.A. was to be a body wielding great executive power.

It must always be remembered that the Board of Consultants who drew up the Lilienthal Plan were mainly concerned with the technical possibilities of the control of atomic energy—and this they certainly successfully demonstrated. The political difficulties of instituting such a control system were clearly recognized, but were held to be mainly outside their terms of reference. For instance, we read in the Report:

> In the field of raw materials as in other activities of the Authority, extremely difficult policy questions, with the most serious social, economic, and political implications, will arise. How shall nations and individuals be compensated for reserves taken over by the Authority? As between several possible mines in different areas, which shall be operated when it is clear that the output of all is not presently required? How can a strategic balance be maintained between nations so that stock-piles of fissionable materials will not become unduly large in one nation and small in another? We do not suggest that these questions are simple, but we believe that practical answers can be found.

A serious difficulty is the question of the stages by which the plan is to come into being. In fact, a major defect of the Report, in the writer's view, is the failure to analyze objectively how the various proposed stages would affect the military security and economic progress of the Soviet Union. It is evident that the early stages of the Plan would involve an appreciable weakening of the Soviet military position. Then the suggestion in the Plan that the atomic plants should be located on strategic grounds was likely to clash with the economic needs of countries such as Russia, which are deficient in power resources.

It would seem self-evident that the basis of any feasible agreement between America and Russia must involve a series of stages at the completion of each of which both countries will have gained

123

something substantial. It is, of course, possible that no such scheme is actually discoverable at the present moment; but this possibility must not be allowed to obscure the fact that any agreement that both sides can be reasonably expected to accept must have this symmetrical property. For, in the existing state of the world, with no super-government over and above the Great Powers, one must always bear in mind the possibility that an agreement may be terminated by one side or the other. This is clearly recognized in the Report, but from one angle only—though a very natural one— that of insuring that, in the event of a failure to proceed with the later stages of the Plan, the United States shall not have lost any of her present advantageous position.

One of the essential conditions for an effective system of safeguards is stated thus: "The plan must be one that if carried out will provide security; but such that if it fails, or the international situation collapses, any nation such as the United States will be in a relatively secure position, compared with any other nation." The same point is made again later. "The significant fact is that at all times during the transitional period such facilities (stock piles of bombs and plants to produce fissile material) will continue to be located within the United States. Thus should there be a breakdown in the plan during the transition, we shall be in a favorable position with regard to atomic weapons." These considerations, entirely explicable from the American standpoint, are not followed by any similar discussion of what the Russian position would be in the case of a breakdown.

The details of the stages by which the full scheme should come into operation is not discussed very fully in the Report, but the order of certain steps is given definitely. For instance one reads: "The first major activity of the Authority must be directed to obtaining cognizance and control of raw materials. The raw materials control will bring the Authority face to face with problems of access, which is both a technical and political problem." It is clear that at the outset Russia, for instance, would hand over control of her nuclear raw materials and her atomic development work to A.D.A. What she would get in exchange at this early stage is not clear.

The disclosure of valuable technical information is mentioned as a possibility, but nowhere is it suggested that any appreciable disclosure should precede or be contemporary with the imposition of raw materials control. Disclosure is discussed in rather general terms in the Plan, and reference is made to three categories of secret information laid down by the Manhattan District Committee on Declassification. "It divided our secret information into three categories, the first of which it recommended for immediate, and the second for eventual declassification in the interest of long-term national security; while the third should not be declassified in the absence of effective international control." Without knowing the intention of the authors of the Plan as to what categories should be declassified and when, nor what actual information the three categories contained, it is not possible to estimate what new information (i.e., over and above that already published) the U.S.S.R. would have received by the time raw materials control would be in full operation on her territories. But the Report does attempt to estimate the effect of complete release of all three categories:

> One of the elements of the present monopoly of the United States is knowledge all the way from theoretical matters to practical details of know-how. It is not possible to give a reliable estimate of how much its revelation would shorten the time needed for a successful rival effort. It is conceivable that it would not be significantly shortened, or that it might be shortened by a year or so. It is, of course, clear that even with all theoretical knowledge available, a major program, surely lasting many years, is required for the actual production of atomic weapons. . . . Our monopoly on knowledge cannot be, and should not be lost at once.

Taking the estimate for an unassisted program as five years, the above estimate of the Report is that a gain in time through full disclosure of all secret American information would lie between a year or so and no gain at all. So the time saved by the very partial disclosure envisaged can be taken to be less than a year, say, 20 per cent of the time required to carry out the whole project. One can conclude the U.S.S.R. would be correct in estimating that any possible gain by disclosure of scientific and technical information would be small compared with the immediate loss of military security and from possible interference with their general atomic development program for industrial power.

Serious as some of these difficulties were likely to be, the Lilienthal Plan did represent at the time a constructive effort to solve the problem of atomic energy on an international basis, and so stood in marked contrast with the drive for a purely national control and development by America alone, which was sponsored by the opposing groups. And, at the time of its appearance, less than a year after the death of President Roosevelt and the end of World War II, it did not seem impossible that modifications might have been put forward to make it more acceptable to the Soviet Union. For some of the warmth of the wartime alliance had not yet cooled, and there was still room for hope that the Plan might have been made the starting point to a mutually acceptable scheme.[4]

Clearly the modifications would have to have been designed (a) so as to reduce to a minimum the possible interference by A.D.A. in the economic affairs of a country; (b) to arrange the stages by which the Plan was to come into operation, so as to give adequate and reciprocal advantages to each of the major nations from the start and at each stage, and (c) that the Charter was not modified so as to make possible a legalized third world war. Even with such modifications, the acceptance of the Plan would have been dependent on the existence of a favorable atmosphere between the Great Powers, and of their obvious determination to make the Charter of the United Nations work on the basis of the recognition of their mutual interests.

How the Lilienthal Plan was, in fact, modified by the American Government before it was put forward as their official policy will be told in Chapter 11. The argument will be interrupted for a space by a chapter describing the circumstances of the dropping of the two bombs on Japan. In the writer's opinion, the circumstances in which the bombs were dropped had not only more important political consequences after the war than they had military consequences during the war, but they had a particularly important effect on the course taken by the campaign for control. It will be remembered that the *Franck Report*, from which we have already quoted, was primarily concerned with the arguments as to the circumstances in which it appeared to the authors that the use of

[4] The background to the Lilienthal Plan, as seen by an atomic scientist who clearly contributed greatly to the formulation of the Plan, is told by Dr. Oppenheimer (*B.A.S.*, Feb., 1948).

the bomb would be justified, and when it would not. Many of the forebodings first expressed by the *Franck Report* as likely to occur if atomic bombs were dropped without warning on Japanese cities appear to have been only too well founded.

10. THE DECISION TO USE THE BOMBS

THE origin of the decision to drop the bombs on two Japanese cities, and the timing of this event, both in relation to the ending of the Japanese war and to the future pattern of international relations, has already given rise to intense controversy and will surely be the subject of critical historical study in the future. The story has, however, great practical importance if one is to understand aright many aspects of American policy and opinion, and of the Russian reaction thereto.

It has already been pointed out in the last chapter that the scientists on the Franck Committee, in a memorandum to the President in June, 1945, strongly deprecated the first use of the bomb against Japanese cities on the grounds chiefly that the gain resulting from the expected shortening of the war would be offset by the inevitable worsening of international relations. Doubts have often been expressed as to the justification for using the bombs in the way they were used, and many American scientists undoubtedly felt morally distressed at finding the results of their brilliant scientific work used in a way which seemed to many of them to lack adequate moral or military justification. Before the bomb was used, most scientists probably felt that the only justification for its use against Japan would be one of overriding military necessity, and there seems definite evidence that, earlier in the summer of 1945, the American authorities did not anticipate such a situation arising. For instance, the Washington correspondent of the *London Times* wrote in the issue of August 8, 1945, as follows:

> The decision to use the new weapon was apparently taken quite recently and amounted to a reversal of previous policy. A correspondent in the *Baltimore Sun*, writing from an authority which

seems unimpeachable, says that, until early in June, the President and military leaders were in agreement that this weapon should not be used, but a reversal of this High Command policy was made within the last sixty and, possibly the last thirty, days. There is, he says, much speculation about what caused this change of policy, but in the view of some highly placed persons those responsible came to the conclusion that they were justified in using any and all means to bring the war in the Pacific to a close within the shortest possible time.

It will be one of the objects of this analysis to elucidate the origin of this presumed change of policy. President Truman stated in a speech on August 9, 1945, three days after the first bomb was dropped: "We have used it in order to shorten the agony of war, in order to save the lives of thousands and thousands of young Americans." Then, on October 3rd, in a message to Congress, he said: "Almost two months have passed since the atomic bomb was used against Japan. That bomb did not win the war, but it certainly shortened the war. We know it saved the lives of untold thousands of American and Allied soldiers who otherwise would have been killed in battle."

In an article published in the *Atlantic Monthly,* in December, 1946, under the title "If the Bomb Had Not Been Dropped," Dr. Karl T. Compton gave his reasons for believing the decision to have been right. Dr. Compton writes: "I had, perhaps, an unusual opportunity to know the pertinent facts." At General MacArthur's headquarters, he learned of the invasion plans and of "the sincere conviction of the best-informed officers that a desperate and costly struggle was still ahead. . . . Finally, I spent the first month after VJ day in Japan, where I could ascertain at first hand both the physical and psychological state of the country. . . . From this background I believe with complete conviction, that the use of the atomic bomb saved hundreds of thousands—perhaps several millions—of lives, both American and Japanese; that without its use the war would have continued for many months." Dr. Compton quotes General MacArthur's staff as expecting 50,000 American casualties in the landing operations planned for November 1st, and a far more costly struggle later before the homeland was subdued. Dr. Compton's final views are as follows: "If the bomb had not been used, evidence like I have cited points to the practical certainty that there would have been many more months of deaths and destruction on an enormous scale."

On December 16th, President Truman wrote to Dr. Compton as follows:

DEAR DR. COMPTON,

Your statement in the *Atlantic Monthly* is a fair analysis of the situation except that the final decision had to be made by the President, and was made after a complete survey of the whole situation had been made. The conclusions reached were substantially those set out in your article. The Japanese were given fair warning, and were offered the terms which they finally accepted, well in advance of the dropping of the bomb. I imagine the bomb caused them to accept the terms.

Sincerely yours,

HARRY S. TRUMAN.

The next contribution of importance was an article in *Harper's Magazine,* in February, 1947, by Henry L. Stimson, who in 1945 was Secretary of War. This article is worthy of very close study. Mr. Stimson states that the President relied for advice on the "Interim Committee" under his Chairmanship and having, as scientific members, Vannevar Bush, Karl T. Compton and James B. Conant. This Committee was assisted in its work by a Scientific Panel whose members were A. H. Compton, Fermi, Lawrence and Oppenheimer. Mr. Stimson's article reads:

On June 1, after discussions with the Scientific Panel, the Interim Committee unanimously adopted the following recommendations.

(1) The bomb should be used against Japan as soon as possible. (2) It should be used on a dual target—that is, a military installation or war plant surrounded by or adjacent to houses and other buildings most susceptible to damage, and (3) It should be used without prior warning of the nature of the weapon. One member later changed his view and dissented from the recommendation (3).

In reaching these conclusions the Interim Committee carefully considered such alternatives as a detailed warning or a demonstration in some uninhabited area. Both these suggestions were discarded as impracticable. They were not regarded as likely to be effective in compelling a surrender of Japan, and both of them involved serious risks. Even the New Mexico test would not give final proof that any given bomb was certain to explode when dropped from an airplane. Quite apart from the generally unfamiliar nature of atomic explosives, there was the whole problem of exploding a bomb at a predetermined height in the air by a complicated mechanism which could not be tested in the static test of New Mexico.[1]

Nothing would have been more damaging to our effort to obtain surrender than a warning of a demonstration followed by a dud— and this was a real possibility. Furthermore, we had no bombs to waste. *It was vital that a sufficient effect be quickly obtained with the few we had* (Author's italics).

Later on in the article Mr. Stimson writes: "The two atomic bombs which we had dropped were the only ones we had ready, and our rate of production at that time was very small."

Why this necessity for speed? What was it in the war plans of the Allies which necessitated rapid action? Mr. Stimson's article makes it clear that there was nothing in the American-British military plan of campaign against Japan which demanded speed in dropping the bombs in early August, 1945.

Mr. Stimson describes the American war plans as follows:

> The strategic plans of our armed forces for the defeat of Japan, as they stood in July, had been prepared without reliance on the atomic bomb, which had not yet been tested in New Mexico. We were planning an intensified sea and air blockade and greatly intensified air bombing, through the summer and early fall, to be followed on November 1 by the invasion of the southern island of Kyushu. This would be followed in turn by the invasion of the main island of Honshu in the spring of 1946. We estimated that if we should be forced to carry the plan to its conclusion, the major fighting would not end until the latter part of 1946 at the earliest. I was informed that such operations might be expected to cost over a million casualties to American forces alone.

Since the next major United States move was not to be until November 1, clearly there was nothing in the Allied plan of campaign to make urgent the dropping of the first bomb on August 6 rather than at any time in the next two months. Mr. Stimson himself makes clear that, had the bombs not been dropped, the intervening period of eleven weeks between August 6 and the invasion planned for November 1 would have been used to make further fire raids with B29's on Japan. Under conditions of Japanese air

[1] However, a trial explosion at a predetermined height could of course equally well have been made over open country.

defense at that time, these raids would certainly have led to very small losses of American air personnel.

Mr. Stimson's hurry becomes still more peculiar since the Japanese had already initiated peace negotiations. In his own words: "Japan, in July, 1945, had been seriously weakened by our increasingly violent attacks. It was known to us that she had gone so far as to make tentative proposals to the Soviet Government, hoping to use the Russians as mediators in a negotiated peace. These vague proposals contemplated the retention by Japan of important conquered areas and were not therefore considered seriously. There was as yet no indication of any weakening of the Japanese determination to fight, rather than accept unconditional surrender."

On July 20, the Big Three Conference at Potsdam was in session and an ultimatum was sent to the Japanese Government on July 26. This was rejected by the Premier of Japan on July 28 "as unworthy of public notice." Unfortunately, Mr. Stimson does not give either the exact date or details of the Japanese approach for mediation through Russia, or the content of their proposals. So the exact relation between this *secret* approach for mediation and the *public* refusal of the Potsdam terms is not clear. At any rate, the reason for the immediate necessity of dropping the bomb seems no clearer.

A plausible solution of this puzzle of the overwhelming reasons for urgency in the dropping of the bomb is not, however, hard to find. It is, in fact, to be found in the omissions from both Dr. Compton's and Mr. Stimson's articles. As already shown, both give a detailed account of the future plans for the American assault on Japan planned for the autumn of 1945, and the spring of 1946. But neither makes any reference in detail to the other part of the Allied plan for defeating Japan; that is, the long-planned Russian campaign in Manchuria. We can, however, fill in this information from other sources; for instance, from Elliott Roosevelt's book, *As He Saw It*, published in September 1946.

In the chapter on the Yalta Conference (February, 1945) Mr. Roosevelt writes: "But before the Conference broke up, Stalin had once more given the assurance he had first volunteered in Teheran in 1943: that, within six months of VE day, the Soviets

131

would have declared war on Japan; then, pausing in thought, he had revised that estimate from six months to three months."

The European war ended on May 8, so the Soviet offensive was due to start on August 8. This fact is not mentioned either by Mr. Stimson or Dr. Compton in the articles from which we have quoted. The first atomic bomb was dropped on August 6 and the second on August 9. The Japanese accepted the Potsdam terms on August 14.

The U.S.S.R. declared war on Japan on August 8, and their offensive started early on August 9. On August 24, the Soviet High Command announced that the whole of Manchuria, Southern Sakhalin, etc., had been captured and that the Japanese Manchurian army had surrendered. No doubt the capitulation of the home government on August 14 reduced the fighting spirit of the Japanese forces. If it had not taken place, the Soviet campaign might well have been more expensive; but it would have been equally decisive. If the saving of American lives had been the main objective, surely the bombs would have been held back until (a) it was certain that the Japanese peace proposals made through Russia were not acceptable, and (b) the Russian offensive, which had for months been part of the Allied strategic plan, and which Americans had previously demanded, had run its course.

In a broadcast to the American people on August 9, President Truman described the secret military arrangements between the Allies made at the Potsdam Conference. "One of those secrets was revealed yesterday when the Soviet Union declared war on Japan. The Soviet Union, before she had been informed of our new weapon, agreed to enter the war in the Pacific. We gladly welcome into this struggle against the last of the Axis aggressors our gallant and victorious ally against the Nazis."

Further details of the events which led up to the capitulation of Japan are given in *United States Strategic Bombing Survey 4*, the Summary Report on the Pacific War.

In the section significantly entitled "Japan's Struggle to End the War," we read:

> By mid-1944, those Japanese in possession of basic information saw with reasonable clarity the economic disaster which was inevitably descending on Japan. Furthermore, they were aware of

132

the disastrous impact of long-range bombing on Germany, and with the loss of the Marianas, could foresee a similar attack on Japan's industries and cities. Their influence, however, was not sufficient to overcome the influence of the Army which was confident of its ability to resist invasion.

The Report then outlines the Allied plan for the final defeat of Japan by staging a heavy air attack on Japan throughout the summer, to be followed by a large-scale landing on Kyushu in November, 1945. The Report, however, states that "certain of the United States commanders and the representatives of the Survey who were called back from their investigations in Germany in early June, 1945, for consultation, stated their belief that by the coordinated impact of blockade and direct air attack, Japan could be forced to surrender without invasion." The Report continues:

Early in May, 1945, the Supreme War Direction Council [of Japan] began active discussion of ways and means to end the war, and talks were initiated with Soviet Russia, seeking her intercession as mediator. The talks by the Japanese Ambassador in Moscow and with the Soviet Ambassador in Tokyo did not make progress. On June 20, the Emperor on his own initiative called the six members of the Supreme War Direction Council to a conference and said it was necessary to have a plan to close the war at once, as well as a plan to defend the home islands. The timing of the Potsdam Conference interfered with a plan to send Prince Konoye to Moscow as a special emissary with instructions from the Cabinet to negotiate for peace on terms less than unconditional surrender, but with private instructions from the Emperor to secure peace at any price. . . .

Although the Supreme War Direction Council, in its deliberations on the Potsdam Conference, was agreed on the advisability of ending the war, three of its members, the Prime Minister, the Foreign Minister and the Navy Minister, were prepared to accept unconditional surrender, while the other three, the Army Minister and the Chiefs of Staff of both Services, favored continued resistance unless certain mitigating conditions were obtained. . . .

On August 6, the atomic bomb was dropped on Hiroshima and on August 9 Russia entered the war. In the succeeding meetings of the Supreme War Direction Council, the difference of opinion previously existing as to the Potsdam terms persisted as before. By using the urgency brought about by the fear of further bombing attacks, the Prime Minister found it possible to bring the Emperor directly into the discussion of the Potsdam terms. Hirohito, acting as the arbiter, resolved the conflict in favor of unconditional surrender. . . .

It seems clear that even without the atomic bomb attacks, air supremacy over Japan could have exerted sufficient pressure to bring unconditional surrender and obviate the need for invasion. . . . Based on a detailed investigation of all the facts, and supported by the testimony of the surviving Japanese leaders involved, it is the Survey's opinion that certainly prior to December 31, 1945, Japan would have surrendered even if the atomic bombs had not been dropped, even if Russia had not entered the war, and even if no invasion had been planned or contemplated.

General Henry H. Arnold expressed the view[2] that "without attempting to deprecate the appalling and far-reaching results of the atomic bomb, we have good reason to believe that its use primarily provided a way out for the Japanese Government. The fact is that the Japanese could not have held out long because they had lost control of the air. They could offer effective opposition neither to air bombardment nor to our mining by air and so could not prevent the destruction of their cities and industries and the blockade of their shipping."

This account of the situation[3] is, of course, based on information much of which was available only after the surrender of Japan. Thus some of it, for instance, the detailed instructions of the Emperor to Prince Konoye, could not have been known to the Allied Command at the time the decision to drop the first bombs was made. It is also quite possible that in July, 1945 the Allied High Command may have genuinely misjudged the real situation in Japan and have greatly overestimated the Japanese will to resist.[4] But all this information was naturally available to Mr. Stimson and Dr. Compton when they wrote their articles justifying the dropping of the bombs.

As far as our analysis has taken us we have found no compelling military reason for the clearly very hurried decision to drop the first atomic bomb on August 6, rather than on any day in the next

[2] In Masters and Way (Editors), *One World or None,* p. 28.

[3] Paul Nitze, Vice-Chairman of the U.S.S.B.S., repeated the view in the Senate Committee Hearings (Senate Resolution 179, p. 530). "It is our opinion that Japan would have surrendered prior to November 1 in any case; the atomic bomb merely accelerated the date at which Japan surrendered."

[4] It is not in dispute that had the invasion of Kyushu taken place as planned in November, and had the Japanese military forces fought as determinedly as they had previously, the American casualties would have been very heavy.

six weeks or so. But a most compelling diplomatic reason, relating to the balance of power in the post-war world, is clearly discernible.

Let us consider the situation as it must have appeared in Washington at the end of July, 1945. After a brilliant, but bitterly-fought campaign, American forces were in occupation of a large number of Japanese islands. They had destroyed the Japanese Navy and Merchant Marine and largely destroyed their Air Force and many divisions of their Army: but they had still not come to grips with a large part of the Japanese land forces. Supposing the bombs had not been dropped, the planned Soviet offensive in Manchuria, so long demanded and, when it took place, so gladly welcomed (officially), would have achieved its objective according to plan. This must have been clearly foreseen by the Allied High Command, who knew well the great superiority of the Soviet forces in armor, artillery and aircraft, and who could draw on the experience of the European war to gauge the probable success of such a well-prepared offensive. If the bombs had not been dropped, America would have seen the Soviet armies engaging a major part of Japanese land forces in battle, overrunning Manchuria and taking half a million prisoners. And all this would have occurred while American land forces would have been no nearer Japan than Iwo Jima and Okinawa. One can sympathize with the chagrin with which such an outcome would have been regarded. Most poignantly, informed military opinion could in no way blame Russia for these expected events. Russia's policy of not entering the Japanese war till Germany was defeated was not only military common sense but part of the agreed Allied plan.

In this dilemma, the successful explosion of the first atomic bomb in New Mexico, on July 16, must have come as a welcome aid. One can imagine the hurry with which the two bombs—the only two existing—were whisked across the Pacific to be dropped on Hiroshima and Nagasaki just in time, but only just, to insure that the Japanese Government surrendered to American forces alone. The long-demanded Soviet offensive took its planned victorious course, almost unheralded in the world sensation caused by the dropping of the bombs.

Referring to these events, a British military historian wrote:[5]

[5] Strategicus, *The Victory Campaign*, p. 242 (London, 1947).

Two days later, Russia declared war on Japan; but so great an impression was made on the world by the first atomic bomb, that very few people took any notice of this important step. . . . The atomic bombs undoubtedly contributed to bring about the Japanese decision. So, also, to a lesser extent, did the swift and skilful overrunning of Manchuria by the Russians. But it is impossible to hold that either, or both together, brought it about. The atomic bombs provided an excuse, a face-saving event that was seized upon to justify a surrender which was as abject as that of Germany and much less explicable.

The last four words of that sentence cannot have been intended as a serious judgment.

Of particular interest is the following quotation from the *New York Times* of August 15, 1945. Under the headline, "Chennault Holds Soviet Forced End: Russia's Entry Decided War With Japan Despite Atomic Bomb, An Air General Says," appears a report of an interview by the newspaper's Rome correspondent, containing the following passage:

> Russia's entry into the Japanese war was the decisive factor in speeding its end and would have been so, even if no atomic bombs had been dropped, is the opinion of Major General Claire Chennault, who arrived en route home via Germany. The founder of the American Volunteer Group (Flying Tigers) and former Air Force Commander in China said that the Soviet armies had been alert for the invasion of Manchuria as far back as VE day. He added that their swift stroke completed the circle around Japan that brought the nation to its knees.

Strong support for the validity of this interpretation of these events is found in an account of the relation between the dropping of the bomb and the planned Soviet offensive, given in an article by two American writers, Norman Cousins and Thomas K. Finletter, originally published in the *Saturday Review of Literature,* June 15, 1946. They refer in detail to the report of the committee under James Franck from which we have already quoted. "This report, not made public by the War Department at the time, is one of the most important American documents of recent years—even though it is virtually unknown to the American people." After analyzing and approving in general the arguments in the report against an initial use of bombs against Japan, and in favor of a demonstration to be witnessed by the United Nations, they write as follows:

> Why then did we drop it? Or, assuming that the use of the bomb was justified, why did we not demonstrate its power in a test under the auspices of the United Nations, on the basis of which an ultimatum would be issued to Japan—transferring the burden of responsibility to the Japanese themselves? . . .
>
> Whatever the answer, one thing seems likely: there was not enough time between July 16, when we knew at New Mexico that the bomb would work, and August 8, the Russian deadline date, for us to have set up the very complicated machinery of a test atomic bombing involving time-consuming problems of area preparations, etc. . . .
>
> No; any test would have been impossible if the purpose was to knock Japan out before Russia came in—or at least before Russia could make anything other than a token of participation prior to a Japanese collapse.
>
> It may be argued that this decision was justified; that it was a legitimate exercise of power politics in a rough-and-tumble world; that we avoided a struggle for authority in Japan similar to that we have experienced in Germany and Italy; that, unless we came out of the war with a decisive balance of power over Russia, we would be in no position to checkmate Russian expansion.

This interpretation by Cousins and Finletter substantially confirms our own analysis.[6] The hurried dropping of the bombs on Hiroshima and Nagasaki was a brilliant success, in that all the political objectives were fully achieved. American control of Japan is complete, and there is no struggle for authority there with Russia.

Two other theories of the timing of the dropping of the bomb are worth a brief notice. The first is that it was purely coincidental that the first bomb was dropped two days before the Soviet offensive was due to start. This view explains Mr. Stimson's statement,

[6] Particular interest attaches to these articles as one of the authors was later chosen by the President to be Chairman of "The Air Policy Committee," whose report, under the title *Survival in the Air Age,* is reviewed in the Appendix. Quite recently Mr. Finletter has been appointed head of the Marshall Plan Mission in London.

"It was vital that a sufficient effort be quickly obtained with the few we had," as referring to the universal and praiseworthy desire to finish the war as soon as possible. Another variant of this interpretation is that which emphasizes the compulsion felt by many Americans to make immediate use of any new gadget, irrespective of the consequences. The difficulty about this view is that it makes the timing of the dropping a supreme diplomatic blunder. For it must have been perfectly clear that the timing of the dropping of the bombs, two days before the start of the Soviet offensive, would be assumed by the Soviet Government to have the significance which we have assumed that it, in fact, did have. If it was not intended to have this significance, then the timing was an error of tact, before which all the subsequent "tactlessness" of Soviet diplomacy in relation to the control of atomic energy pales into insignificance. That the timing was not an unintentional blunder is made likely by the fact that no subsequent steps were taken to mitigate its effects.

The second view relates, not to the timing, but to the choice of an unwarned and densely populated city as target. This view admits that there was no convincing military reason for the use of the bombs, but holds that it was a political necessity to justify to Congress and to the American people the expenditure of the huge sum of two billion dollars. It is scarcely credible that such an explanation should be seriously put forward by Americans, but so it seems to have been, and rather widely. Those who espouse this theory do not seem to have realized its implications. If the United States Government had been influenced in the summer of 1945 by this view, then perhaps at some future date, when another two billion dollars had been spent, it might feel impelled to stage another Roman holiday with some other country's citizens, rather than 120,000 victims of Hiroshima and Nagasaki, as the chosen victims. The wit of man could hardly devise a theory of the dropping of the bomb, both more insulting to the American people, or more likely to lead to an energetically pursued Soviet defense policy.

Let us sum up the three possible explanations of the decision to drop the bombs and of its timing. The first, that it was a clever and highly successful move in the field of power politics, is almost certainly correct; the second, that the timing was coincidental, convicts the American Government of a hardly credible tactlessness; and the third, the Roman holiday theory, convicts them of an equally incredible irresponsibility. The prevalence in some circles of the last two theories seems to originate in a curious preference to be considered irresponsible, tactless, even brutal, but at all costs not clever.

There is one further aspect of the dropping of the bomb which must be mentioned. There were undoubtedly, among the nuclear physicists working on the project, many who regarded the dropping of the bombs as a victory for the progressively minded among the military and political authorities. What they feared was that the bombs would *not* be dropped in the war against Japan, but that the attempt would be made to keep their existence secret and that a stock pile would be built up for an eventual war with Russia. To those who feared intensely this latter possible outcome, the dropping of the bombs and the publicity that resulted appeared, not unplausibly, as far the lesser evil. Probably those whose thoughts were on these lines did not reckon that the bombs would be dropped on crowded cities.

The motive behind the choice of targets remains obscure. President Truman stated on August 9, 1945: "The world will note that the first atomic bomb was dropped on Hiroshima, a military base. That was because we wished in the first instance to avoid, in so far as possible, the killing of civilians." On the other hand, in the official Bombing Survey Report we read: "Hiroshima and Nagasaki were chosen as targets because of their concentration of activities and population." There seem here signs of a lack of departmental coordination.

So we may conclude that the dropping of the atomic bombs was not so much the last military act of the second World War, as the first major operation of the cold diplomatic war with Russia now in progress. The fact, however, that the realistic objectives in the field of *Macht-Politik*, so well achieved by the timing of the bomb, did not square with the advertised objective of saving "untold numbers" of American lives, produced an intense inner psychological conflict in the minds of many English and American people who knew, or suspected, some of the real facts. This conflict was particularly intense in the minds of the atomic scientists themselves, who rightly felt a deep responsibility at seeing their brilliant scientific work used in this way. The realization that their work had been used to achieve a diplomatic victory in relation to the power politics of the post-war world, rather than to save American lives, was clearly too disturbing to many of them to be consciously admitted. To allay their own doubts, many came to believe that the dropping of the bombs had in fact saved a million lives. It thus came about that those people who possessed the strongest emotional drive to save the world from the results of future atomic bombs, had in general a very distorted view of the actual circumstances of their first use.

It can never be repeated often enough that the first maxim of the scientific study of current events is that one should not attempt to predict the future until one has attempted to understand the past. All attempts to control atomic energy involve predictions about the course of future events and, in particular, prediction of the probable part that atomic bombs will play in future wars. It is certainly necessary to make such estimates in order to approach the problem of their control in a rational manner. Inaccurate views as to the historical facts of their first use are a poor basis on which to plan for the future.

Perhaps the most important consequence of this situation, and of the inner personal conflicts to which it gave rise, is the firm belief among many Americans that it is certain that atomic bombs will be used against civilian populations at the outset of future wars as a matter of course and in all circumstances. Dr. J. R. Oppenheimer, with his characteristic clarity of expression, explains the origin of this view: "Every American knows that if there is another major war, atomic weapons will be used. We know this because in the last war, the two nations which we like to think are the most enlightened and humane in the world—Great Britain and the United States—used atomic weapons against an enemy which was essentially defeated." In the place of a rational attempt to understand in detail the part that atomic bombs are likely to play in future world affairs, and of the circumstances in which they would be likely to be used again, an atmosphere of imminent world destruction arose in which clear thinking was at a discount and emotion triumphant. The world became regaled with authoritative statements which departed wildly from the realm of probability. Of particular importance is the strand of thought represented by the well-known statement of Mr. Stimson, who wrote:[7] "The future may see a time when such a weapon may be constructed in secret and used suddenly and effectively with devastating power by a wilful nation or group against an unsuspecting nation or group of much greater size and material power. With its aid even a very *powerful and unsuspecting nation might be conquered within a very few days by a very much smaller one* . . ." (Author's italics).

This view has two most important consequences. Firstly, it implies that an unsuspecting United States itself might be defeated in a few days by a very much smaller nation. The obvious result has been to stimulate a hysterical search for 100 per cent security from such attack. Since there can be no such complete security for America, except through world hegemony imposed by America, Mr. Stimson's view, which is very widely accepted, justified a drive towards world hegemony by America in one form or another.

Secondly, the inescapable conclusion from the assumption that a small nation with atomic bombs could defeat a great nation without them in a few days, was that a great nation with bombs (America) could defeat another great nation (Russia) in a few hours, and consequently very cheaply. The justification for a cheap preventive war, of the "push-button" variety, became complete. The logic of the Irishman in the story was applied to the bomb. On seeing a stove advertised to save half one's fuel, he bought two to save it all! If two bombs could save a million American lives in a war with Japan, then a hundred would save them all in a war with Russia.

In all this discussion the question of the military effect of atomic bombs and their effect on warfare is of paramount importance; a full discussion has already been attempted in earlier chapters. From the point of view of the present discussion, the significant point is obvious. Atomic bombs will be used in future wars when the potential user estimates that great gains will result, at any rate

[7] *B.A.S.*, Feb., 1947.

for some years, over the whole military, political and economic field. As has already been shown, this condition was fulfilled in the views of the American, and presumably also the British statesmen in August, 1945. But this commonsense view shows up in its provocative nonsense such a remark[8] as "If Russia had atomic bombs, they would already have been dropped on the United States."

In the atmosphere created by such statements, the drive for one hundred per cent security from atomic bombs becomes understandable, but none the less highly dangerous. For perfect security from any of the dangers besetting humanity is clearly not attainable. If one drives an automobile, complete security against the danger of being killed in a collision with another car can only be attained by prohibiting anyone but oneself from driving a car—that is, by the abolition of road transport. It is to be noticed that there are strong tendencies in America today which strive for the illusory goal of 100 per cent security from atomic bombs,[9] by attempting to prevent anyone else using atomic energy for any major purpose.

The story behind the decision to drop the two atomic bombs on Hiroshima and Nagasaki, as far as it is possible to unravel it from the available published material, has been told in this chapter not with the intention of impugning motives of individuals or of nations, but for a much more practical reason. This is to attempt to offset as far as possible some of the disastrous consequences resulting from the promulgation of the official story that the bombs were dropped from vital military necessity and did, in fact, save a huge number of American lives. For this story is not believed by well-informed people who therefore have to seek some other explanation. Since they reject the hypothesis that they were dropped to win a diplomatic victory as being too morally repugnant to be

[8] Mr. Bullitt, ex-Ambassador at Moscow, quoted by the *New Republic*, April 7, 1947. A still wilder expression of self-induced fear or deliberate provocation is Walter Winchell's remark, quoted by the *London News Chronicle* on October 20, 1947. "Russia is going to make war on America. The cholera epidemic in Egypt is suspected of being the first Soviet experiment in mass killings by germs."

[9] Dr. Oppenheimer has recently written: "In fact, it appears most doubtful if there are now any courses open to the United States which can give to our people the sort of security they have known in the past. The argument that such a course *must* exist seems to be specious; and in the last analysis most current proposals rest on this argument."

entertained, the only remaining resort is to maintain that such things just happen, and that they are the "essence of total war." Believing therefore that America dropped atomic bombs on Japan for *no compelling military or diplomatic reason*, the belief comes easily that other countries will, when they can, drop atomic bombs on America with equal lack of reason, military or diplomatic. This is a belief that provides the breeding ground for hysteria.

In decisive contrast are the consequences of believing what the writer holds to be the truth, that is, that the bombs were dropped for very real and compelling reasons—but diplomatic rather than military ones. For though the circumstances did then exist in which a great diplomatic victory could be won by annihilating the population of two cities, these circumstances were of a very special character and *are not very likely to recur*. If they did recur, few nations would perhaps resist the temptation to employ these means to attain such an end. But if we are right in supposing that a repetition of such special circumstances is unlikely, then the world is less in danger of more Hiroshimas than is generally believed.

11. THE BARUCH PLAN

WHEN the Atomic Energy Commission first met, the auspices for a successful outcome were not good. On the one hand stood Russia, fully conscious of the reasons behind the first use of the atomic bombs by America, and clearly also keenly aware of the immediate danger to her military security and the long-range danger to her economic development underlying the idealistic phraseology of the Lilienthal Plan. On the other hand, America was seeking an unattainable hundred per cent security from the weapon she was so proud to have developed and so ashamed to have used. The diplomatic initiative in the matter of atomic energy inevitably lay in American hands, as the only nation with the know-how, the plants and the bombs. The world waited anxiously for

American leadership which would offer some hope of an agreed solution.

At the first meeting of the Commission, which took place in New York on June 13, 1946, Bernard Baruch put forward, on behalf of the American Government, proposals for international control of atomic energy. At the second meeting on June 19, Andrei Gromyko presented the Soviet proposals. These rival proposals have been the subject of endless debate and the cause of intense mutual national recriminations during the two years that have elapsed since their first presentation. In spite of minor changes from time to time in the tactics of both major contestants, the essential clash of viewpoints revealed by these two documents persists in essentially the same form today and is clearly the cause of the present impasse. It would neither be profitable, nor possible within the compass of a small book, to attempt to follow in detail the course of the debate. It is, however, essential to study the two proposals as they were originally put forward; to analyze the motives of their authors, and to attempt to predict the consequences to the world, had either been accepted.

In essence, the American proposals amounted to the adoption of the recommendations of the Acheson-Lilienthal Report, with the important addition that decisions relating to atomic energy and to the imposition of sanctions against violation of any agreement reached between the Powers, should not be subject to the unanimity rule of the permanent members of the Security Council. Nothing was added to the Lilienthal Plan which would have reduced the essential asymmetry as between America and Russia inherent in the early stages of the Plan.

Extracts from Mr. Baruch's statement are reproduced below.

"My fellow-members of the United Nations Atomic Energy Commission, and my fellow-citizens of the world. We are here to make a choice between the quick and the dead. That is our business.

"Behind the black portent of the new atomic age lies a hope which, seized upon with faith, can work our salvation. If we fail, then we have damned every man to be the slave of Fear. Let us not deceive ourselves: We must elect World Peace or World Destruction.

"Science has torn from nature a secret so vast in its potentialities that our minds cower from the terror it creates. Yet terror created by weapons has never stopped man from employing them; for each new weapon a defense has been produced, in time. But now we face the condition in which adequate defense does not exist.

"Science, which gave us this dread power, shows that it *can* be made a giant help to humanity, but science does *not* show us how to obviate that peril by finding a meeting of the minds and the hearts of our peoples. Only in the will of mankind lies the answer.

"It is to express this will and make it effective that we have been assembled. We must provide the mechanism to assure that atomic energy is used for peaceful purposes and preclude its use in war. To that end, we must provide immediate, swift and sure punishment of those who violate the agreements that are reached by the nations. Penalization is essential if peace is to be more than a feverish interlude between wars."

Then in his closing remarks:

"All of us are consecrated to making an end of gloom and hopelessness. It will not be an easy job. The way is long and thorny, but supremely worth travelling. All of us want to stand erect, with our faces to the sun, instead of being forced to burrow into the earth like rats.

"The pattern of salvation must be worked out by all for all.

"The light at the end of the tunnel is dim, but our path seems to grow brighter as we actually begin our journey. We cannot yet light the way to the end. However, we hope the suggestions of my government will be illuminating.

"Let us keep in mind the exhortation of Abraham Lincoln, whose words, uttered at a moment of shattering national peril, form a complete text for our deliberation. I quote, paraphrasing slightly:

"We cannot escape history. We of this meeting will be remembered in spite of ourselves. No personal significance or insignificance can spare one or another of us. The fiery trial through which we are passing will light us down in honor or dishonor to the latest generation.

"We say we are for Peace. The world will not forget that we say this. We know how to save Peace. The world knows that we do. We, even we here, hold the power and have the responsibility.

"We shall nobly save, or meanly lose, the last best hope of earth. The way is plain, peaceful, generous, just—a way which, if followed, the world will forever applaud."

Some of the most important concrete proposals of the report are reproduced below:

"The United States proposes the creation of an International Atomic Development Authority, to which should be entrusted all phases of the development and use of atomic energy, starting with the raw material and including:

1. Managerial control or ownership of all atomic energy activities potentially dangerous to world security.

2. Power to control, inspect, and license all other atomic activities.

3. The duty of fostering the beneficial uses of atomic energy.

4. Research and development responsibilities of an affirmative character intended to put the Authority in the forefront of atomic knowledge and thus to enable it to comprehend, and therefore, to detect, misuse of atomic energy. To be effective, the Authority must itself be the world's leader in the field of atomic knowledge and development and thus supplement its legal authority with the great power inherent in possession of leadership in knowledge.

"I offer this as a basis for beginning our discussion.

"But I think, the peoples we serve would not believe—and without faith nothing counts—that a treaty, merely outlawing possession or use of the atomic bomb constitutes effective fulfillment of the instructions to this Commission. Previous failures have been recorded in trying the method of simple renunciation, unsupported by effective guarantees of security and armament limitation. No one would have faith in that approach alone.

"Now, if ever, is the time to act for the common good. Public opinion supports the world movement toward security. If I read the signs aright, the peoples want a program not composed merely of pious thoughts but of enforceable sanctions—an international law with teeth in it.

"When an adequate system for control of atomic energy, including the renunciation of the bomb as a weapon, has been agreed upon and put into effective operation and condign punishments set up for violations of the rules of control which are to be stigmatized as international crimes, we propose that:

1. Manufacture of atomic bombs shall stop.

2. Existing bombs shall be disposed of pursuant to the terms of the treaty, and

3. The Authority shall be in possession of full information as to the know-how for the production of atomic energy.

"Let me repeat, so as to avoid misunderstanding: my country is ready to make its full contribution toward the end we seek, subject, of course, to our constitutional processes, and to an adequate system of control becoming fully effective, as we finally work it out.

"Now as to violations: in the agreements, penalties of as serious a nature as the nations may wish and as immediate and certain in their execution as possible, should be fixed for:

1. Illegal possession or use of an atomic bomb.

2. Illegal possession, or separation, of atomic material suitable for use in an atomic bomb.

3. Seizure of any plant or other property belonging to or licensed by the Authority.

4. Wilful interference with the activities of the Authority.

5. Creation or operation of dangerous projects in a manner contrary to, or in the absence of, a license granted by the international control body.

"It would be a deception, to which I am unwilling to lend myself, were I not to say to you and to our peoples, that the matter of punishment lies at the very heart of our present security system. It might as well be admitted, here and now, that the subject goes straight to the veto power contained in the Charter of the United Nations so far as it relates to the field of atomic energy. The Charter permits penalization only by concurrence of each of the five great powers—the Soviet Union, the United Kingdom, China, France and the United States.

"I want to make very plain that I am concerned here with the veto power only as it affects this particular problem. There must be no veto to protect those who violate their solemn agreements not to develop or use atomic energy for destructive purposes. The bomb does not wait upon debate. To delay may be to die. The time between violation and preventive action or punishment would be all too short for extended discussion as to the course to be followed."

Then later on we read:

"But before a country is ready to relinquish any winning weapons, it must have more than words to reassure it. It must have a guarantee of safety, not only against the offenders in the atomic area, but against the illegal users of other weapons—bacteriological, biological, gas—perhaps—why not? against war itself?"[1]

The publication of the Baruch Plan, as it came to be called, was received with wide acclaim by all members of the Atomic Energy Commission except the Soviet Union and Poland. Typical comments were the following:

General McNaughton (Canada):
    . . . At the first meeting of the Commission on Friday last, we had the privilege of listening to the constructive and imaginative proposals which were put before us by Mr. Baruch on behalf of the Government of the United States.
    I am now authorized to say that the Canadian Government welcomes this approach to the problems before the Commission and that Canada supports the principles on which those proposals have been based. We are well aware that proposals so novel and far-reaching will encounter many difficulties. Some of these, no doubt, will be hard to overcome, but we should not be deterred; for on the success of our efforts the future of the world depends.

Sir Alexander Cadogan (U.K.):
    His Majesty's Government in the United Kingdom warmly welcome the statement by the United States Representative and are grateful to the United States Government for providing so broad and constructive a basis for the Commission's work.
    Consequently, His Majesty's Government fully endorse the emphasis laid in the United States statement on the need for condign, immediate and effective penalties against violation of

[1] This last paragraph merits careful study. Its explicit meaning seems clearly that the U.S. did not then contemplate relinquishing its atomic bombs, until a firm guarantee was obtained against *all* weapons of mass destruction. Thus even if the U.S.S.R. accepted the full American plan for control of atomic bombs, Mr. Baruch's statement implies that America would be justified in refusing to dispose of her bombs till a satisfactory system of control, say, of biological warfare had also been accepted. On this basis, the Russians might argue that some new weapon could always be found to justify postponement of the dispersal of atomic bombs to "the Greek calends."

the future international scheme of control. The greatest deterrent value against any such violation will be the knowledge that punishment will be inevitable and overwhelming.

For example, there is the question of the actual weapons with which penalties[2] would be enforced on a transgressor and this is one of the crucial points in the scheme which will require particular study. Peace has been defined as depending always on there being overwhelming power behind just law.

Dr. Quo (China):

I wish to express on behalf of my Government, our keen appreciation of the great contribution that Mr. Baruch has already made at this initial stage of our labors. This is indeed a source of inspiration and encouragement to us all and to an anxious world.

Dr. Vallarta (Mexico):

. . . In the name of the Mexican Delegation I wish to state first that explicit instructions have been received from my Government to approve the elimination of the veto power as far as the questions coming under jurisdiction of the Atomic Energy Commission are concerned, as proposed by the Representative of the United States.

Let us first consider the probable effect of the Baruch Plan, if carried out, on the use of atomic energy for peaceful purposes. It has been shown in Chapter 8 that the potential effect of atomic power in raising living standards must certainly have been rated very high in such a country as the U.S.S.R., which is still very deficient in power compared with America. So it is useful to inquire, firstly, to what extent the adoption of the Baruch Plan would have led to a situation in which the Atomic Development Authority would have had the power to slow down or stop the development of atomic energy for industrial purposes in the U.S.S.R.; secondly, whether this body would have so acted; and thirdly, if it had, what would have been the consequences.

A careful reading of Baruch's speech makes inevitable the conclusion that the Atomic Authority would have had the power to hold up atomic energy development where it desired. It is clear

---

[2] It would appear that the British Government believed that there now exists a preponderance of force in the world by which "condign, immediate and effective penalties" can be imposed on a transgressor without precipitating a long and major war. The reference to "the actual weapons with which penalties would be enforced" suggests that the British Government did actually envisage the feasibility of imposing sanctions with a limited variety of weapons (and what else but atomic bombs could have been meant?) rather than by a major campaign of all arms.

that the production of power on a large scale was to be classed, following the Lilienthal Plan, as a dangerous operation to be entrusted only to A.D.A., and that only minor power plants were to be under national control. In fact, one of the essential features of the Baruch Plan, as it was of the Lilienthal Plan, was that large-scale power production should be removed from national control, owing to the ease of adaptation of the plants to bomb production.[3] Without this provision the plan would certainly not have been put forward. Thus we conclude that the A.D.A. would under certain conditions have had the right to stop or slow down actual power production or even the technical development of power production in, say, the U.S.S.R.

Moreover, it is clear that any reasonable guess at the probable national members of the A.D.A. over the next ten or twenty years would give a majority of members voting in favor of such a course, if the United States considered the matter to be of great importance.[4] Increased power resources in the U.S.S.R. would mean not only an increased standard of living, but increased economic and military strength. The Soviet leaders might well consider that the American Government, out of fear of the economic and political consequences of a possible rapid economic advance, would be most unwilling to permit the Soviet Union to develop atomic energy on a large scale, even if this was done without danger of diversion to bomb production. Even if the American Government were not influenced by this motive, the very nature of the proposed control system implied that the development of atomic power would be based not primarily on the economic needs of the various countries, but would be subordinated to the needs of military security. It will be remembered that in the Lilienthal

[3] According to the Lilienthal Plan, about half the power output would be in A.D.A. hands and half in national hands. But the former would be the key plants on which the others would be completely dependent for supply of fissile materials.

[4] Some countries which might themselves benefit greatly by the development of atomic energy, might well be susceptible to the security argument, and so would oppose its development in the U.S.S.R.

President Truman's confidence that the majority of the United Nations would support what the United States considered her just demands is shown clearly by the following passage from his Address to the Nation on August 9, 1945. ". . . though the United States wants no territory or profit or selfish advantage out of this war, we are going to maintain the military bases necessary for the complete protection of our interests and of world peace. Bases which our military experts deem to be essential for our protection, and which are not now in our possession, we will acquire. We will acquire them by arrangements consistent with the United Nations Charter."

150

Plan the major atomic plants were to be located on strategic grounds, not according to need. How would the number of plants, allocated, say, to America and Russia be determined? If it was according to relative need, America, with her already high standard of living and ample supplies of coal and oil, would receive few or none! If A.D.A. made such a decision, America would certainly repudiate the whole scheme. But allocation on strategic grounds would lead equally to grave injustices. For instance, Russia might find herself allotted the same number of plants as America; the result, of course, would be to tend to stabilize the present inequality of living standards.

These conditions make it probable that the United States Government would not have proposed a scheme such as the A.D.A. if they had not every confidence that the Western Powers would be assured of a majority on A.D.A.[5]

To answer our third question as to the probable consequences, if the A.D.A. had attempted to slow down or stop atomic energy developments for industrial purposes in the Soviet Union, it is necessary to consider the proposed stages by which the Plan was to come into operation and the proposed punishments for violations.

Let us suppose that the Charter was drawn up to cover, say, a period of ten years, in such detail as to specify just what plants or what power output should be erected in what countries and at what dates. This would be a formidable task, especially in a field of technology in extremely rapid development. But let us suppose this were done to the mutual satisfaction of the Great Powers. Is it not perfectly clear that clashes of interest would later be bound to arise, either due to questions of interpretation of the Plan (perhaps brought about by some technological advance made in the meantime), or perhaps by some large change in the overall economic situation of one of the nations?

[5] It is clear that Mr. Baruch's proposals were such as to insure that, at any rate for the first few years of its operation, the operating and inspection personnel of the Atomic Development Authority would be predominantly American. For Mr. Baruch in his original speech said: "The personnel of the Authority should be recruited on a basis of proven competence, but also so far as possible on an international basis." It must be remembered that America undoubtedly has at the present time far greater numbers of scientists and technicians of "proven competence" in nuclear energy than any other country, and possibly more even than all other countries put together. It will be noticed that the international character of the personnel was only to be implemented "as far as possible."

The problem now arises how such a dispute would be handled by the UN. According to the Baruch Plan, the decision would not be governed by the unanimity rule, so that a decision adverse to some Great Power, say the Soviet Union, could be taken against its opposition. If the Soviet Union considered, as well it might, that the issue was an important one and the decision unjust, it would have to repudiate the agreement unless it was willing to abandon an industrial project that might be vital to its productive development.

On what would happen then, Baruch is quite explicit. In the list of crimes, which would merit immediate and condign punishment is not only "the illegal possession of an atomic bomb," but "creation or operation of dangerous projects in a manner contrary to, or in the absence of, a license granted by the international control body." Since large-scale power supply is essentially, in the sense of the Lilienthal Plan, a dangerous project, a country such as the U.S.S.R. which attempted to develop atomic energy for power production—even with the most peaceful of intentions, but against a majority decision of A.D.A.—might find itself convicted of the crime of "wilful interference with the activities of the Authority," and so become liable to have instant and condign punishment imposed on her. The Baruch Plan might have transformed a program of social betterment into an international crime.[6]

Apart from the possibility of interference by A.D.A., by a majority vote, with a long-term Soviet plan to use atomic energy to strengthen the U.S.S.R. economically (and hence militarily), the putting into operation of the Baruch Plan would undoubtedly have led to an immediate reduction of Russian military strength relative to America, uncompensated by any clear reciprocal gain. For the first stage of the Baruch Plan—and here it followed the *Franck Report* of 1945 and the Lilienthal Plan—was to consist of a world-wide survey for the raw materials of atomic energy. The operation of such an unlimited survey in the U.S.S.R. would have given the UN inspectors—and hence the American Chiefs of Staff—a fairly complete target map of the U.S.S.R., even if it

---

[6] Mr. Bullitt goes so far as to use the expressed determination of the Soviet Union to raise her steel production to sixty million tons per year, as one of the proofs of Soviet aggressive imperialism, so stigmatizing as provocative the attempt of another country to reach the American level of prosperity.

did not develop into a complete system of military and industrial espionage. In the present situation in the world, with America in possession of a stock of atomic bombs and explicitly espousing their use as a normal means of war, the Soviet military authorities would rightly consider that secrecy about the exact locations of military and industrial plants and even of new industrial areas would be a considerable military asset.[7] On the other hand, the American authorities would be correct in assuming no comparable worsening of American military security from the acquisition by the Soviet Government of a target map of America. For there is at present little secrecy about the location of essential plants in America; thus, not much would be lost on this score by the admission of UN (including Soviet) inspectors to American territory. If America undertook a dispersal of essential plants, out of fear of atomic bombs—a possible step which has been very fully discussed—then America would judge that secrecy as to the location of her newly dispersed plants would be of military importance.

Moreover, even if the degree of present geographical secrecy were the same in the U.S.A. and in the U.S.S.R., which it is not, the present differences in the positions of the two countries in relation to atomic bombs would make the effects of an unlimited international inspection system far more detrimental to the Soviet Union than to the U.S.A. For the former has, presumably, no atomic bombs, nor the means of delivering them to targets in America, while the latter has not only a large stock pile, but has access to bases from which they can probably be delivered on targets in Russia.

It is certain, therefore, that the early stages of the operation of the Baruch Plan would be definitely detrimental to immediate Soviet security. There is nothing in the Plan which suggests that the U.S.S.R. would gain anything immediate and substantial in exchange. All the potential benefits to the U.S.S.R.—release of

[7] The military significance of secrecy as to geographical locations is well brought out by the remark of Field-Marshal von Rundstedt about the campaign in Russia.

"I realized soon after the attack was begun that everything that had been written about Russia was nonsense. The maps we were given were all wrong. The roads that were marked nice and red and thick on a map turned out to be tracks, and what were tracks on the map became first-class roads. Even railways which were to be used by us simply didn't exist. Or a map would indicate that there was nothing in the area, and suddenly we would be confronted with an American-type town with factory buildings and all the rest of it." Shulman, *Defeat in the West*, p. 66.

know-how, scrapping of American bombs, etc.—are to come only after an adequate system of atomic energy control has been set up, and a system of effective sanctions for violations have been agreed upon. The Baruch Plan proposes to fix the various stages by which the Plan should come into operation; but the decision at any time as to the degree to which the envisaged stages had been achieved, would rest on a majority vote of the Atomic Energy Commission. Hence at any time the Commission could decide that some country had not fulfilled her obligations under the earlier stages of the control plan, and so could decide against the implementation of the later stages. Russia would rightly expect that the possible gain accruing to her in the later stages would be dependent on a majority vote of an international commission on which the U.S.S.R. and her supporters would surely be in a minority.[8]

No explicit time scale for the implementation of the various stages was given in the report. But in the War Department document submitted to Congress in the spring of 1947, the view is expressed that a period of five years would elapse after international control is achieved before the final destruction of the American stock pile of bombs.

Even were the Soviet leaders convinced that the present American Government is sincerely determined to implement all the proposed schedule of stages, including the eventual destruction and outlawing of the bombs, they would inevitably consider that another Administration might come into power with different views. They would anticipate the possibility that some technical pretext might be used to justify the non-implementation of the final stages, so leaving America in possession of her stock pile and Russia with nothing gained but some, possibly inconsiderable, technical know-how.

It is interesting to speculate on what would have happened if the roles of America and Russia in relation to atomic bombs had been reversed. Suppose that Russia had produced bombs first and used them, say, on June 4, 1944—two days before D-day—to induce German capitulation to the Soviet Armed Forces alone. Britain and America would have been bitterly critical, and justi-

[8] A further discussion of this point will be found in Chapter 13, in connection with the majority report of the Atomic Energy Commission.

fiably so. Then, suppose that the Soviet Union had proposed a plan of control like the Baruch Plan but in reverse, with immediate international ownership and inspection, but with the outlawing of the use of the bombs and their destruction postponed for several years, and even then made dependent essentially on Soviet acquiescence. Suppose this had happened, would such a plan have been hailed by the Western Powers as "one of the most generous gestures of history"?

When we turn to consider the nature of the condign punishment to be inflicted on violators of an A.D.A. decision, we are bound once more to consider the general problem of how and in what circumstances one group of nations can in fact impose its will on another. If the offending nations are small and weak, no problem arises since the remaining nations would possess such an overwhelming preponderance of force as to make capitulation probable without the actual use of force; or, if force were needed, the resulting war would be short and decisive. If, however, the offending nation were great and powerful, no such overwhelming force could be brought to bear on it, and the outcome of the attempt to use force would be a major war which would almost certainly develop into a third world war.

It was clearly considerations of this kind that led to the incorporation in the Charter of the United Nations of Article 27, which demands unanimity of the Great Powers on all matters other than procedural matters; that is, in particular when the enforcement of sanctions is in question. The Baruch proposals explicitly recommend that the unanimity rule should be waived in matters concerning atomic energy. If these proposals had been adopted, it would have been possible for the United Nations, by a majority vote, to order all member nations to impose armed sanctions against any nation which had taken some action in the field of atomic energy—such as the setting up of an atomic power station without a license from A.D.A.—which the same majority of the United Nations considered to be a serious violation of the atomic energy agreement. If the Baruch Plan had been adopted, it would have created a situation in which any violation, real or suspected, of the agreement, could by a majority vote be used to precipitate the third World War.

When one tries to understand how it was that such proposals were ever put forward and should have been received in so many places with such wide acclaim, one can detect several main strands of thought.

Much of the support for the Baruch Plan was clearly derived from the belief that the advent of the atomic bomb had in fact made it possible to impose sanctions on a Great Power without precipitating a long and major war of all arms. That this should be the implicit view of the general public and particularly of the atomic scientists, who had been morally and mentally stunned by the effects of the bombs on Japan and who were without professional military knowledge, is fully understandable. But more explanation is needed as to why responsible statesmen like Mr. Stimson and Sir Alexander Cadogan should have definitely supported this view, in the statements quoted already in Chapters 9 and 10. As Secretary of War, Mr. Stimson was certainly fully advised as to the professional views of his military staff. As had been shown in detail in Chapters 5 and 6, the gist of the American Army and Navy thinking about the military effects of the atomic bomb is that, important as the bomb certainly is as a weapon, the time is certainly not in sight—and it is doubtful if it will ever come—when a quick and cheap military decision can be achieved even with atomic bombs in a war against a Great Power. It is impossible to believe that Mr. Stimson was not informed of these views of the military. When therefore, in February 1947, Mr. Stimson stated that with the aid of atomic bombs "even a very powerful unsuspecting nation might be conquered within a very few days by a very much smaller one," he was clearly contradicting the views of his own military advisers. Whatever the reason for Mr. Stimson's remarks, they certainly had the result of increasing markedly the already very considerable fear existing in the United States as to the danger of a sudden atomic bomb attack by the U.S.S.R., and so strengthening the American determination to insist on no retreat from the full Baruch Plan.[9]

[9] Official sanction to the expectation that such an attack on American cities by Soviet atomic bombers is likely to take place as soon as the Soviet Government has the bombs and the carriers, is found in the *Compton* and *Finletter Reports* (reviewed in Appendix V).

It is important to bear in mind the essentially complex strands of thought that went to make up the prevailing opinion of American political, military and public circles relating to atomic energy control. There always has been a large group which never wanted any international control at all and who bitterly opposed the Lilienthal Plan as idealistic, and as giving away the security which they believed the possession of more or better bombs than any other nation gave them. Once, however, the United Nations had adopted the principle of international control, the obvious tactics of this group was to demand a form of control which was so one-sided as to be clearly unacceptable to the Soviet Union. Thus some of the support for the Baruch Plan may have had its origin in an attempt to block any kind of control at all.

Still, even to people of this way of thinking, there was always the attractive chance, or so it may have seemed to them, that the Russians might have accepted the Plan. As has already been pointed out, this would have entailed an immediate weakening of the Russian military position and an eventual weakening of her economic position also. To those who have convinced themselves of Russian aggressive expansionism, such a weakening would have had the effect of discouraging acts of expansion which might have led to war. So support for the Baruch Plan falls into place as a consistent part of the Anglo-American policy of "containing" Communism at all possible points.[10] In this sense the Baruch Plan was a forerunner of the explicit Truman doctrine, of which the theoretical formulation has been given by George F. Kennan, Director of the Policy Planning Staff of the Department of State and expert on Russian affairs, in *Foreign Affairs* for July 1947.[11]

[10] A more extreme form of this view which was current in certain Washington circles in the autumn of 1946, took the form of a belief that the adoption or operation of the Baruch Plan would have led to such drastic social changes in Russia as to cause the actual disruption of the Soviet regime. What was not clear in this view was whether it was believed that drastic alteration to the social structure of the Soviet Union would be an essential preliminary to a Soviet acceptance of the Baruch Plan, or a necessary consequence of having accepted it. In either case, it is hardly to be credited that such drastic alteration in the Soviet system as was envisaged could have come about without a social and political upheaval in Eastern Europe and Russia which would almost certainly have led to widespread civil war.

[11] This article was published anonymously but was stated later by Walter Lippmann in his book *The Cold War* to have been written by Mr. George F. Kennan. It is of interest to note that Mr. Kennan expresses the view that Russia is in reality rather weak: "Soviet power bears within itself the seeds of its own decay, and the sprouting of these seeds is well advanced."

There were, of course, many supporters of the Baruch Plan who would not, at least at the time, have subscribed to this view, but on the contrary sincerely believed the Plan to be so equitable and even generous that its rejection by the U.S.S.R. could only be attributed to their willful neglect of their own self-interest. It is unlikely that many hard-headed statesmen or military men held that opinion, but undoubtedly many idealists and liberals in England and America did so. Such people, on seeing the U.S.S.R. reject these "generous" proposals, tended in many cases passionately to implore the Russian leaders to realize the danger in which they stood from American atomic bombs. "The central element in the Russian attitude towards the bomb is *ignorance of its significance....* Their recalcitrance is evidence that they have not understood the political and psychological significance of the atomic bomb. . . ."[12] A recurrent theme is that the Russians have committed the unforgivable sin of not being as frightened of atomic bombs as the Americans.

In the long run, the Baruch Plan, in spite of its rejection by the U.S.S.R., must be considered historically as an astute move and a very considerable victory for American diplomacy. For so great was the success with which this specious plan was put across in most countries as a wise and generous measure, that it became possible to brand the Soviet Union, by her rejection of it, as the sole obstacle to world peace. But, leaving aside motive and intention, and considering the Plan for the moment as a serious attempt to solve the problem of atomic energy—and so it certainly appeared to many individuals whose sincerity was undoubted—one is able, on the basis of the analysis of the former chapters, to detect its essential fallacy. The Baruch Plan would have failed even if all its supporters had been sincere in their intentions, because it attempted the impossible. The attempt to find complete security was bound to fail in the field of atomic energy as in all other fields of life.

In detail, the Plan failed because, in its attempt to secure nearly complete security for America, it was inevitably driven to propose a course of action which would have put the Soviet Union in a situation where she would have been subservient to a group of

[12] E. A. Shils, *B.A.S.*, Sept., 1947.

nations dominated by America. Since America would keep her atomic bombs till a late stage in the process of setting the control scheme in operation, the Soviet Union could have no firm guarantee that, when the stage was reached at which the bombs should be disposed of, some technical point would not be raised to justify retaining them. In the meantime, she would have thrown her land and economy open to inspection and so inevitably to military espionage.

The dangers to the world of the uncontrolled use of atomic energy are indeed great. The arguments of the Lilienthal Plan—that the processes of power production are nearly identical with those of bomb production—are sound. In so far as the intention was to make available for humanity, as soon as possible, all possible peaceful benefits of atomic energy it was praiseworthy. But as the Lilienthal Plan took more concrete shape in the form of the Baruch proposals, it became clear that its most likely outcome would have been to subordinate the development of atomic energy for peaceful purposes to the desire for security from atomic bombs. Under the slogan: "Is Atomic Power Worth the Risk?" the view that it isn't seems to be rapidly gaining ground in America.

To conclude, however, that mankind must be prepared to forego the beneficial use of atomic power for fear of the destructive use of atomic bombs, is like counselling men never to fly because they may crash, never to swim because they may drown, never to light a fire lest they burn down their house; or perhaps, more aptly, to propose the abolition of medical inoculation lest bacteriological weapons are made on the sly. This way lies the road to anxiety neurosis and the madhouse. There are some marked symptoms of anxiety neurosis among Americans today. Some, but by no means all, can be attributed to the possession by the U.S. of atomic bombs, and the consequent dilemma in which Americans feel gripped. As has already been pointed out, the very effective campaign, largely initiated by the atomic scientists themselves, to make the world aware of the terrible dangers of atomic bombs, played an important part in bringing pressure to bear on the American Government to propose measures to control atomic weapons and to take them out of the hands of the military. The

159

very success of this campaign was in the end one of the major causes of the failure of the plans for control. For the American public became so frightened that nothing but the prospect of 100 per cent safety became acceptable.

The only possible way in which the American people can obtain complete safety from atomic bombs is by effective American control of all other nations. The attempt to reach such a state of world hegemony clearly means taking steps which are likely to lead to a third world war, and so to the probability, in their own way of thinking, of atomic bombs being used eventually on America. So the widespread publicity to the real "Horrors of Hiroshima" unwittingly gave impetus to a drive to attain as great a security as America had enjoyed in the past. Clearly this could only be attained by measures which were themselves likely to provoke a third world war and so to increase the likelihood of more Hiroshimas. Here, as in ordinary life, the only real safety lies in taking reasonable risks. But to the overcharged imagination and the uneasy conscience of the American public no risks appear reasonable.

In the present state of the world only world hegemony of some Power or Powers provides *absolute* security from more Hiroshimas. And even this only provides it precariously and in the short run. For, in the long run, world hegemony by one nation, even if initiated by consent, could only be maintained by force. It seems, therefore, certain that any control system for atomic energy which attempts to reach too high a degree of security from atomic bombing is likely to increase, rather than decrease, the danger, through the international tension that will be set up. To date, the American plans for control, strongly supported by Great Britain and most of the Western nations, have undeniably led to worsened relations between Russian and the West. It has already been argued, and will be argued in still more detail in Chapter 15, that the deterioration would have been still greater if the plans had been accepted. It is to Russian stubbornness that the non-acceptance of the Baruch Plan is due. In the next chapter we will consider the Russian attitude in detail.

12. THE SOVIET ATTITUDE TO ATOMIC ENERGY AND MR. GROMYKO'S PROPOSALS

THE first authoritative Russian comments on the implications of atomic energy available to the writer were a series of articles in the fortnightly periodical *New Times*, published in Moscow in many languages. In the issue of September 1, 1945, a well-documented review of world press reactions to atomic bombs was given by Modest Rubinstein. Some of the main themes outlined were the following:

(*a*) The claim that atomic bombs have revolutionized warfare is based on insufficient evidence. On the contrary, the lessons of the last war "have clearly shown that success in war is not achieved by the one-sided development of one or another weapon, but by the perfection of all arms and their skilful coordination."

(*b*) Two main strands in Anglo-American opinion are distinguishable. On the one hand is a "comparatively small though very vociferous group of reactionaries," who see in atomic bombs a means by which America could dominate the world. The Hearst, McCormick and Patterson newspapers are said to demand that the United States should establish its domination over the world by the threat of the atomic bomb. The *London Observer* is quoted as stating that "the policy of monopoly use of the atomic bombs is not only an American but a British-American policy" and that "possession of the atomic bomb makes American and British power preponderance for the time being a fact." Mr. L. S. Amery is quoted as writing in the *Sunday Chronicle* that the United States "in terms of power politics can dominate the world. In comparison, Russia is only a vulnerable second-class Power." Mr. Rubinstein stresses, however, that progressive papers, such as the *Daily Herald*, strongly opposed the attempt to maintain the monopoly of the bomb as being both impossible and dangerous.

(*c*) On the other hand, the author of the article stresses that "much more prevalent are vague arguments to the effect that atomic bombs put all international problems on a new footing

161

and that accordingly earlier Allied agreements . . . are out of date." The article continues: "It is obvious that such arguments, because of their ambiguity can only cause harm. Unless it is clearly specified in what respect recent decisions have become out of date, such statements are only calculated to cause unnecessary confusion and to bewilder credulous minds. It must not be forgotten that the problems relating to the maintenance of peace are political problems. They cannot be examined only from the military technical aspects, ignoring the political, economic and social factors."

(d) Tendencies are noted in the American press to dampen hopes of the peaceful use of atomic energy, and mention is made of the fear expressed by American public utility companies at the potentiality of the new invention.

The final section of the article bears quotation in full:

> The utilization of atomic energy inaugurates a new era, one fraught with momentous and incalculable consequences, in the subjugation of the forces of nature to man, a process which, under the social system which prevails in the majority of the countries of the world, assumes complex and antagonistic forms.
>
> The practical utilization of atomic energy is one more striking demonstration of the fact that modern science and technology hold out prospects of unparalleled expansion of productive forces and of man's mastery over nature. However, formidable obstacles stand in the way of the utilization of these advances for the benefit of the masses. If atomic energy is applied on a big scale to industry, it would, owing to the predominance of capitalist monopoly, result in stupendous unemployment, in the permanent displacement of millions of miners and other workers, and in further enhancing the power of the monopolies, not to mention the awful peril involved if this formidable weapon should fall into the hands of aggressors.
>
> The invention of the atomic bomb renders it still more imperative to mobilize all the forces of progress for the maintenance of enduring peace and reliable security for nations, big and small. At the same time it should be clear to all thinking men that this discovery cannot solve political problems, either nationally or internationally. Those who harbor illusions on this score are doomed to disappointment.
>
> On the other hand, the discovery that it is possible to utilize the inexhaustible resources of atomic energy makes it likewise impera-

tive to speed the organization on a broad scale of genuine international scientific cooperation which is one of the most effective methods of promoting mutual understanding among the freedom-loving nations of the world.

A second survey of the foreign press appeared in the same paper on November 1 by Colonel M. Tolchenov. The main feature of this article was an analysis of the world reactions to President Truman's message to Congress on October 3 (quoted in Chapter 10). Referring to the analysis of the previous article showing the cleavage in America and Britain between the progressive section of the press, with its advocacy of international cooperation to prevent new wars, and the reactionary press, with its insistence on keeping the secrets of the bomb as a means of dominating the world, new quotations are given to show that both groups claim that Mr. Truman's speech confirmed their viewpoints. An explanation is offered in the view of American radio commentator Johannes Steel that the President's message "was obviously a compromise between demands and pressure from the Army and Cartel group upon the one side, and scientists under the leadership of Secretary of Commerce Wallace and former Secretary of War Stimson on the other." In the concluding paragraph of the Tolchenov article we again find emphasis on the theme that: "history convincingly proves that the attempt of any country to attempt world domination with the aid of new weapons is doomed to failure."

In the *New Times* of June 12, 1946, Mr. Rubinstein reviews the book, *One World or None*, the collective work of a group of American scientists published in March 1946, from which we have already quoted. In a discussion of the theme of much of the book, that "there is no defense to atomic bombs," Rubinstein writes:

> Such disquisitions on the relative efficiency of attack and defense are customary whenever a new offensive weapon is devised. We need only recall the theories of the Italian fascist, General Douhet, on the impossibility of defense against air attack, theories which were completely shattered by the second World War. Such, too, was the fate of General Fuller's theory of the overwhelming superiority of the tank offensive and the German strategists' theory of submarine warfare, not to mention others.

Without denying that the immense destructive effect of the atomic bomb introduces factors of an entirely new category, one cannot but remark that the authors of the above-mentioned articles seem involuntarily to have accepted the adventurist *blitzkrieg* doctrine preached by the Nazi strategists. In spite of their best intentions, the learned physicists have unwittingly become tools of the tactics of intimidation which are an integral part of that doctrine. By declaring that "there is no defense," they may be said to be furthering the tactics of psychological warfare. This is the case to an even greater extent in other chapters, those dealing with the military aspects of the atomic bomb.

Then, on the subject of atomic power, Professor Urey is quoted: "The postponement of the use of atomic energy for power plants would make for easier control of the atomic bomb. It is a small price to pay for the accomplishment of this most desirable end."

A passage in an article by Walter Lippmann, advocating the setting up of a world state, by force if necessary, is quoted and criticized. "The United States is at the zenith of its power and for the time being at least is the sole possessor of the most devastating weapons ever manufactured on earth. . . . We can use the pre-eminence of our military power so that an ideal for all mankind, not the United States of America as a national state, may dominate and conquer the world." Rubinstein expresses the view that "the florid talk about a 'World State' is actually a frank plea for American imperialism."

In summing up his view of *One World or None*, Rubinstein comes to the following conclusion:

1. Many of the writers are inclined to accept the theory of a *blitzkrieg* with the help of the atomic bomb.

2. Anxious to secure effective international control of the use of atomic energy at the earliest possible date, many of them lay the colors on too thick, and, however well-intentioned the scientists may be, the effect is to hold up a bogy to the reader. The overt and covert imperialists skillfully exploit this for their own ends.

3. Nearly all the writers, although they consider the utilization of atomic energy for peaceful purposes quite feasible and in certain fields, moreover, in a comparatively short time, nevertheless plead for its postponement, fearing that it may be prejudicial to international control.

4. All the writers evade the important question of the role of the capitalist monopolies in the utilization (or rather non-utiliza-

164

tion) of atomic energy for peaceful purposes and in subordinating all the work in this field to military ends.

In spite of these mistakes (and partly because of them) the book deserves serious attention.

Professor Peter L. Kapitza, the well-known Soviet physicist, in a statement published by *Soviet News* in July 1946 said:

> If the basic problem of nuclear physics is not made a matter for international cooperation, if the physicists are split, and attempt to solve the problem in every country separately, the investigation of these important natural phenomena will undoubtedly be delayed. That will be all the more regrettable because the center of gravity of the problem is certainly not the military aspects of the new discovery, but the unprecedented power of the new source of energy now at the disposal of mankind, and which in time, one may surmise, will change the aspect of our culture.

On June 19, 1946, Andrei Gromyko presented the Soviet proposals for international control of atomic energy to the United Nations Commission. Of particular interest is the emphasis placed on the importance of the use of atomic energy for peaceful purposes:

> As a result of developments in the last few years, circumstances have brought it about that one of the most important discoveries of humanity has found its application at the outset in a particular form of weapon, the atomic bomb. However, although, up to the present time, this use of atomic energy is the only known form for its practical application, it is the general opinion that humanity stands at the threshold of a wide application of atomic energy for peaceful purposes: for the good of the peoples as a means of raising their standards of welfare and their living conditions: for the good of and with a view to the development of science and culture.

This point is again stressed in the preamble of the suggested draft convention which reads: "Deeply aware of the extreme importance of the great scientific discoveries connected with the splitting of the atom and with a view to the use of atomic energy for the purposes of raising the welfare and standard of living of the peoples of the world, and also for the development of culture and science for the good of humanity: unanimously desiring universal cooperation as wide as possible for the use of all people of scientific discoveries in the field of atomic energy, for the improvement of the conditions of the life of the peoples of the whole world, the raising of their standards of welfare and further progress of human culture. . . ."

The Soviet plans for control are outlined in the following paragraph:

As one of the primary measures for the fulfillment of the resolution of the General Assembly of January 24, 1946, the Soviet delegation proposes that consideration be given to the question of concluding an international convention prohibiting the production and employment of weapons based on the use of atomic energy for the purpose of mass destruction. The object of such a convention should be the prohibition of the production and employment of atomic weapons, the destruction of existing stocks of atomic weapons and the condemnation of all activities undertaken in violation of this convention. The elaboration and conclusion of a convention of this kind would be, in the opinion of the Soviet delegation, only one of the primary measures to be taken to prevent the use of atomic energy to the detriment of mankind. This act should be followed by other measures aiming at the establishment of methods to ensure the strict observance of the terms and obligations contained in the above-mentioned convention, the establishment of a system of control over the observance of the convention and the taking of decisions regarding the sanctions to be applied against the unlawful use of atomic energy. The public opinion of the whole civilized world has already rightly condemned the use in warfare of asphyxiating, poisonous and other similar gases, as well as all similar liquids and substances, and likewise bacteriological means, by concluding corresponding agreements for the prohibition of their use.

The Soviet proposed a draft international agreement of which the main Articles were as follows:

"Article 1: The high contracting parties solemnly declare that they will forbid the production and use of a weapon based upon the use of atomic energy, and with this in view, take upon themselves the following obligations:

(*a*) Not to use, in any circumstances, an atomic weapon.

(*b*) To forbid the production and keeping of a weapon based upon the use of atomic energy.

(*c*) To destroy within a period of three months from the entry into force of this agreement all stocks of atomic energy weapons whether in a finished or semi-finished condition.

Article 2: The high contracting parties declare that any violation of Article 1 of this agreement shall constitute a serious crime against humanity.

Article 3: The high contracting parties, within six months of the entry into force of the present agreement, shall pass legislation providing severe punishment for the violation of the terms of this agreement.

Article 4: The present agreement shall be of indefinite duration.

Article 5: The present agreement is open for signature to all States whether or not they are Members of the United Nations.

Article 6: The present agreement shall come into force after approval by the Security Council, and after ratification by half the signatory States, including all States Members of the United Nations, as under Article 23 of the Charter. The ratifications shall be placed for safe-keeping in the hands of the Secretary-General of the United Nations.

Article 7: After the entry into force of the present agreement, it shall be an obligation upon all States whether Members or not of the United Nations."

The Soviet delegate proposed a Committee should be set up to prepare recommendations on various subjects (of which the last two are especially relevant to the present discussion):

"1. The preparation of a draft international agreement for the outlawing of weapons based upon the use of atomic energy and forbidding the production and use of such weapons and all similar forms of weapons destined for mass destruction.

2. The elaboration and creation of methods to forbid the production of weapons based upon the use of atomic energy and to prevent the use of atomic weapons and all other similar weapons of mass destruction.

3. Measures, system, and organization of control in the use of atomic energy to ensure the observance of the conditions above-mentioned in the international agreement for the outlawing of atomic weapons.

4. The elaboration of a system of sanctions for application against the unlawful use of atomic energy."

The penultimate paragraph is of great importance:

"Efforts made to undermine the activity of the Security Council, including efforts directed to undermine the unanimity of the members of the Security Council upon questions of substance, are incompatible with the interests of the United Nations created by the international organization for the preservation of peace and security. Such attempts should be resisted. I considered it necessary to make this statement in order that from the very beginning of the work of our Commission I might make clear the position of the Soviet Government as regards the question of the character and basis of the work of the Commission upon the question of the preparation of its recommendations as regards measures of control of atomic energy placed before the Security Council.

"In conclusion, I wish to say that in this statement I aimed chiefly at underlining the extreme importance to be attributed to the conclusion of the above-mentioned agreement for the outlawing of the production and use of atomic weapons. The conclusion of such an agreement would constitute an important practical step in the direction of fulfilling the task which lies before the Commission."

Comment in the Western world on Mr. Gromyko's proposals was unfavorable. They were held to be entirely inadequate to the situation and it was feared that they might even give rise to greater dangers than no control at all. Without a complete system of *unlimited* international inspection, how could the peaceful Powers know that some aggressive Power was not building atomic plants in secret? The proposal to outlaw atomic bombs and other weapons of mass destruction was likened to the ill-fated Kellogg Pact outlawing war.

It is doubtful whether the Soviet Government, with its knowledge of the state of mind of the American public and military departments, expected its proposals to be taken very seriously, since they would have robbed the American Government of what it certainly then considered as its main weapon to weigh against the strength of the Soviet Army. On the other hand, since the American proposals would have left Russia in a very much weakened position, the U.S.S.R. had to play for time. These delaying tactics were particularly important in view of the novelty of the problems, and the doubt that the Soviet Government must have entertained whether all the information necessary for a full understanding of the military and social implications had been made available to them.

That this doubt was justified appears clearly in a recent article[1] by J. R. Oppenheimer, who writes: "One must bear in mind that for reasons of security much that was relevant to an understanding of the problem could not be revealed and cannot be revealed today." This statement implies that if the Soviet Government had signed an agreement for the control of atomic energy they would have done this while ignorant of some essential information.

The Editorial in the *Bulletin of the Atomic Scientists* for July, 1946[2] gives a reasoned appraisal of the Russian and American proposals, laying special stress on the Russian opposition to Mr. Baruch's proposal that the "veto" should not operate so far as sanctions against nations violating any provisions of the Atomic Energy Convention. "Thus the question of sanctions and the veto power became the first point of disagreement in the Atomic Energy Commission—a controversy which may deadlock its deliberations. Since such a deadlock may be tragic, it is essential to approach the veto provisions in their relation to the international control of atomic energy as dispassionately as possible." The article recognizes that the essence of the veto controversy lies, not in the day-to-day working of the control system, but in the applications of sanctions. "If the agreement be violated by a major nation, the other Great Powers will hardly be deterred from action by the veto power of the violator. . . . The question will then be one of war or peace and it will make little difference whether the threatening war is 'legal' or 'illegal' under the veto provisions."

The last sentence is certainly untrue in many important circumstances. Consider, for instance, the position of Russia, if accused of building atomic power plants in excess of her stipulated quota, and threatened with armed sanctions by, say, America and Britain. In the absence of the veto power, the UN could, by a two-

[1] *B.A.S.*, Feb., 1948.
[2] *B.A.S.*, July, 1946.

thirds majority, impose on *all* the member states the *obligation* to participate in armed sanctions against Russia, whereas, under the unanimity rule, each nation would be free to make its own choice whether to do so. For instance, in the former case, a small nation which happened to be suitably placed geographically to provide bases for American atomic bombers would be legally obliged to do so. It can hardly, therefore, be maintained that little difference will result whether the war is legalized by the UN or not.

One finds in most Anglo-American criticism of the Russian objection to the abolition of the veto clear signs of the implicit assumption, which we have already discussed in detail and held to be fallacious, that armed sanctions can be imposed on a major Power without precipitating a third world war.

The *B.A.S.* Editorial continues:

> Appraisal of the Russian proposals must be based first of all on its attitude towards the establishment of an effective International Atomic Energy Authority, with assured rights of research, production, control and inspection. In this respect, all that can be said of the Russian declaration is that it is not entirely negative. The only detailed suggestions in the Russian plan deal with the outlawing of atomic weapons and with the exchange of information. That the Russians would suggest as a first step the outlawing of atomic weapons, and the destruction of existing bombs, could easily have been predicted; that they would also press for rapid release of all atomic information, should not astound anyone. Neither of the two proposals touches upon the most fundamental issues. As pointed out by Walter Lippmann, the insistence on the prohibition of atomic bombs, and the destruction of existing bombs, is a sign of insufficient understanding of what the real danger is. There is no question but that the existence of assembled atomic bombs constitutes a serious problem, but the true long-range threat of atomic energy lies in uncontrolled large-scale production of atomic explosives ("fissionable materials") whether for military or for peacetime application (atomic power).

This last passage underlines very clearly the essential difference in emphasis between the Anglo-American and Russian viewpoints. The threat to Russia from American bombs exists *now*, while the threat to America from Russian bombs is some years *in the future*. When Lippmann implies that Russia has "insufficient understanding of what the real danger is," he is deserting his usually realistic standpoint. Russia knows only too well that the main danger to her now is the short-range danger, due to the American stock pile, and is naturally concerned to remove the threat. On the other hand, America—not immediately threatened—characterizes the long-range danger as the *true* danger.

It is hardly likely that either the American or Russian Governments had serious expectations that their proposals for control would be accepted by the other. As has already been emphasized, the American proposals constituted a very shrewd move in the diplomatic cold war, promising concrete advantages in the event either of their acceptance or their rejection. American diplomacy had maneuvered Russia into the disadvantageous position of having to reject a speciously fair offer. Gromyko's speech was an attempt to retrieve the situation; but, in the eyes of the Western world, the attempt was unsuccessful.

The Soviet Government was diplomatically on the defensive and had little freedom of tactical maneuver in the field of atomic energy itself. Clearly her interests were to attempt to delay any decisions till the real issues became clearer and her bargaining position had improved. If the analysis of this book is accepted, the Soviet Goverment had very good reasons to reject the American proposals. But it was inevitable that these reasons would fail to be appreciated in those circles which held the American proposals to constitute "a generous and equitable plan proposed in good faith."

The key to the widespread failure to understand the Soviet viewpoint, a failure which has led to the constant reiteration of the theme that the Russians neither understand the problem nor realize the danger in which they stand, is the failure to realize that the basic demand for complete security behind the American control plan could not be satisfied within the next decade without revolutionary changes in the political structure of the world. The actual authors of the Baruch Plan presumably believed either that these revolutionary changes could be forced through peaceably, using to the full the threat to the world of atomic weapons, or, failing this, that the possession of bombs by America would allow the changes to be imposed by force without precipitating

171

a long-drawn-out and devastating third world war. The history of the last two years has shown that the first method has not been successful. The military analysis in previous chapters suggests that the second belief is fallacious.

13. THE UNITED NATIONS ATOMIC ENERGY COMMISSION

It would be impossible in a short book to attempt a full survey of the discussions in the United Nations Atomic Energy Commission (A.E.C.) since its first meetings in June, 1946, or of the widespread public comment on the contesting viewpoints revealed there. What will be attempted in this chapter is to bring into relief those aspects of the controversy which, in the writer's opinion, have special significance for the understanding of the present impasse.

Before proceeding to discuss the chief points of controversy, mention must be made of the considerable amount of valuable technical and scientific information[1] on atomic energy processes which was given to the A.E.C. by the American delegation in accordance with the decision to make available sufficient information for a proper understanding of the problem. One of the essential difficulties of negotiating a control agreement on a subject which is still largely secret is that the nations not "in the know" could never be certain that they had been given all the essential information. As has been observed in the previous chapter, Dr. Oppenheimer has recently said that they were not.

Much has been made of the success in getting agreement of all countries, including Russia, on the technical possibility of controlling atomic energy. Though the importance of this must not be underrated, it should be remembered that the *technical* possibilities of the control of other armaments—land forces, navies and air forces—have always existed, and are much easier than the control of atomic energy. Since the most serious danger to the world from atomic bombs lies in their probable employment only

[1] Baruch, *The International Control of Atomic Energy: Scientific Information Transmitted to the United Nations Atomic Energy Commission, 1946*, Vols. I-III.

in combination with powerful other arms, the control of the latter would greatly reduce the danger from atomic bombs. Yet no detailed proposals for the control of other arms have been put forward by the Western Powers.

The main available source of information on the proceedings of the Commission are its First and Second Reports to the Security Council, dated December 30, 1946, and September 11, 1947. Valuable additional light on American policy is to be found in the official American publication[2] entitled *Growth of a Policy*. No later official documents are available to the writer. In the discussion which follows, an attempt will be made to elucidate the real points of difference between the rival policies, rather than the verbal and legal forms in which, inevitably, these differences were actually manifested in the discussions. A careful reading of these documents shows clearly that the fundamental points of difference remained throughout the discussions essentially the same as those which had already emerged in the opening speeches by Mr. Baruch and Mr. Gromyko. It will therefore be legitimate to concentrate mainly on the final position of the contesting groups, as reached in the autumn of 1947, rather than on the steps by which these were reached.

The two official Reports, adopted by a majority of the member nations of the A.E.C. but rejected by the U.S.S.R., follow very closely in their recommendations the lines of argument first outlined in the Lilienthal and the Baruch Plans, and amplified in three memorandums submitted to the Commission by the United States representative early in June, 1946. The views and recommendations put forward in these three American memorandums and those expressed in the First and Second Reports[3] of the A.E.C. show little essential difference. On the other hand, the alternative proposals put forward by the U.S.S.R. on July 11, 1947, differ very

[2] The extent of the divorce of the discussions on control of atomic bombs from any serious military considerations as to their effectiveness in war is shown by the fact that in the 278 pages of this official American book, there is no detailed discussion at all of the military basis of the arguments. This might be taken to imply that there was universal agreement on these military facts. Evidence that this is not the case has been given in earlier chapters.

[3] The *Second Report* was adopted by the Commission on September 11, 1947 by a vote of ten to one, with one abstention. The nations voting for the Report were: Australia, Belgium, Brazil, Canada, China, Colombia, France, Syria, United Kingdom and the United States. The Soviet Union voted against, and Poland abstained.

considerably from the original plan proposed by Mr. Gromyko in June, 1946. The new Soviet proposals were much more detailed and, in fact, incorporated a part of the detailed proposals adopted by the majority of the A.E.C.

The area of agreement reached by September, 1947 was considerable. To demonstrate the extent of this agreement, the General Findings and Recommendations of the First Report, together with the alternative Soviet proposals put forward on June 11, 1947, are reproduced in full in Appendices III and IV.

The extent to which these final Soviet proposals meet the demand for an adequate inspection by an international inspectorate of all national atomic plants is shown clearly in the various sections of the document. The personnel of the Control Commission were to be selected on an international basis, and were, among other things, to have access to all mines, plants and stock piles, and to inspect these periodically. The Commission was itself to be authorized to carry on research and to study production operations to the extent necessary to exercise its control function.

Taken together, these proposals represented a considerable move towards meeting the demands of the majority on the Atomic Energy Commission, and a definite change of Soviet policy. For Mr. Gromyko is reported[4] to have held originally that a system of international inspection was not in conformity with the sovereignty of States, though the actual text of his remarks to this effect does not appear to be available.

The main points of difference between the majority and minority views are brought out by the questions put by the representative of the United Kingdom in a letter to the representative of the U.S.S.R., of which the most important were the following:

(a) Is it to be understood from the last two lines of paragraph 4 [of the Soviet proposals stating that the convention on atomic energy control is to be concluded in accordance with the convention on the prohibition of atomic weapons], that the Soviet Government maintain their view that the prohibition and destruction of atomic weapons must be the subject of a separate agreement to be concluded in advance of any agreement on control? And would the Soviet representative be ready to modify his position to the

[4] In United States State Department, *The International Control of Atomic Energy: Growth of a Policy* (Washington, 1946).

extent of saying that the first convention (on prohibition) shall only come into force following satisfactory implementation of the second convention?

(*i*) Can the Soviet proposals be interpreted as allowing any further consideration of such controls as supervision, management or licensing as defined in the First Report of the Atomic Energy Commission?

(*j*) Should paragraph 6 (*h*) of the Soviet proposals be interpreted as saying that all measures for the prevention and suppression of violations will be subject to the veto in the Security Council? or,

(*k*) Does the Soviet Government agree that at least minor sanctions against violators of an agreement may be decided upon by a majority vote either in the Commission itself or in the Security Council?

The Soviet answers to these questions were as follows:

Answer to question (*a*). The Soviet Government has considered and continues to consider the prohibition of atomic weapons and the conclusion of an appropriate convention to this end as a foremost and urgent task in the establishment of international control of atomic energy. After the conclusion of a convention on the prohibition of atomic weapons, another convention can and must be concluded, to provide for the creation of an international control commission and for the establishment of other measures of control and inspection, ensuring the fulfilment of the convention on the prohibition of atomic weapons.

Answer to question (*i*). No, since supervision, management, and licensing do not follow from the tasks of the establishment of strict and effective international control of atomic energy.

Answer to question (*j*). Item 6 (*h*) of the Soviet proposals should be understood in the sense that the question of sanctions against violators of the convention on the prohibition of atomic weapons is subject to decisions by the Security Council only. As it is known, the procedure of adoption by the Council of decisions on sanctions as well as of other important decisions relating to the maintenance of international peace has been defined in Article 27 of the United Nations Charter.

Answer to question (*k*). In conformity with the United Nations Charter, decisions on all sanctions can be taken only by the Security Council.

The considered conclusions of the A.E.C. on the Soviet proposals are expressed in the following resolution by one of its Committees:

The Committee RESOLVES that these proposals as they now stand and the explanations given thereon do not provide an adequate basis for the development by the Committee of specific proposals for an effective system of international control of atomic energy. They therefore do not call for a change in the program of work of the Committee.

These extracts from the proceedings of the A.E.C. reveal clearly the basic points of difference between the majority view and that of the Soviet Union. The Soviet Government demanded that the first step towards control should be the outlawing of atomic weapons, and the second the setting up of a control system. The majority recommended a treaty embracing the whole program of putting an international control system into effect. These two rival viewpoints clearly reflect the objective differences in the contemporary position of America and Russia in relation to atomic weapons. America naturally does not wish to let go the advantages that the possession of atomic bombs confers on her, before she has cast-iron guarantees that no other country will ever make atomic weapons. Russia, on the other hand, quite as naturally, refuses to agree to proposals, the initial stages of which would be very largely to her strategic disadvantage and from which the reciprocal benefits would be both speculative and remote. The lack of guarantee that the later stages of the majority plan would be carried out is shown by the wording of paragraph 5 of Part III of the majority Report, in which it is stated explicitly that the Atomic Energy Commission itself should determine when a particular stage is completed so that subsequent ones can commence. Since, according to these proposals, the veto would not operate in the Commission, this implies that a two-thirds majority of the members of the A.E.C. could in principle decide, on some pretext, that no further stages of the plan, including destruction of atomic weapons, should be implemented.

Though each plan corresponded to the military and strategic needs of the countries sponsoring them, the responsibility for putting forward a plan acceptable to both certainly rested with England and America, not only because the atomic bomb was invented in these countries, but because both countries had, historically speaking, enjoyed far greater security in the past than had

Russia. President Truman himself recognized this general obligation in his speech on October 27, 1945, when he said: ". . . We must seek to understand the special problems of other nations. We must seek to understand their own legitimate urge towards security as they see it."

That the majority of the member nations of the A.E.C. should have expected their proposals to be acceptable to the Soviet Union (assuming that they did expect this) suggests a failure to appreciate how the early stages of the plan would affect Soviet military security. Of particular importance is the inevitable loss of secrecy about the location of military establishments and industrial plants, due to the activities of the international inspection and aerial survey, which would occur at the very outset of the control plan; that is, several years before the American stock pile of atomic bombs would be dispersed, even on the most optimistic assumption.

The second important point of difference relates to the ownership or management of the atomic plants by the Commission. The Soviet Union's reasons for rejecting the proposals of the majority Report seem likely to have been in part due to the desire to develop atomic power unhindered by control by an international body, on which she would expect to be in a minority. The majority Report explicitly subordinates peaceful development to the requirements of security, and only within the limits set by the latter recommends the Commission to "make power available on a fair and equitable basis to any nation which requires it."[5] Further, the majority plan recommends the location of the primary, and so "dangerous" plants on a strategic basis, so as to "eliminate as far as practical, the possibilities that a nation or group of nations might obtain military supremacy." Only secondary, and so "safe" atomic plants would be free from these considerations. Since about half the total power generated would come from these primary plants, one would not expect the power to be produced at the places where it was most needed.

More generally, the whole conception of the possibility of a *fair and equitable* allocation of such a potentially important economic factor as atomic power by an impartial international body is surely illusory in a world where such great differences exist in the

[5] Atomic Energy Commission, *Second Report to the Security Council* (New York, 1947).

natural resources, degree of industrialization and standard of living of the various nations. Figures for the actual allocation of power today between America and the rest of the world have already been given in Chapter 8. A curious expression of this illusion of impartiality in such matters is to be found in the second memorandum of the American delegation. This characterizes the activities of the proposed Commission, which explicitly would include decisions on the size and location of power plants, as "essentially non-political." Would it be less "political" than the Washington oil lobby? It is difficult to avoid the conclusion that the majority Report was departing from the realms of political reality by its insistence on the ownership and management functions of the proposed Atomic Energy Commission.

The third main point of disagreement is that of the veto. The clash of view is direct and absolute. The majority recommend that "Once the violations constituting international crimes have been defined and the measures and enforcement and punishment thereof agreed to in the treaty and convention, there shall be no legal right, by veto or otherwise, whereby a wilful violator of the terms of the treaty or convention shall be protected from the consequences of violation of its terms." The Soviet representative states ". . . the Soviet proposals should be understood in the sense that the question of sanctions against violators of the convention on the prohibition of atomic weapons is subject to the decision of the Security Council only."

Which view is correct? As has already been emphasized, it is the opinion of the writer that the approach to an answer can only be made by a detailed analysis of the possible meaning in practice of the words "enforcement and punishment" in the majority statement. These words clearly mean the imposition of economic and/or military sanctions against the violator. Now arguments have already been presented in this book which indicate that, in the present state of the world, the application of such sanctions against a Great Power would, in all probability, result in a long-drawn-out third world war. The basis for this conclusion was an analysis of the military strength and strategical and geographical positions of the Great Powers and of their allies. Naturally such an analysis must depend on the assumptions that are made as to the effect on war of new weapons, particularly weapons of mass destruction such as atomic bombs, and the carriers by which they are delivered to their targets. Using as a basis the evidence furnished by the actual history of the 1939-1945 war, it was concluded that sanctions could not, for instance, be applied to the Soviet Union and her allies by all the other member nations of the UN, even though armed with a large number of atomic bombs, without a major war resulting.

If this thesis is accepted, then the arguments that led to the incorporation of the unanimity rule in the United Nations Charter retain their validity today, and the proposal of the Atomic Energy Commission, following the original American proposals, to abolish the unanimity rule in relation to matters concerning atomic energy would have amounted to a revision of the Charter and would have led to the very dangers which the original drafting of the Charter sought to avoid. This clash between the American and the Soviet viewpoints can thus be traced, in part, to a difference of view as to the military effects of atomic bombs. The widely held view that the invention of atomic bombs has made it possible for the UN to impose its will even on a Great Power, which it was held was not possible before their invention, provided the intellectual justification for the revision of the Charter.

How much this thesis was believed by the military experts of the Western Powers is difficult to estimate with certainty. But it appears to have been believed by many statesmen, as for instance by Sir Alexander Cadogan, in his comment on the Baruch Plan already quoted in Chapter 11. He quite clearly implied that he thought that, thanks to the atomic bomb, it was now possible to apply inevitable and overwhelming punishment to Russia without precipitating a major war.

The Soviet Union has consistently taken the opposite view; that is, that the invention of atomic bombs has not the decisive significance in major wars attributed to it by the Western Powers. Hence logically, as well as sensibly from the standpoint of her own interest, the U.S.S.R. has opposed the modification of the Charter. The arguments given in detail in Chapters 5, 6 and 7, in the long run support the Soviet viewpoint.

In the terms of reference of the Atomic Energy Commission,

atomic weapons are linked with "all other major weapons adaptable to mass destruction," but no other weapons than atomic bombs have, in fact, been discussed. This is particularly curious in view of the very great destructive power of ordinary bombs, as used in both the European and Pacific wars, and of the widely held view that biological warfare may prove potentially even more destructive than atomic weapons. Since the manufacture of biological weapons does not, presumably, require any very large and expensive plants, and is not dependent (as are atomic weapons) on certain rare material, it is clearly impossible to control them by any such system as has been proposed for atomic energy. Again, even if atomic energy were brought under complete control, any small nation would be in danger of devastating attacks by the airplanes of a neighboring Great Power using ordinary bombs.

The main arguments of Chapters 6 and 7, that the invention of atomic bombs has not made necessary a fundamental alteration in the structure of the UN, were based on the properties of existing or slightly improved atomic bombs and of the carriers for them that are likely to be available within the next few years. The situation may be altered, however, if far more lethal weapons using bacteria or radioactive poisons are invented. (See last section, Chapter 5.) The introduction of such weapons, which are necessarily extremely indiscriminate in character, and which may easily endanger the forces or populations of the nation using them, bring into play such complicated issues, some of which are discussed in the next chapter, as to make prediction difficult. Three conclusions however seem certain. Bacteria or radioactive poisons would be even more useless than atomic bombs as "police" weapons. If the use of such weapons to destroy a large fraction of the population of any nation is envisaged as a possible decision of the United Nations, it would be far better to dissolve the UN at once and return to open power politics, rather than to camouflage such activities under its moral authority and legal sanction. Lastly, if biological warfare does become as effective a weapon as the official American Report suggests,[6] then the unique concentration of the Atomic Energy Commission on atomic weapons, to the deliberate exclusion of biological weapons, becomes mis-

[6] See Chapter 5, p. 69–70.

guided, and its final conclusions in no way a fulfilment of the terms of reference of the Commission.[7]

These considerations lead one inevitably to envisage the necessity of controlling not only or primarily the weapons themselves, but their carriers, be they long-range aircraft, rockets or other devices. This possibility is attractive, as such carriers are not at all easy to conceal in peacetime, given some system of international inspectorate; a long-range bombing force would be particularly difficult to hide.

In the First Report of the Commission the decision to limit the inquiry initially to atomic weapons is recorded in the following words:

> The Commission has however proceeded on the assumption that inquiry into the matter of atomic energy and recommendations for its control were the most urgent problem before it. Accordingly it has occupied itself first, and thus far exclusively, with that subject. Further, if a satisfactory solution to that problem could be found, it might furnish a guide for "the elimination from national armaments . . . of all other major weapons adaptable to mass destruction."

This hope is clearly illusory in view of the danger of biological warfare and ordinary bombs. The essential basis for the Atomic Energy Commission's proposals for the control of atomic energy is the special feature of the present methods of making atomic bombs; these are that very large industrial plants are required which would be difficult to conceal, and that the essential raw material, uranium, is only found in a relatively few places in the world. If atomic bombs could be made out of light elements only, though this is in fact unlikely, the A.E.C. system of control would be inapplicable. It is certainly inapplicable to the control of biological weapons and of ordinary bombs.

In addition, of course, the novelty of the subject of atomic energy and the uncertainty of its military and social implications, and the marked concentration of scientific knowledge and technical know-how in the hands of one nation, made it about as unsuitable a subject matter for such an experiment as could be imagined.

[7] See, for instance, Ernest Oppenheimer on the possible effects of a "preventive" war against Russia, Chapters 5 and 14.

It would seem that this decision of the A.E.C. had very unfortunate consequences, in that it led to a very narrow approach to the problem of security, by undue concentration on a single weapon. In any further attempts to break the present deadlock on the Atomic Energy Commission, it would seem essential to renew the discussions[8] on the basis of its original terms of reference, by including other weapons of mass destruction also. The same question, whether to broaden or narrow the basis of the discussions, arises in connection with the General Assembly Resolution of December 14, 1946, on General Disarmament.

Though one cannot fail to see the attractive simplicity in the idea that a single weapon could be isolated from all others, and from the general problem of armaments and war potential, it is very difficult not to conclude now that the attempt to do so has been disastrous. The Soviet view on the matter was clearly expressed by Mr. Gromyko in his speech of July 8, 1947, in which he said, referring to the Assembly Resolution:

> It is necessary first to point out that this plan correctly combines the question of a general reduction of armaments and armed forces with the question of prohibiting atom bombs and other weapons of mass destruction. The linking of these two questions represents the basic difference between the Soviet proposals and the American plan, which in no way links the question of a general arms reduction with that of prohibiting atom bombs and other weapons of mass destruction.
>
> The Soviet plan is based on the principles established by the General Assembly in its above-mentioned decision, in which the prohibition of atomic weapons not only is not contrasted with the general problem of disarmament, but, on the contrary, is regarded as a component part of this general problem. The Soviet plan thus derives from the understanding that the successful solution of these problems is possible only on condition that concerted measures are taken with regard to a general reduction of arms, together with the prohibition of atomic and other weapons suitable for mass extermination.

It is by no means easy to understand the full import of the at-

[8] There is some evidence that the British Government opposed this isolation of atomic from other weapons. For instance, Thomas J. Hamilton, in the *New York Times* of Dec. 6, 1946, described Mr. Baruch's speech of Dec. 5 as "a rejection of a recent British demand that the prohibition of the atomic bomb should be coupled with the prohibition of other weapons of mass destruction."

tempt by the American Government to isolate atomic weapons from all other armaments, in contradiction to the terms of reference of the Atomic Energy Commission and against the reported opposition of the British Government. But if we cannot be sure of the motive, we can at least estimate the probable consequences of the policy. The arguments of earlier chapters have led us to believe that, if the Baruch Plan had been accepted, Russia would have been so weakened as to make less important to America the control of other armaments. Alternatively, it might have happened that Russia would have soon become a violator of the agreement and so would have been quickly destroyed (according to the current military thinking of the time) by sanctions inflicted on her by all the other nations. If this had happened, there would have remained no Power in the world strong enough to be a potential threat to the U.S.A., and so the control of other weapons of mass destruction may have appeared quite unnecessary.

Further explanation is required also of the hope expressed in the A.E.C. Report that the plan would "furnish a guide for the elimination . . . of ordinary bombs or of all other weapons adaptable to mass destruction." For clearly the hope cannot be fulfilled in the case of biological weapons, and for the control of the carriers—that is, long-range aircraft, etc.—other methods than international ownership are quite adequate.

Whatever were the motives behind the isolation of atomic bombs from other weapons, there is no doubt of the decisive diplomatic success of the American Government in getting the Atomic Energy Commission to incorporate the main features of the Baruch Plan in their Second Report to the Security Council. For this shrewd move in the field of power politics to have any chance of success, two things were essential. The plan of control had to appear a fair and generous one, and the Soviet Government had to be thoroughly frightened.

The theme of the generosity of the Plan had been taken up many times by the spokesmen of many countries. Mr. Evatt, Australian representative on the A.E.C., said: "In his opinion the United States proposal was a gift which should not be refused." Mr. Warren R. Austin, American delegate, stated that the United States proposals were acclaimed "for unprecedented boldness, generosity and fairness." Then Sir Alexander Cadogan said of the American plan: "This is a very great offer to make."

The campaign to frighten the U.S.S.R. into accepting the Plan has developed in intensity since the Baruch Plan was first put forward. To a considerable extent, however, the campaign overreached itself. For by its emphasis on the thesis that weapons of mass destruction are the essence of modern war, and on the expectation that a small nation with one devastating new weapon can defeat a great nation, it implied that even the full acceptance of the A.E.C. proposals by the U.S.S.R. would not bring security to any country. This is so because of the danger of such weapons as bacteria, which could be prepared in secret even by a small country, even though such a country was thoroughly inspected by the A.E.C. atomic energy inspectors. It will be remembered that Mr. Baruch covered this point in his original speech by stating that the United States would not be prepared to relinquish *atomic bombs* till it had a guarantee of safety against *bacterial and other weapons as well*.[9] However, this statement is in complete conflict with the policy of the United States Government in treating atomic bombs separately.

In July, 1946, Mr. Henry Wallace, former Vice-President of the United States, wrote a letter to President Truman in which he sharply criticized his Government's handling of the atomic energy question. Apart from a general attack on its policy as likely to fail in its objective and to be disastrous for the world, Mr. Wallace drew attention to several important points, which have subsequently been the subject of much controversy. Of particular importance to our argument is the controversy on the stages by which the plan should come into being. Mr. Wallace wrote:

> There is, however, a fatal defect in the Moscow statement, in the Acheson (Lilienthal) Report and in the American plan recently presented to the United Nations Atomic Energy Commission. That defect in the scheme, as it is generally understood, of arriving at international agreements by "many stages," of requiring other nations to enter into binding commitments not to conduct research into the military uses of atomic energy and to disclose their uranium and thorium resources while the United States retains its right to withhold its technical knowledge of atomic energy until

[9] Chapter 11, p. 148.

the international control and inspection system is working to our satisfaction.

In other words, we are telling the Russians that if they are "good boys" we may eventually turn over our knowledge of atomic energy to them and to the other nations. But there is no definite standard to qualify them as being "good" nor any specified time for sharing the knowledge. . . .

It is perfectly clear that the "step by step plan" in any such one-sided form is not workable. The entire agreement will have to be worked out and wrapped up in a single package. This may involve certain steps or stages, but the timing of such steps must be agreed to in the initial master treaty.

Mr. Baruch replied to this attack in a memorandum to the President on September 24, in which he stated that Mr. Wallace was quite mistaken as to the American proposals which did in fact conform to those recommended by Mr. Wallace. To establish this point he quoted from his original speech on June 14 and from the first and second American memorandums to the A.E.C. The following are some of the relevant passages:

The treaty should contain provisions governing the sequence and timing of the steps in the transition from the present conditions to the conditions which will prevail once the authority is in effective control of atomic energy.

Obviously, the controls outlined in the memorandum cannot spring into existence full-grown and complete upon the legal establishment of the Authority. The process of putting them into effect will necessarily extend over a considerable period of time. It will have to be done in stages provided in the treaty or charter and according to prearranged schedules based on sound and logical sequence leading to full and effective establishment of all controls.

Mr. Baruch had won his point—on paper—but not in substance.

For on December 31, 1946, the A.E.C. issued its First Report, containing the General Findings and Recommendations, which are reproduced in Appendix III. The gist of Mr. Wallace's criticism of the American proposals certainly applies to the majority report of the A.E.C., except in so far as it was not the Americans alone who would decide when a given stage was completed, but a *majority* of the A.E.C. This can be seen from the following sentences: "In order that the transition may be accomplished as rapidly as possible and with safety and equity to all, this Commission should supervise the transitional process as prescribed in the treaty or convention, *and should be empowered to determine when a particular stage or stages have been completed and subsequent ones are to commence*" (Part III, par. 5) (Author's italics). When referring to the setting up of the proposed Control Agency, the report says:

> Its rights, powers and responsibilities, as well as its relation to the several organs of the United Nations, should be clearly established and defined by the treaty or convention. Such power should be sufficiently broad and flexible to enable the international control agency to deal with new developments that may hereafter arise in the field of atomic energy. The treaty shall provide that the rule of unanimity of the permanent members, which in certain circumstances exists in the Security Council, shall have no relation to the work of the international control agency. (*Part III, par. 3 (a)*)

There is no ambiguity here. Though the *sequence* of steps is to be laid down in advance, the *date* on which a particular stage will be deemed to have been completed, and the next stage begun, is to be determined by the Commission without the operation of the unanimity rule; hence presumably by a majority, or a two-thirds majority, vote. So we cannot but conclude that one or two small nations, who happened at the time to be members of the Security Council, could determine by their votes whether the next stage should be proceeded with or not.[10] It is hardly to be expected that the U.S.S.R. would consider such a situation to differ in essentials from one in which the United States of America was explicitly given the sole right to determine the timing of the stages.

A further point of importance is that recognized in the passage of the majority report quoted above, which emphasizes that the power of the Commission must be flexible enough to deal with the new developments which must inevitably arise in a technical field in such rapid change. Sensible as is such a provision, one must not underestimate the power it would give to the Commission. For one can only too well imagine that new technical developments will arise which will bring new dangers not envisaged explicitly in the treaty, but which could "legitimately" be used to postpone the commencement of the next of the scheduled phases.

---

[10] For instance, in 1947, Colombia or Syria could have so held the balance.

Though the Commission never got as far as to specify precisely what the various stages would be, it did make clear that the early stages would include control of the mining of uranium, geological and aerial surveys, while the later stages would include the release of information and finally the disposal of the American stock of bombs. So, to repeat the point already made several times before, the early stages would be all to Russia's immediate disadvantage, and only in the later stages would she get something in return. Whether the later stages would actually be implemented or not would depend ultimately on a vote of the A.E.C., and thus would be determined by the votes of a chance selection of the smaller Powers.

Mr. Wallace had undoubtedly put his finger on one of the major defects, not only of the American plan, but of the wording of the original Moscow agreement. It would be possible to argue that the Soviet leaders made a tactical error in subscribing to this wording, which was taken verbatim from the Attlee-Truman-King statement, and that some of the tactical difficulties in which the U.S.S.R. found herself on the A.E.C. resulted from this mistake. The American Government may equally have felt embarrassed at having committed itself to eliminate not only atomic bombs but other weapons of mass destruction also.

Essentially the same issue kept arising in subsequent discussions. Mr. F. H. Osborn, deputy representative of the United States on the A.E.C., discussed it in an article[11] on August 3, 1947, in which he wrote:

> The Soviet Union states that under such a treaty as is proposed, the economic life of their nation might be interfered with by a hostile majority in control of the atomic energy agency. Such a fear is very naturally in the minds of every nation trying to work out the terms of a treaty. . . . To meet this objection, the working papers propose that the general plan for the strategic balance of atomic materials and facilities be written into the treaty, so that the agency will have no arbitrary powers. The Soviets have shown interest in this proposal. The treaty must be so written that every nation must be protected from every sort of iniquity, and have the right to appeal whenever it thinks it is not being fairly treated.

It is first to be noted that the distribution of atomic material is

[11] Quoted in *B.A.S.*, p. 799, Oct., 1947.

to be made on *strategic*, not *economic* grounds. It has already been pointed out that the existing inequality in the distribution of power throughout the world (Chapter 8) makes it certain that a strategic distribution would lead to economic inequity and so could be characterized as itself an iniquity—to use Mr. Osborn's word. Apparently Mr. Osborn thinks it possible to lay down in a treaty drawn up in 1948 precisely how atomic power will be distributed to the various countries in 1958 or 1968, from plants not yet designed, and working on scientific principles not yet worked out. Imagination boggles at such a task. Even if such a treaty were ever satisfactorily composed, interminable disputes as to its interpretation would be inevitable. Mr. Osborn's "right of appeal" would presumably be to a majority vote of the Security Council, since the unanimity principle is not to hold for matters concerning atomic energy. In spite of these difficulties Mr. Gromyko and the Polish delegate are reported[12] to have accepted the idea of a quota system.

Most public spokesmen in America have continued to back the A.E.C. plan to the full. A few regrets have been expressed at some of the tactics of the American delegation, and particularly at the great emphasis on abolishing the veto, but very little suggestion has been made that anything less than the whole plan would be acceptable to American public opinion. Mr. Baruch has stated[13] that "the United States delegation cannot consider modification in those fundamental principles of its plan, which in our judgment must be maintained to meet the mandate given the Commission by the United Nations General Assembly last January."

On the other hand, the Editorial of the *Bulletin of the Atomic Scientists* for September, 1947, emphasizes the extent of the Soviet concessions:

> Since the negotiations began fourteen months ago, the Russians have conceded step by step: that international control of atomic energy is necessary, and should include both atomic armaments and atomic power for peaceful purposes; that it should be exercised by an international personnel, having unrestricted access to all mines, plants and laboratories engaged in atomic activities; that the control agency must sponsor international research, and that the

[12] *B.A.S.*, pp. 247, 249, Sept., 1947.
[13] "Memorandum to the President," *B.A.S.*, Oct., 1946.

atomic energy developments in each country should be subject to a quota system.

The Russian system is still far from satisfactory. Two crucial questions remain to be answered. First, how does the Soviet Union propose to satisfy other countries that no illegal mining and processing occurs on its territory? Second, can efficient (but not unlimited) inspection be organized without international management of major atomic activities, as envisaged in the Lilienthal Plan?

The Russians have certainly produced no convincing answer to the first question. Probably there is, in fact, no complete answer, given the present organization of the world into hostile blocs. Moreover, it is likely that only through a third world war could such changes occur as would make a really water-tight system possible by leading to the effective hegemony of one or another group of Powers. Given the present deadlock, the problem before the world is whether there is any control system which, though falling short of the demands for complete security, does offer something better than nothing.

The second question reveals, as does the A.E.C. report itself, a somewhat strange emphasis on the functions of ownership and management, the true import of which it is a little difficult to grasp, except in terms of open power politics.

The relation between the ownership of power plants and the exercise of political power is well brought out by the following remark attributed by George Seldes, in *One Thousand Americans*, to Mr. Newton D. Baker: "Before many years have passed, it will be necessary for us to use water power wherever possible and conserve coal. Our water powers are therefore our great unexhausted and inexhaustible national assets. Whoever owns them in a large sense may be said to own the United States, industrially and commercially. . . . If I were greedy for power over my fellowmen, I would rather control Muscle Shoals than to be continuously elected President of the United States." One notes that the A.E.C. plan would have led to the ownership of all major atomic energy power plants in the U.S.S.R. by an international body on which Russia would expect to be in a minority.

It is easy to see the dangerous consequences of this emphasis on ownership in the A.E.C. plan. If mankind can only be safe from atomic bombs through the international ownership of all atomic

189

energy plants, then mankind can only be safe from ordinary bombs or biological weapons through the international ownership of all air forces and all bacteriological laboratories. But this is clearly impossible so long as separate States exist. In fact, the insistence that atomic bombs can only be controlled through international ownership leads to the conclusion that "other weapons adaptable to mass destruction" cannot be controlled at all, and so to the conclusion that the terms of reference of the Atomic Energy Commission can never be carried out.

The British Government strongly supported the Baruch proposals when they were first put forward, and has continued to support them in their final form as incorporated in the majority Report of the Atomic Energy Commission. In this attitude they have been followed by the bulk of the British press and by many public pronouncements by individuals. On the other hand, sharp criticism of some of the detailed proposals in the Baruch Plan have been expressed by the British Atomic Scientists' Association, although the general conception of the Atomic Development Authority was supported. In January, 1947 this body issued a statement which starts as follows:[14]

> The most important objection to the Baruch Plan from the point of view of other nations is probably that it envisages in its first stages measures which may be construed as maintaining the dominance of the United States in the field of atomic energy, whereas the concessions which are to be made by that country appear mostly in the later stages. If these later stages are not ratified until the previous ones have been achieved, technically Congress could withhold ratification at any stage.

Suggestions follow for mitigating this difficulty. The essential points at issue are those already covered in our discussion of the Wallace-Baruch controversy. The statement raised doubts as to the necessity of "ownership" of atomic plants by the A.D.A., and pointed out the danger of the control plan allowing interference in the economic life of a country to an extent not necessary for the control of atomic energy. Part of its final paragraph reads: "It must be admitted that an effective system of control acceptable to all concerned is a very doubtful proposition in the present

[14] Reprinted in *B.A.S.*, Feb., 1947.

state of distrust between nations, since it must contain, at least in embryonic form, a measure of world government."

In the autumn of 1947, Professor N. F. Mott, President of the Atomic Scientists' Association, issued a statement expressing his own view of the position of Britain in the likely event of failure to attain any agreement. After referring to the high hopes which were raised by the Lilienthal Plan, that "great and inspiring document," Professor Mott stresses many points of acute difficulty in the Baruch Plan. Referring to the power of the A.D.A. to allocate uranium and to distribute atomic piles between the countries concerned, he writes: "It is therefore hopeless to expect their (i.e., the Soviet) Government to accept as binding any decision of an international body on such a vital matter. The United States would take the same view if the number of States voting consistently with the U.S.S.R. exceeded the number voting for them." Mott emphasizes the very great lessening of suspicion which would result from an international inspection system of national plants, and that the degree of security so obtainable would be not much less than under the full Lilienthal Plan. Finally, stress is laid on the peculiarly dangerous position of Great Britain in a future war in which weapons of mass destruction are used.

A rather similar line is taken in a statement by the Association of Scientific Workers of Great Britain. Emphasis is here laid on the danger of demanding an unattainable perfect system of security. "Perfection is just as illusory in this field as in any other field of international relations." The wide measure of agreement that already exists between the Soviet and the majority viewpoint is stressed and the importance of widening the field of discussion is emphasized. "Since America is the only country producing fissionable materials, the concessions she makes in the field of the production of atomic weapons could not be matched by concessions by other Powers that would be considered by the American electorate to compensate her. If, however, the whole field of disarmament were brought into the question, agreement should be easier since, with the U.S.S.R. possessing the greatest Army in the world, concessions in the field of atomic energy could be matched by concessions in other fields."

The Royal Institute of International Affairs has published a pamphlet containing a number of individual and mainly unco-ordinated contributions on the various aspects of atomic energy, and a useful bibliography. In the concluding article Lord Hankey, after recommending that work on atomic bomb control should be temporarily suspended, recommends that: "In the meantime, as a token of good intention, there should be a ban on the use of atomic weapons in war, but on the analogy of gas and bacteri-ological weapons, national research and development should not be forbidden."

In general, the majority of those expressing views about the Baruch Plan emphasize its generosity. A recent debate in the House of Lords on February 18, 1948, provides many examples. The Archbishop of York said: "I am not quite sure if, till re-cently, I quite appreciated the magnitude of this offer which has been made by the United States. It is a very great offer. We were told in the Press the other day that they are perfecting the bombs. It means that that nation at this moment has supremacy in arma-ments over any other nation in the world. And yet, for the sake of international peace, they are prepared to give up that suprem-acy. It is a very great offer made by a great people." In the same debate Lord Cherwell stated: "As has been stressed, we had the extraordinarily generous offer by the United States of the so-called Baruch Plan. . . . Anyone would have imagined that they (the Russians) had everything to gain and nothing to lose by accepting the Baruch Plan and trying to work it. It is strange that they did not accept it." He added, however: "Nor can we really isolate this atomic form of warfare from others which are equally horrible to contemplate. Germ warfare, as we all know, has the extraordinary unpleasant characteristic that it spreads catalytically; a few germs in favorable circumstances may go on generating more and more. Modern poisons are excessively potent; one pound of them prop-erly distributed would be enough to poison the whole of the in-habitants of the globe."

The Chancellor of the Duchy of Lancaster (Lord Pakenham), replying for the Government, said: "May I say, on that subject, how heartily I echo the words used by the most reverend Primate, when speaking about the generosity of the whole American atti-tude in this matter? When all is said, it is a very remarkable thing to find a country ready to throw away such a colossal advantage provided that agreement can be arrived at regarding terms."

The virtual end of attempts to negotiate an agreement came with the rejection of the Soviet control proposals by a Working Committee on April 5, 1948. The three main headings under which the Soviet proposals were considered as inadequate are given[15] as follows:

I. The powers provided for the International Control Commission by the Soviet proposals, confined as they are to periodic inspection and special investigations, are insufficient to guarantee against the diversion of dangerous materials from known atomic facilities, and do not provide the means to detect secret activities.

II. Except by recommendations to the Security Council of the United Nations, the International Control Commission has no powers to enforce either its own decisions or the terms of the convention or conventions on control.

III. The Soviet Government insists that the convention establishing a system of control, even so limited as that contained in the Soviet proposals, can be concluded only after a convention providing for the prohibition of atomic weapons has been "signed, ratified and put into effect."

As we have seen, the first point is a legitimate criticism of the Soviet plan, but is probably a less fundamental difficulty than the last two. It seems not unlikely that the U.S.S.R. might have agreed to continuous inspection by resident inspectors if a solution of the other two much more serious difficulties could be formed. It will be remembered too that we have emphasized that the danger of illicit leakages of fissile material is not as dangerous as was thought in the days when a few atomic bombs were held to be militarily decisive in wars between major Powers. Moreover, the value of periodic inspection seems underrated. For this would give to the inspectorate such detailed knowledge not only of the scientific personnel of each country but of its scientific and technical organization, that the organization of illicit operations would become appreciably more difficult, though not entirely impossible. Moreover, it must be remembered that it is quite impossible to invent an inspection system which would be certain to detect secret activities such as the making of bacterial weapons.

[15] *B.A.S.*, May, 1948, p. 130.

193

The second point brings one back again to the veto controversy. If, as recommended in the majority Report, the proposed International Control Agency had powers to enforce its own decisions and the terms of the conventions against a Great Power, it must be able to impose sanctions and so, in effect, to declare war. To give this power to a two-thirds majority vote of the International Control Agency would be to modify profoundly the Charter, and in a very dangerous way.

The third point alone would lead to the decisive rejection of the Soviet proposals by the Americans. For, when the convention providing for the outlawing of atomic weapons and for the destruction of stocks had been put into effect, there could be no guarantee that the Soviet Union would in fact agree to an adequate system of control. This defect of the Soviet plan is of course paralleled by the defect of the majority plan arising from the possibility, already discussed, that the later stages of the control plan might never be implemented.

So, in essentials, the deadlock remained to the end much as it was in the beginning. For sound objective reasons, Russia and America put forward proposals appropriate to their own interests. Owing to the great difference between the strategic situations of the two Powers and between the level of their atomic energy developments, these proposals were completely antagonistic, and each completely unacceptable to the other.

14. THE PRESENT SITUATION

IN THE first chapters of this book, an attempt has been made to give a realistic view of how the military situation of the Great Powers has been affected by the invention of atomic bombs. In later chapters the course of the international negotiations for the control of atomic energy has been described in some detail and the essential causes of the breakdown have been emphasized. As the last chapters were being written, the negotiations on the Atomic Energy Commission were suspended on the initiative of the

Western Powers. The task now remains of analyzing the possible courses of action of the Great Powers, taking as a basis the view of the strategical situation given in Chapter 6.

Any such analysis of possible future events must inevitably have a very tentative character. Real historical processes are so complex and depend on such a variety of causative factors, that all one can hope to do is to provide a rather schematic analysis as a guide to making more concrete analyses in the light of future developments.

In this chapter we will attempt to outline the possible courses of action open to the Western and Eastern Powers. We will begin with an account of the situation as it may appear through American eyes.

The main possibilities of action as stated by many authoritative American spokesmen, can be grouped under two main headings: to wage preventive war before the Soviet Union has accumulated an appreciable stock of atomic bombs, or to pursue a policy of containment of Soviet power wherever possible, but without forcing deliberately an actual armed struggle. What is meant here by an American preventive war is the initiation, perhaps, on some substantial ground, of armed action against the Soviet Union, before the Soviet Union has taken armed action against any of the Western Powers. Possible events in Persia, Turkey, Greece, Germany, Austria or any other area of dispute between the Eastern and Western Powers might provide a suitable pretext.

Many statements have been made by American and British spokesmen suggesting that the failure of the Soviet Union to agree to the Control plan of the Atomic Energy Commission should constitute an act of aggression justifying preventive war. Senator McMahon[1] said: "I assert that for the first time in human history, the failure to agree to a sane, effective and righteous control of weapons of war constitutes in and of itself an act of aggression," and Mr. George Earle[2] said: "Every nation must permit inspectors, or be atom-bombed."

In addition, there have been many statements and reports which

[1] McMahon, "Speech to U.S. Senate, May 21, 1947." B.A.S., July, 1947.
[2] Earle, quoted by New Republic, April 7, 1947.

though not explicitly mentioning a preventive war, do make it clear that the writers consider one as likely.[3]

Many eloquent arguments against the initiation by America of a preventive war have been voiced. Mr. Ernest Oppenheimer[4] has recently expressed them thus: "What would be the real consequences of such a 'preventive war'?" "In all probability," says Oppenheimer, "United States Air Squadrons could devastate most of Russia's cities and destroy a large part of her industry. However, even under the most 'favorable' circumstances, this would not eradicate more than forty million people (which would still leave Russia a population larger than that of the U.S.A.) nor could the assault destroy more than 50 per cent of her industries. Moreover, the Russian armies, could hardly be wiped out by atomic bombs; they would have sufficient reserves of supplies and equipment to engage in large-scale military activities for some time at least. That time would probably be sufficient to enable them to overrun Europe, the Near East, the Middle East and most of the Far East,[5]

[3] The following is a typical example of American discussion of preventive war:
"How Byrnes Vetoed Plan to Send Atom Bombs to Europe in Tito Crisis.
—Washington, Sept., 28, 1946.
It's just coming to light—and certainly won't be officially confirmed even now—that the U.S. was on the verge of sending a supply of atomic bombs to Europe as a 'big stick' gesture in last month's dispute with Yugoslavia.
And one of the most interesting aspects of the story is the fact that it was Secretary of State Byrnes who intervened personally at the eleventh hour, to veto such a gesture.
It was at the height of the diplomatic crisis with Yugoslavia over the shooting down of U.S. planes in mid-August, that plans were virtually completed to send Superfortresses and a supply of A-bombs to the American occupation zone in Germany.
Four groups of B29's were ordered activated for the mission at Smoky Hill Army Air Field, Salina, Kan. Simultaneously, Army personnel and scientists attached to the atomic bomb stock pile depot in New Mexico received an A.A.F. alert to be ready to load an unspecified number of bombs.
'Destination, Germany' was more or less freely discussed, both at Salina and in New Mexico, in connection with the Yugoslavia crisis.
Plans for the dispatch of the A-bomb force to Germany may never have received final official sanction, since President Truman was on vacation at the time and Byrnes was in Paris.
Preparations were well advanced, however, before they were finally vetoed by Byrnes, who rightly argued that the U.S. should neither appear 'timid nor trigger-happy' in its relations with Russia."—New York Post, Sept. 28, 1946.
If this report has a basis of fact in the wishes of certain sections of American military opinion, it is clear that the real intention was probably to drop bombs on the U.S.S.R., not Yugoslavia. But whichever was intended, the gist of the article was that a preventive war would have broken out but for Mr. Byrnes' intervention at the last minute.
[4] Ernest Oppenheimer, B.A.S., Dec., 1947. See also H. C. Urey, B.A.S., Nov., 1946.
[5] Confirmation that Dr. Oppenheimer's view on this point is shared by the American Armed Services is found in a recent statement by General Omar Bradley before a Committee of the House of Representatives, quoted by the Manchester Guardian, June 3, 1948:
"The precipitation of armed hostilities, either by a deliberate or accidental incident, is a plausible possibility so long as our forces face each other on opposing frontiers in

especially, since they can count on the support of strong 'fifth columns' in all these regions. The U.S.A. would have to atom-bomb cities and industrial centers in the areas overrun by the Soviet, lest the latter obtain new sources of supplies. This will not endear the United States to the people of Eurasia; many of whom may well make common cause with Russia.

"Moreover," Oppenheimer continues, "a mass destruction of cities will not be sufficient to guarantee safety for the U.S.A.; American forces would have to conquer and hold vast spaces of Eurasia. Regular and guerilla warfare of unsurpassed magnitude would face them. At the same time Russian air fleets may attack American cities with ordinary bombs and with bacteriological weapons. Consequently Americans may die of plague while Russians die of radioactivity. Finally a 'preventive war' would alienate large segments of public opinion at home necessitating in all probability the institution of a totalitarian regime in order to prevent internal collapse."

It is interesting to note that, in this highly colored statement,[6] the chief danger to the U.S.A. is stated to lie in the biological weapons which the United States Government has taken the initiative in preventing the Atomic Energy Commission from considering, in spite of its terms of reference, which implicitly included them with other weapons of mass destruction.

If, however, in spite of the cogency of such arguments, America did contemplate preventive war, there are at least two reasons why the Armed Forces might want to wait for a few years. The first is the lack at present of suitable carriers for atomic bombs. In Chapter 5 it was shown that the only possible long-range carriers at present are piloted heavy bombers and that those now in service are extremely vulnerable to existing fighters. Possibly jet-engined bombers of much higher performance may soon be available, but the figures for American aircraft production for 1945-1947, given in the *Finletter Report*,[7] show that there cannot possibly be an

---

this strained atmosphere of distrust and tension. Soviet armed forces, with an approximate total of 4,000,000 men and 14,000 planes, provide a substantial iron fist for the aggressive policies of Moscow. These forces are capable of swiftly overrunning most of Europe, the Near and Middle East, Korea and even China."

[6] Some comments on the extremely high Russian casualties (assumed) have been given in Chapter 5.

[7] *Finletter Report*, p. 57.

operationally decisive number in existence today.[8] To attempt to maintain for many months a long-range atomic bomb attack on Russia with existing heavy bombers against the fighter defense system that the Soviet Air Force may reasonably be expected to possess, would be a great military gamble.

On the other hand when American air rearmament has taken place and a first-line strength of many hundreds of long-range jet bombers are in existence, no one can be quite certain that marked parallel improvements in active defense measures may not also have occurred. Furthermore, Russia would be able to use the delay to improve her defense arrangements, and disperse her essential plants.[9]

But more important than these technical considerations is the essential difficulty pointed out by Walter Lippmann and others that if America initiates an atomic war in the near future, she is likely to find herself militarily unable to prevent Russia overrunning Europe, the Middle East and much of the Far East. The fact that Russia might be now able militarily to overrun these countries, by no means implies that she would do so even if America did drop atomic bombs on Russian cities. Russia would probably only do so for very solid military and economic reasons. There would be a considerable possibility that countries which proclaimed a strict neutrality, and were prepared to defend it to the best of their ability, would in fact be able to maintain their neutrality.

Even though Russia might not attack the countries of Western Europe, the American planners must reckon with the possibility that she would. Since there are not in Europe now, nor are likely to be in the near future, adequate American land forces to stop the Russian armies, the American staffs would have to prepare to

[8] "The B29's at least exist; the jets are still on paper." *Economist*, May 8, 1948.

[9] Quite recently Alexander Werth, the Moscow correspondent of the *Manchester Guardian*, wrote: "Not that the atom bomb is as much of a bogy to the average Russian as it tended to become at one time. Among diplomatists in Moscow the theory is strongly held that, whether the Russians have atom bombs or not, they have, in any case, some formidable retaliatory weapons. The Americans in particular speak of Russian bacteriological weapons with some concern; and it is also estimated that jet planes— such as we saw over the Red Square on May Day—are being produced on a very large scale and that the number of these planes already runs into a thousand or more. Therefore, so the argument runs, war would mean immense destruction and death to both sides, compared with which the last war was a mere drunken brawl." *Manchester Guardian*, June 24, 1948.

carry on the war either with Europe and the Middle East in Russian hands (or at least in a state of civil war) or to rely initially on the defense that could be put up by the land armies of France, Italy, Benelux and Great Britain.

The second reason why the American sources are likely to advise against precipitating an armed conflict in the next year or two relates to the effect of the Marshall Plan on the economies and military strength of the Western Powers, including Western Germany. It is no doubt believed in America that by the end of the envisaged four years of financial help, the national economies of the Western Powers will be markedly strengthened, so as to make much more feasible than at present their active participation in a third world war. Along with the financial aid, it is presumably envisaged that the Western European powers will be rearmed on a large scale with American arms and equipment. But all this will take time, and till this economic and military strengthening has occurred, England, France, Italy and Western Germany can hardly be considered as likely to be either very efficient or very willing participants in a major war. The social tension existing today in France and Italy is likely to be sufficient to deter rational Americans from following policies which cannot but augment it dangerously.

Then again, a land war against Russia is hardly conceivable without the active participation of Western Germany. Not only, however, will it be many years before Western Germany has recovered enough to be a military asset rather than a liability, even with generous economic and military assistance, but the political difficulties likely to be encountered in Europe as a result of the rearmament of Western Germany are likely to be formidable. European memories of the German occupation and of Maidanek and Auschwitz must grow dimmer by the elapse of a number of years, before armies of France, Holland and Belgium can be expected to fight enthusiastically alongside a reborn Wehrmacht.

In the end, therefore, the military and moral arguments against the initiation of a preventive war by America in the near future are very strong. There remains the dilemma that if America waits too long, she may be faced with the alternative of fighting a war when Russia also has atomic bombs, and restarting negotiations for the control of atomic energy, but in a far weaker bargaining position than she is at present.[10]

If war broke out between the Eastern and Western Powers, and if for some reason the latter did not use atomic bombs at the outset, the Soviet Government would probably find it to its advantage to keep mainly to the defensive. Since the Western Powers could not quickly invade Russia and are assumed not to be able to drop atomic bombs on her, the main change from the present situation would be that the cold war would become a phony war. As soon, however, as American atomic attacks from European bases took place, or seemed likely to take place, Russia might be forced to take the offensive to remove the threat. But even so her offensive action would probably be limited as far as possible to the immediate objective of removing the atomic bomb threat, rather than to attempt to occupy all of Western Europe. For, not only might such operations prove unexpectedly expensive militarily, as in Finland in 1939-1940, but the cost of the occupation of the country attacked and its subsequent defense would prove a very heavy burden and might lead to a dangerous dissipation of effort. One can assert with some confidence, for instance, that extreme military necessity would be needed to make Russia attack Italy. For even if successful, its subsequent defense against Anglo-American forces based on North Africa and holding command of the Mediterranean would be extremely expensive, if possible at all.

Let us now consider the situation as it must appear to the Soviet leaders. Even if they consider an armed clash with the West inevitable, which is not at all certain, they must certainly consider that on both military and industrial grounds they have much to gain and little to lose by delaying the clash as long as possible. However much Russia may be credited with long-term expansionist tendencies, it cannot possibly be supposed that the Soviet leaders are so blind to their own interests as to precipitate a major war before Russia and her Eastern Allies have recovered from their

[10] In a recent House of Representatives debate, Defense Secretary James Forrestal was quoted as saying that the international situation had deteriorated and "time flows against us." *Manchester Guardian*, June 3, 1948.

huge war losses,[11] and till Russia herself has accumulated a stock of bombs.

A further consideration of importance is that in Soviet political thought, America is probably now near the height of power relative to the rest of the world, and moreover is likely to meet increasingly severe internal difficulties within the next few years due to the nature of her economic system. If an economic crisis developed which did not find relief by external adventures, then Russia would expect to be strengthened relatively. If, on the other hand, an internal crisis developed in such a way as to lead to a preventive war as an outlet, then Russia would have the political advantage of becoming the victim of aggression. In 1941, Russia was incontrovertibly the victim of German aggression, and this fact was of considerable value to her. She is bound to rate very high the political advantage of not being the initiator in turning the cold war into a shooting war. If no crisis develops, Russia at least gains time, both to strengthen her economy and to make military preparations. The Soviet leaders are probably convinced that in the next few years the economic and military strength of the Soviet Union and her Eastern Allies is likely to increase relatively to that of America and the Western Powers, partly because of the healing of the heavier wounds of war and partly because of the carrying out of their national plans of economic and industrial development. They probably believe that Marshall Plan aid will quicken the pace of Western European recovery, but not to such an extent as to cause a reversal of the trend of time in their favor.

It is certainly not only in Russia that an economic crisis in America is held to be likely. There is a gnawing fear in the minds of thoughtful Americans that their economic system may fail to produce stability, and may lead as in 1929 to an economic crisis in which social tensions will rise high, so weakening the country industrially and militarily. The atmosphere in America has been vividly described recently in the following words:[12] "Meanwhile the atmosphere of foreboding which overhung most of 1947—has returned. Americans who are profiting look gloomy lest they cease

[11] The extent of the losses to be recovered from is shown in Appendix II.
[12] *Economist*, Feb. 21, 1948.

to profit, and those who are not look gloomy by reflection. But even this is not so much depression as a raincoat worn out of superstition to ward off a disaster whose inevitability has become a national fetish. So far, it shows no signs of becoming a national and hence an international fact." One might add that the inevitability of an atomic bomb attack on the U.S.A. has also become a national fetish.

All these arguments reinforce the view that Soviet Russia will be very careful to avoid precipitating a military showdown, while at the same time she will do her best to increase her defensive strength. The more successfully she succeeds in this twin policy, the more acute does the problem facing the Western Powers become. It becomes especially acute for America, just because of the widespread acceptance of the view, however false the view may be, that Russia will drop atomic bombs on American cities just as soon as she has any to drop, irrespective of any possibility of a subsequent invasion and occupation. The "horrors of Hiroshima" propaganda, and the thesis that "weapons of mass destruction are the essence of modern war," have come full circle, and have faced Americans with the dilemma of having to choose between waging preventive war and, according to their own way of thinking, of waiting to be annihilated.

If the analysis of the previous chapter is valid, there is little substance in the expectation that if America waits too long she will be annihilated one day by Soviet atomic bombs. On the other hand the analysis equally proves that the longer America waits, the weaker her *relative* power position in the world will become.

If Russia gives no pretext for a war, and if America does not initiate a preventive one, the time must come when Russia also has a stock pile of bombs. Even though America has a very much larger one, America will be in a much weaker position than now, unless she has very greatly increased her general armaments and has created a large land army either already overseas, or ready to go there. For Russia's already great military strength will be markedly increased by the possession of bombs, whereas America's stock pile becomes an effective weapon only when backed by large conventional armed forces to hold the bases from which they are to be used and to follow up their use by invasion on a continental scale.

Meanwhile the cold war continues, and the Soviet Union has not made the diplomatic retreat expected by the advocates of the use of threats of destruction by atomic bombs.[13]

This brings one to the important but difficult problem of the extent to which the possession by one power of weapons of mass destruction such as atomic bombs, normal bombing, or biological weapons do or do not act as a deterrent to the actions of a rival Power. There is clearly no general answer, but only a number of particular answers for particular cases.

If Russia and America both had atomic bombs and were equally vulnerable, each might be deterred from using them on the other. In Mr. Oppenheimer's view, America may be already feeling the deterrent effect of possible use by Russia of biological weapons as reprisals for an American attack on Russia with atomic bombs. So the undeniable diplomatic value to America of atomic bombs may be already weakened by the possible existence of other weapons of mass destruction.

On the other hand the threat of the use of weapons of mass destruction may prove far less a deterrent than an incitement of the rival power to strengthen its position by relatively unprovocative means. In fact, the obvious counter to the diplomatic use of the threat of atomic and similar weapons is the intensification of political warfare, or the actual waging of a guerilla type of war.

A weapon only has a deterrent effect on the actions of a given nation if there is a reasonable chance of its being used and if its actual use would produce serious hurt. The Communist armies of China are not deterred by America's stock pile of bombs because they know that even if they were used against them, they would not be effective. The Arabs were not deterred from waging war against the Jews in Palestine by the possibility that atomic bombs might be dropped on Amman because they know that this was extremely unlikely to happen.

If one looks back over the last three years, it is not possible on the

[13] An interesting example of the view that Russia is likely to be more conciliatory the more she is threatened, is found in an article by E. A. Shils, Associate Professor in Social Thought at the University of Chicago, and Reader in Sociology at the London School of Economics: "The Soviet Union, despite its clamor about 'American atomic bomb imperialism' also does not seem to regard the United States as an immediate threat. Otherwise, how can one account for the unconciliatory line taken by the Russians on so many minor issues?"

basis of available information to determine whether the possession by America of atomic bombs has in the end restrained rather than encouraged the expansion of Soviet influence. Certainly the use of the bombs as a weapon of power politics to stop the advance of Communism has not been uniformly successful. It has, however, undoubtedly played a large part in sharpening the clash between East and West.[14]

The following passage gives Mr. Lippmann's formulation of what the Anglo-American policy was since 1945:[15]

"The British and the Americans, of course, could not accept the permanent division of the European continent along the Yalta line. They could not accept a settlement in which Poland, Czechoslovakia, Yugoslavia, Hungary, Rumania and Bulgaria would lose all independence and become incorporated as Soviet republics in the U.S.S.R. They had a debt of honor to the countless patriots in those lands. They realize that if the frontiers of the Soviet system were extended as far west as the middle of Germany and Austria, then not only Germany and Austria but all Western Europe might fall within the Russian sphere of influence and be dominated by the Soviet Union. . . . Thus for the best of reasons and with the best of motives they came to the conclusion that *they must wage a diplomatic campaign to prevent Russia from expanding her sphere, to prevent her from consolidating it, and to compel her to contract it*" (Author's italics).

The italicized words form as good a definition as could be desired of the objectives of the "cold war." It is to be noted that it included not only the stopping of further Russian expansion, but the forcing of the withdrawal of Russian influence from areas where it was strong at the end of the war. In fact, Lippmann's account of the cold war gives it more an offensive than a defensive character.

So long as the atomic bomb was considered an all-powerful weapon able, if need be, to defeat Russia quickly and cheaply, the

[14] Dr. Jan Bêlahrádek, formerly Rector of Charles University in Prague and a Socialist member of the Czechoslovak Parliament, said recently:

"In my country we cannot escape the conclusion that the discovery of the atomic bomb has produced the division of the world into two halves. Ideological differences cannot be denied or neglected, but it was only after the birth of atomic energy that this separation gained an efficient material basis . . ." *B.A.S.*, Feb., 1948, p. 62.

[15] Walter Lippmann, *The Cold War*, p. 28 (New York, 1947).

diplomatic campaign to make Russia contract her sphere of influence seemed possible of achievement.[16] When, however, after the initial success at Hiroshima, it came to be recognized that atomic bombs would be only generally useful as an adjunct to mass armies and other conventional weapons, the difficulties began to appear. They are, for instance, forcibly described by Mr. Lippmann. "We have a relatively small population, of which the greater proportion must in time of war be employed in producing, transporting and servicing the complex weapons and engines which constitute our military power. The United States has, as compared with the Russians, no adequate reserves of infantry."[17] The countries of Western Europe must clearly provide the mass armies, while America provides the arms. Mr. Lippmann sees the implications with great clarity:[18]

> "The failure of our diplomatic campaign in the borderlands, on which we have staked so much too much, has conjured up the specter of a third world war. The threat of a Russian-American war, arising out of the conflict in the borderlands, is dissolving the natural alliance of the Atlantic community. For the British, the French, and all the other Europeans see that they are placed between the hammer and the anvil. They realize, even if we do not realize it, that the policy of containment, in the hope that the Soviet power will collapse by frustration, cannot be enforced and cannot be administered successfully, and that it must fail. Either Russia will burst through the barriers which are supposed to contain her, and all of Europe will be at her mercy, or, at some point, and at some time, the diplomatic war will become a full scale shooting war. In either event Europe is lost. Either Europe falls under the domination of Russia, or Europe becomes the battlefield of a Russian-American war.
>
> "Because the policy of containment offers these intolerable alternatives to our old allies, the real aim of every European nation, including Great Britain, is to extricate itself from the Russian-American conflict. While we have been devoting our energies to lining up and

[16] Two years ago there may have been some excuse for such military wishful thinking. It is surprising to find that the responsible British newspaper *The Observer* can write in June 1948 in relation to the controversy over Berlin: "In the wider sphere of inter-governmental diplomacy, however, it is we who hold the overwhelming trump cards. It is our side, not Russia, which holds atomic and post-atomic weapons and could if sufficiently provoked, literally wipe Russia's power and threat to the world's peace from the face of the earth." Bluff may be a legitimate element in power politics, but it is useful to remember that to win at cards, it is best to start by gauging the strength of one's own hand, before guessing that of one's opponent.

[17] Lippmann, *The Cold War*, p. 13.

[18] *Ibid.*, pp. 19, 20.

bolstering up the Chinese Nationalists, the Iranians, the Turks, the Greek monarchists and conservatives, the anti-Soviet Hungarians, Rumanians, Poles, the natural alignment of the British, French, Belgians, Dutch, Swiss and Scandinavians has been weakened.

"And so in any prudent estimate of our world position they are no longer to be counted upon as firm members of a coalition led by the United States against the Soviet Union. We must not deceive ourselves by supposing that we stand at the head of a world-wide coalition of democratic states in our conflict with the Soviet Union.

"The aim of the leading democratic states of Europe and probably also of the Americas is at best to hold the balance of power between Russia and America, and thus to become mediators of that conflict. At worst, their aim is to isolate themselves in some kind of neutrality which will spare them the dual catastrophe of being overrun by the Red Army and bombed by the American air forces."

If such a war between East and West developed within the next few years, there is no room for doubt that civil war would be widespread. A recent authoritative article in the *Observer* emphasizes this point in a rather oversimplified form:

"A war between Russia and the West would be even more ideological and less nationalistic than the last. Every country occupied by one side would therefore be added, with its man-power and resources, to the active war-making forces of the occupier. The imposition of Communist Government on Western Europe would soon add vast new armies and resources to Russia's own, and America would for obvious reasons hardly be able to attack them with atomic weapons."[19]

It is certain that atomic bombs and other weapons of mass destruction are preeminently weapons for nationalist wars and are likely to be often unusable in the confused situation of a civil war.[20] It follows that a latent or actual civil war situation acquires in itself a defensive value against weapons of mass destruction. For instance, a city which was half in the hands of sympathizers of

[19] *Observer*, April 25, 1948.
[20] cf. a letter by Archibald Robertson in the *New Statesman and Nation* of Jan. 10, 1948. "Hitherto it has always been assumed that the cruellest of all wars is civil war. So long as war was fought with weapons that dealt destruction only to individuals or small bodies of combatants, that was no doubt true. But with the advent of weapons of mass destruction the reverse is the case. No side in a civil war can afford to use atomic bombs or bacteria, for the simple reason that it would thereby deal mass destruction to its partizans as well as its enemies—not to mention the country which it aspires to control. But in a foreign war, where everyone the other side of no man's land is presumed to be an enemy, no such scruples need deter the belligerents. It follows that of all probable wars civil war is now the least destructive."

each of two contending Great Powers might reasonably hope to escape annihilation by either.

The only offensive action open to America which does not involve a participation either in a European civil war or the actual commitment to a major land war in Europe with American troops, would seem to be the staging of a long-range atomic bomb offensive against Russian cities from bases, say, in North Africa, which could be reasonably expected to be held with relatively small land forces. That this may be the only feasible offensive action, no more proves that it would be a decisive one, than the inability of Britain to take any other offensive action against Germany in 1940-1941 made the area bombing offensive a decisive operation.

The validity of the argument as so far developed depends on the assumption that the number of atomic bombs America is likely to possess within the next few years, and such means of delivering them as she may produce, will not be adequate to defeat the Soviet Union quickly or cheaply without a major land campaign. This assumption was itself based on data for the performance of existing or somewhat improved atomic bombs and aircraft. It is, however, possible that these technical assumptions are wrong and that such improved weapons or carriers for existing weapons may be invented as will materially alter the conclusions. The most likely "improved"—that is, more devastating—weapons, are the super-atomic bomb, the use of radioactive poisons, and biological weapons. These have been discussed in Chapter 5, as far as the very little published data allow.

Let us look into the situation that would arise supposing that the United States will soon possess a vastly more devastating weapon than the atomic bomb and the power to deliver it where she wants. As shown in Chapter 5, there is internal evidence in Mr. Oppenheimer's recent remarks that he expects that the use of radioactive poisons and biological weapons will, or perhaps already has, provided such weapons. These weapons are so indiscriminate as to be only usable on targets very far from any friendly populations. They could not be used in any area which the troops of the Western Powers intended to occupy, and therefore their use would presumably be limited to the Soviet homeland. Perhaps the major cities of Russia would be destroyed and a belt of country from the Baltic to the Black Sea sprayed with radioactive and biological poisons. Such a belt might well impede an advance westward by the Russian armies, but it would also impede the invasion of Russia by the armies of the Western nations—assuming, of course, that these armies were available and ready. To prevent what was left of Russia from recovering, the attack with weapons of mass destruction would have to be continued more or less indefinitely, and extended over the whole of the vast spaces of Asiatic Russia. Numberless reasons, military, economic and moral in character, would serve eventually to call a halt to such a war without end. Once it stopped, however—and even while it lasted—America would fear that some day Russia would reply in kind. This fear, which would grow with the efficacy and lethality of the weapons, would eventually prevent the maintenance of America's traditional way of life. The killing of 120,000 Japanese with two atomic bombs in Japan has already produced severe symptoms of anxiety neurosis in numberless Americans. To continue to slaughter millions of Russians without any visible end in view, would be to complete the collapse of professed American moral standards, and the necessary defense measures would be likely to force profound change in her economic system.

So we conclude that the bigger and better the weapons of mass destruction in the hands of America and Great Britain, the less and less opportunity may there be to obtain useful results by their use. The greater the threat, the more will individuals, classes and nations in Western Europe attempt to withdraw from the struggle by any and all means that may present themselves.

Paralleling the objective dilemma facing Britain and America in search of a foreign policy, is the personal dilemma facing the atomic scientists themselves. In Chapter 10 we have already outlined some aspects of the mental conflict arising from the use of the bombs on Japan, and have referred to the gradual discovery that the weapons that they had developed had been used by their Government not so much to end the second World War, as to inaugurate a third cold one. Their warnings as expressed in the *Franck Report* had gone unhindered and the evils prophesied, before even the experimental bomb had exploded, had duly come to pass. The appointment by the President of the Board of Consultants under David Lilienthal gave them another opportunity to retrieve the situation. This was brilliantly taken. This "bold and inspiring" document was essentially the atomic scientists' attempt to wipe away the stain of Hiroshima and Nagasaki and to turn the atomic bomb into a boon rather than a curse for mankind.

Triumphantly successful at first—or so it appeared from the universal acclaim with which it was received in the Western world —the clearer-sighted among them gradually perceived their idealistic plan metamorphosed before their eyes into its opposite. The Lilienthal Plan, the creation of the atomic scientists themselves,[21] became the chief ingredient of the Baruch Plan and so of the Atomic Energy Commission proposals. What was intended by the atomic scientists to bring cooperation with Russia became an instrument in the hands of the American Government to coerce her. It is doubtful if the American Government would have succeeded so well in convincing the world of the purity of its heart in all matters relating to atomic energy and of the blackness of that of the Russians, if they had not had ready at hand the fine phrases and genuine idealism of the Lilienthal Plan, with which to clothe with specious generosity the hard-bitten *Realpolitik* of the Baruch Plan. In short, the atomic scientists were outmaneuvered—for a second time.

The extent of this defeat is not widely enough understood, nor has there yet been time enough for American atomic scientists to rally their forces for a third round. However serious for the postwar world have been the effects of the use of the bombs on Japan and of the conduct of the campaign for control, the harm done is not yet irretrievable. How a new start might perhaps be made is told in the final chapter. It will be an essential condition for any such new start that it must eschew the mixture of hysterical fear and apocalyptical fervor in which so much of the earlier discussions were conducted. To those steeped in this Spenglerian mood of the end of civilization, the future steps may seem prosaic and even dull.

[21] See Oppenheimer, *B.A.S.*, Feb., 1948.

15. A WAY OUT?

UNLESS our analysis has been greatly in error, the danger of a third world war in the next few years is much less than is generally thought. The reason for this belief is on the one hand that it seems overwhelmingly to Russia's advantage to avoid a war, and on the other, that America is for a number of reasons rather unlikely to precipitate one. So in the long run it seems likely that the world will remain at peace, at any rate for some years.[1]

Meanwhile America's stock pile of bombs will continue to grow ever bigger and bigger, and at some uncertain date Russia's will start to grow too. Responsible American statesmen will be bound to weigh very carefully the delicate question of when to begin again negotiations for the control of atomic energy, which they have just broken off. For the danger of waiting too long is great. When Russia has accumulated a stock pile of a few thousand bombs, her military strength, already very great by the size and efficiency of her armies, will be much enhanced. We have already noted that atomic bombs may prove valuable tactical weapons and even a hundred or so would be of great military value when used in conjunction with large-scale land operations, whereas such a number would bring no decisive results if used for area bombing of cities unrelated to the course of other military operations. If negotiations do not start till this situation has arisen, Russia will hold most of the cards.

Let us consider what are the essential conditions for future negotiations to have a reasonable chance of success. It is undeniable that any settlement between America and Russia must be based

[1] This has recently been reported to be a commonly held view in Russia, as expressed, for instance, by Alexander Werth in the *Manchester Guardian* of June 24, 1948: "Another reason why Russians think there will be no war is that Europe is now, in fact, split into two blocs, and neither side will run any serious risks by budging. Agreements—or further friction—may be possible on some secondary questions like Austria or Berlin. But, in the main, the map of Europe is considered to have been drawn and accepted *de facto* by both sides. Whether a real halt can be called to the 'cold,' or 'ideological,' war may be seriously doubted; but that there will develop, for some years, a *de facto* armistice, the Russians consider quite possible."

essentially on a bargain between the two States. The bargain must be one in which both sides make comparable sacrifices and reciprocally receive comparable advantages at all stages. If America continues to insist, as she appears to have done in the past, on treating atomic energy in isolation, then clearly there will be no possibility of a bargain, and so none for an agreement, till Russia has drawn more nearly even with America in the field of atomic energy.

If, however, atomic energy is not again treated in isolation, if, that is, atomic bombs are considered along not only with other weapons of mass destruction, but with conventional armaments and land armies as well, then it is easy to see the possibilities of an agreement acceptable to both America and Russia at a much earlier date.

On this broader basis, Russia with her strong land army has something to bargain against America's atomic bombs. By taking conventional weapons and armed forces into consideration at the same time, it should not be impossible, though undeniably it would not be easy, to reach an agreement to reduce armaments generally. Even if it is not found possible at first to abolish and outlaw the use of all weapons of mass destruction, a general limitation of armaments including a limitation of numbers of atomic bombs would nevertheless represent a great advance on the present situation.

Clearly an essential basis for an agreement must be not only a realistic appreciation both of the actual power position in the world at the time the agreement is negotiated, and of the effect on this power position of the proposed limitation of armaments. The negotiations will be stillborn if conducted as in the last two years. If an agreement is really desired the future negotiators will at least have the advantage of being able to learn from the proceedings of the Atomic Energy Commission how not to conduct such negotiations. For instance, the exaggeration of the efficacy in major wars of a particular weapon used, in isolation of other arms, and of the efficiency of existing methods of delivering it to its target, and the world-wide campaign to prove the Baruch Plan as the most generous of gifts, were, it seems, part and parcel of the Anglo-American diplomatic offensive, commonly called the cold war, rather than part of a genuine attempt to reach agreement.

In the future, however, the circumstances may be different. For, if negotiations for the limitation of all armaments, including atomic bombs, are begun in the next few years, then each nation will wish to retain adequate supplies of such armaments as it considers most useful to its particular situation. For instance some kind of bargain might be struck between America and Russia, in which so many American atomic bombs and their carriers are held to be the military equivalent of so many Russian divisions. In these circumstances it would pay each country to depreciate the potency of its own chosen arms and to exaggerate those of its opponent, so as to be in a position to argue for a bargain favorable to itself. Consequently the United States would need to depreciate the military value of the atomic bomb, so as to be able to make a case for the retention of a large number of bombs to balance militarily a given number of Soviet divisions.

At a somewhat later stage it should be possible and useful to return to the distinction between weapons of mass destruction and other weapons introduced into the contemporary scene by the Attlee-Truman-King statement in the autumn of 1945. Though this statement, with its reference to all weapons adaptable to mass destruction, was incomparably more sensible than the actions of the Atomic Energy Commission in restricting discussion to atomic bombs alone, it is an essential part of our argument that the time is not ripe to treat weapons of mass destruction separately from other armaments. The main reason for this is the wide difference in the geographical situation, and in the state of industrialization of America and Russia, which gives different weapons and armed forces a markedly different value to the two States. When Russia has approached more nearly to the level of industrialization of America, there will be a better chance of reaching an agreement within the single field of weapons adaptable to mass destruction. For the present it seems more hopeful to tackle the problem of general disarmament, even though this means the continued existence in the world of some limited number of atomic bombs, rather than to attempt to abolish all atomic bombs, leaving all other arms uncontrolled.

Probably a more valuable distinction than that between weapons adaptable to mass destruction and those that are not, is the much older one of the distinction between the use of a given weapon against the armed forces of the enemy and against civilian populations. For most weapons, certainly including the atomic bomb, but probably not bacteriological weapons, can be used effectively against either one or the other. Of course, there are also well-known difficulties in the application of this distinction, but the historical account given in Chapters 2 and 3 of the use of air power in the last war shows that that is a useful one. The air forces of America and Britain are at present loath to abandon a method of warfare which they seem curiously proud to have initiated, but the situation may change when the citizens of their countries become fully aware of the danger to their countries involved in this military theory.

This brings one to the important question of the limitation of long-range carriers, aircraft and rockets. Since these are much more difficult to conceal than the weapons, bombs, atomic bombs or bacteria which they may carry, their limitation and control should be relatively easy. A general limitation on numbers of long-range military aircraft and rockets would bring both a reduction in the burden of armaments and, more important, a reduction in fear of long-range attack, provided it is accompanied by an adequate inspection system.

When the Powers start within a few years to discuss in detail the nature of a suitable inspection system, it is reasonable to assume that the international ownership and management of armed forces, weapons and their carriers, will not commend itself as useful. For the world of a few years hence—we are assuming no third World War breaks out in the meantime—will still be a world of separate States and groups of States, with radically diverse social organizations. The ownership and management themes of the Lilienthal and Baruch Plans must be considered as a legacy of the days of the fallacious belief in the decisive character of a single weapon.

Moreover, it is clear that the infliction of sanctions against violators of the disarmament agreement must remain, as in the present Charter of the UN, the prerogative of the Security Council with its rule demanding the unanimity of the Great Powers.

It is easy to see that a control system for armaments which satisfies these requirements is likely to be based primarily on adequate inspection by an international inspectorate of all major armaments as well as atomic bombs, rather than on international ownership and management.

At some later stage of the world's history, however, the American plan of control of armaments through ownership and management, might become feasible. The conditions for this to happen are that some form of world state was already in being, or that the relations between separate states were entirely friendly. It might be doubted whether, under such conditions, a plan of this type would be necessary in which atomic power plants, and so inevitably other types of power plants also, would be allocated, owned and administered by an international body. Units of production on a national scale are already so large as to make efficient administration difficult. The necessary coordination and supervision could probably be most efficiently achieved by an international coordinating body, and an international inspection system, but with the "ownership" and administration left in the hands of local national authorities. Though it is, of course, impossible to predict the form that any system of world government might take in the future, or how it will come into being, it is easy to predict that it will not begin with world government in one weapon and one commodity, which was the essence of the majority report of the Atomic Energy Commission of the United Nations.

APPENDIX I

THE ALLIED BOMBING OFFENSIVE IN EUROPE
(1939-1945)

THE following statistics and quotations are taken from the reports of the United States Strategic Bombing Survey (*Overall Report, European War, U.S.S.B.S. 1; The Effect of Bombing on Health and Medical Care in Germany, U.S.S.B.S. 2; The Effect of Strategic Bombing on the German War Economy, U.S.S.B.S. 3*).

"The total weight of bombs dropped on all targets by the Anglo-American forces was 2,700,000 tons. The total loss of planes (bomber and escorting fighters) was 40,000, and the personnel lost in action was 160,000. The total service personnel engaged in the European Air War reached 1,300,000 in 1944 and 1945" (*U.S.S.B.S. 1*).

TABLE I

Total Weight of Bombs on Countries

		per cent
Germany	1,350,000 tons	50.3
France	590,000 "	21.8
Italy & Sicily	370,000 "	13.7
Austria & Balkans	180,000 "	6.7
Other targets	200,000 "	7.5
Total	2,690,000 "	

TABLE 2

Weight of Bombs on Germany Alone in Each Year

	Weight of bombs	No. of killed	No. of killed per ton
1940	10,000 tons	350	0.03
1941	30,000 ”	2,800	0.1
1942	40,000 ”	4,300	0.1
1943	120,000 ”	103,000	0.9
1944	600,000 ”	201,000	0.3
1945 (4 months)	500,000 ”	110,000	0.2
	1,300,000 ”	app. 500,000[1]	0.38

TABLE 3

Division of the Total Weight of Bombs Dropped for All Countries Between Types of Targets (U.S.S.B.S. 1)

Target	Tons	per cent
Land Transportation	800,000	32.1
Industrial Areas	640,000	23.7
Military	300,000	11.1
Oil and Chemicals	250,000	9.3
Airfields	190,000	6.9
Aircraft Factories	48,000	1.8
Others	410,000	15.1

TABLE 4

Index of Total German War Production from Figures Given by Kaldor[2]

	Total War Production
1940	100
1941	101
1942	146
1943	229
1944	285

[1] *U.S.S.B.S. 2.* A lower figure, 300,000, is given in *U.S.S.B.S. 1.*
[2] *Review of Economic Studies, 1945-1946,* Vol. 13, p. 33.

TABLE 5

Yearly Production of Aircraft and Tanks in Germany[3] and the United Kingdom

Year	Aircraft		Tanks	
	Germany	U.K.	Germany	U.K.
1940	10,200	15,000	1,500	1,400
1941	11,000	20,100	3,800	4,800
1942	14,200	23,600	6,300	8,600
1943	25,000	26,200	12,100	7,500
1944	39,600	26,500	19,000	4,600
Total	100,000	111,400	42,800	26,900

Productions of synthetic rubber and oil reached their peak in the spring of 1944, after which they suffered a rapid fall due to very successful attacks on the plants.

TABLE 6

Fall of Oil Production in 1944

	per cent
Jan.	100
March	100
May	80
July	20
Sept.	5
Nov.	20

Very similar trends are shown by the German rail transport,[4] which remained roughly constant throughout the war till the spring of 1944, after which it fell precipitately to nearly a complete stoppage in early 1945. It was the breakdown of transport due to the bombing which was mainly responsible for the final collapse of overall production in the autumn of 1944, not the actual destruction of the factories or the cities.

[3] *U.S.S.B.S. 3.*
[4] A detailed analysis of the effects of these attacks is given by Tedder, *Air Power in War*, p. 110 et seq.

The "area bombing" of 61 German cities having a population of 100,000 or more, on which over half a million tons were dropped (80 per cent by British night bombers) was very effective in destroying them. It is estimated that 3,600,000 dwelling units (about 70 per cent of all residential units in these cities) were destroyed, some 500,000 civilians were killed, and 7,500,000 rendered homeless.[5] It is not clear from the published analyses what portion of the total number of civilian killed arose from the area bombing, and how much from the bombing of other targets. (See Table 3 for relative weight of attacks.)

On the other hand, the effect on production was relatively small; the estimated figures for the loss of production due to the mass attacks on cities are as follows:

TABLE 7

Loss of Production Due to Area Bombing of German Cities (U.S.S.B.S. 1)

	Tonnage	*Loss as per cent of annual Reich production*
1942	38,000	2.5
1943	135,000	9.0
1944	255,000	17.0
1945 (Jan. to April)	97,000	6.5
Total	525,000	

Lord Tedder[6] states that during 1943 the bombing offensive as a whole reduced German total production by 10 per cent and armament production by 5 per cent.

Chart 1, Chapter 2, showed the actual production of armaments annually (*Curve B*), together with what it would have been in the absence of the *city bombing* (*Curve A*), using the estimated loss of production given above. *Curve C* showed the *total* weight of bombs on Germany in half-yearly intervals.

Chart 2 gives the German Armament production in three monthly intervals (Kaldor and *U.S.S.B.S. 3*).

[5] *U.S.S.B.S. 1*, p. 72 and *U.S.S.B.S. 4*, p. 11.
[6] *Op. cit.*, p. 106.

An indirect effect of the campaign not fully shown in the quoted figures lay in the diversion of some 4,500,000 workers to other activities, amongst which were debris clearance and reconstruction (1,000,000), replacement of civilian goods (1,000,000), and manning and production of anti-aircraft munitions (1,000,000).

APPENDIX II

WAR CASUALTIES OF THE POWERS (1939-1945)

Germany

No FIGURES for the total German casualties up to the end of the war appear to be available, but figures from September 1, 1939, to

TABLE I

German War Casualties Up to November 30, 1944

Campaign	Killed	Missing	Total
West (till June 6, 1944)	66,000	3,000	69,000
West (June 6-Nov., 1944)	54,000	338,000	392,000
N. Africa	12,000	90,000	102,000
Italy	48,000	97,000	145,000
Balkans	24,000	12,000	36,000
Germany	64,000	1,000	65,000
Russia	1,419,000	907,000	2,326,000
Total	1,687,000	1,448,000	3,135,000

November 30, 1944, are given in great detail in a document found in the house of General Reinicke, head of the German High Command Propaganda Department. Extracts from these documents were published in British and American newspapers, July 30, 1945.

From these figures it can be estimated that up to D-Day, that is, up to June 6, 1944, about 85 per cent of all German casualties had been incurred on the Eastern Front. Up to November 30, 1944, this fraction was still about 75 per cent.

Total Casualties of the Powers

The following rough figures for the total casualties (killed, missing and wounded, both military and civilian) are taken from *The*

219

World Almanac 1948, p. 551 et seq. The pre-war population figures are taken from *Whitaker's Almanack 1936*, p. 185 et seq.

Country	Casualties (millions)	[1935] Population (millions)	Casualties as Percentage of Population
U.S.A.	1.04	137	0.8
U.K.	0.57	45	1.3
France	0.75	41	1.8
Germany	9.5	66	14.3
Japan	6.5	84	7.7
Poland	5.6	32	17.5
Czechoslovakia	0.5	14.7	3.4
Yugoslavia	1.7	14	12.2
U.S.S.R.	13.5	162	8.3

These rough figures can be supplemented by rather more detailed and somewhat different estimates from various sources, for the collection of which I am indebted to the Information Department of the Royal Institute of International Affairs, Chatham House, London.

France[1]
160,000 military deaths
160,000 civilians killed
300,000 deaths of prisoners, deportees and compulsory workers in Germany.
Total 620,000

Poland[1]
600,000 killed by direct war action
3,900,000 lives lost by execution and liquidation of the ghetto
1,400,000 lives lost in concentration camps and enforced work.
Total 5,900,000

Czechoslovakia[2]
245,000 mainly civilian, i.e. 1.25 per cent of pre-war population, compared with 3.5 per cent given in *World Almanac*.

[1] Economic and Social Council, *Report of Temporary Sub-Committee on Economic Reconstruction of Devastated Areas*, Sept., 1946.
[2] International Committee for the Study of European Questions, *Memorandum on the Results of the War (1939-45)*.

220

Yugoslavia[2]	1,660,000 including 1,380,000 civilian, i.e. 10.5 per cent of pre-war population.

U.S.S.R. Mr. Molotov at the Paris Peace Conference stated that 7,000,000 Soviet soldiers fell in battle. In addition the Paris Institute for Research in the Soviet Economy estimate the civilian losses to be 10,000,000, of which one half were killed and one half dead from cold, starvation or deportation.

APPENDIX III

EXTRACT FROM THE FIRST REPORT OF THE ATOMIC ENERGY COMMISSION TO THE SECURITY COUNCIL, DECEMBER 31, 1946

General Findings and Recommendations[1]

. . . the Commission has made the following findings of a general nature:

1. That scientifically, technologically, and practically, it is feasible:

(*a*) To extend among "all nations the exchange of basic scientific information on atomic energy for peaceful ends";

(*b*) To control "atomic energy to the extent necessary to ensure its use only for peaceful purposes";

(*c*) To accomplish "the elimination from national armaments of atomic weapons," and

(*d*) To provide "effective safeguards by way of inspection and other means to protect complying States against the hazards of violations and evasions."

2. That effective control of atomic energy depends upon effective control of the production and use of uranium, thorium, and their fissionable derivatives. Appropriate mechanisms of control to prevent their unauthorized diversion or clandestine production and use and to reduce the dangers of seizure—including one or more of the following types of safeguard: accounting, inspection, supervision, management, and licensing—must be applied through

[1] The text reproduced is taken from the Atomic Energy Commission *Second Report to the Security Council,* dated Sept. 11, 1947 (p. 88), (New York, 1947).

221

the various stages of the processes from the time the uranium and thorium ores are severed from the ground to the time they become nuclear fuel and are used. Ownership by the international control agency of mines and of ores still in the ground is not to be regarded as mandatory.

3. That whether the ultimate nuclear fuels be destined for peaceful or destructive uses, the productive processes are identical and inseparable up to a very advanced state of manufacture. Thus, the control of atomic energy to ensure its use for peaceful purposes, the elimination of atomic weapons from national armaments, and the provision of effective safeguards to protect complying States against the hazards of violations and evasions must be accomplished through a single unified international system of control and inspection designed to carry out all of these related purposes.

4. That the development and use of atomic energy are not essentially matters of domestic concern of the individual nations but rather have predominantly international implications and repercussions.

5. That an effective system for the control of atomic energy must be international, and must be established by an enforceable multilateral treaty or convention which in turn must be administered and operated by an international organ or agency within the United Nations, possessing adequate powers and properly organized, staffed and equipped for the purpose.

Only by such an international system of control and inspection can the development and use of atomic energy be freed from nationalistic rivalries with consequent risks to the safety of all peoples. Only by such a system can the benefits of widespread exchange of scientific knowledge and of the peaceful uses of atomic energy be assured. Only such a system of control and inspection would merit and enjoy the confidence of the people of all nations.

6. That international agreement to outlaw the national production, possession, and use of atomic weapons is an essential part of any such international system of control and inspection. An international treaty or convention to this effect, if standing alone, would fail: (*a*) "to insure" the use of atomic energy "only for peaceful purposes," and (*b*) to provide "for effective safeguards by way of inspection and other means to protect complying States

against the hazards of violations and evasions," and thus would fail to meet the requirements of the terms of reference of the Commission. To be effective, such agreement must be embodied in a treaty of convention providing for a comprehensive international system of control and inspection and including guarantees and safeguards adequate to ensure the carrying out of the terms of the treaty or convention and "to protect complying States against the hazards of violations and evasions."

Recommendations (Part III)

The Commission makes the following recommendations to the Security Council:

1. There should be a strong and comprehensive international system of control and inspection aimed at attaining the objectives set forth in the Commission's terms of reference.

2. Such an international system of control and inspection should be established, and its scope and functions defined, by a treaty or convention in which all nations, members of the United Nations, should be entitled to participate on fair and equitable terms. The international system of control and inspection should become operative only when those Members of the United Nations necessary to assure its success by signing and ratifying the treaty or convention have bound themselves to accept and support it. Consideration should be given to the matter of participation by non-members of the United Nations.

3. The treaty or convention should include, among others, provisions for:

(a) Establishing in the United Nations an international control agency possessing powers and charged with responsibility necessary and appropriate for the prompt and effective discharge of the duties imposed upon it by the terms of the treaty or convention. Its rights, powers, and responsibilities, as well as its relations to the several organs of the United Nations, should be clearly established and defined by the treaty or convention. Such powers should be sufficiently broad and flexible to enable the international control agency to deal with new developments that may hereafter arise in the field of atomic energy. The treaty shall provide that the rule of unanimity of the permanent members, which in certain circum-

223

stances exists in the Security Council, shall have no relation to the work of the international control agency. No government shall possess any right of "veto" over the fulfilment by the international control agency of the obligations imposed upon it by the treaty nor shall any government have the power, through the exercise of any right of "veto" or otherwise, to obstruct the course of control or inspection.

The international control agency shall promote among all nations the exchange of basic scientific information on atomic energy for peaceful ends, and shall be responsible for preventing the use of atomic energy for destructive purposes, and for the control of atomic energy to the extent necessary to insure its use only for peaceful purposes.

The international control agency should have positive research and developmental responsibilities in order to remain in the forefront of atomic knowledge so as to render the international control agency more effective in promoting the beneficial uses of atomic energy and in eliminating its destructive ones. The exclusive right to carry on atomic research for destructive purposes should be vested in the international control agency.

Research in nuclear physics having a direct bearing on the use of atomic energy should be subject to appropriate safeguards established by the international control agency in accordance with the treaty or convention. Such safeguards should not interfere with the prosecution of pure scientific research, or the publication of its results, provided no dangerous use or purpose is involved.

Decisions of the international control agency pursuant to the powers conferred upon it by the treaty or convention should govern the operations of national agencies for atomic energy. In carrying out its prescribed functions, however, the international control agency should interfere as little as necessary with the operations of national agencies for atomic energy, or with the economic plans and the private, corporate, and State relationships in the several countries;

(*b*) Affording the duly accredited representatives of the international control agency unimpeded rights of ingress, egress, and access for the performance of their inspections and other duties into, from and within the territory of every participating nation, unhindered by national or local authorities;

(*c*) Prohibiting the manufacture, possession, and use of atomic weapons by all nations parties thereto and by all persons under their jurisdiction;

(*d*) Providing for the disposal of any existing stocks of atomic weapons and for the proper use of nuclear fuel adaptable for use in weapons;

(*e*) Specifying the means and methods of determining violations of its terms, setting forth such violations as shall constitute international crimes, and establishing the nature of the measures of enforcement and punishment to be imposed upon persons and upon nations guilty of violating the terms of the treaty or convention.

The judicial or other processes for determination of violations of the treaty or convention, and of punishments therefor, should be swift and certain. Serious violations of the treaty shall be reported immediately by the international control agency to the nations parties to the treaty, to the General Assembly and to the Security Council. Once the violations constituting international crimes have been defined and the measures of enforcement and punishment therefor agreed to in the treaty or convention, there shall be no legal right, by "veto" or otherwise, whereby a wilful violator of the terms of the treaty or convention shall be protected from the consequences of violation of its terms.

The enforcement and punishment provisions of the treaty or convention would be ineffectual if, in any such situations, they could be rendered nugatory by the "veto" of a State which had voluntarily signed the treaty.

4. In consideration of the problem of violation of the terms of the treaty or convention, it should also be borne in mind that a violation might be of so grave a character as to give rise to the inherent right of self-defense recognized in Article 51 of the Charter of the United Nations.

5. The treaty or convention should embrace the entire program for putting the international system of control and inspection into effect, and should provide a schedule for the completion of the transitional process over a period of time, step by step, in an orderly and agreed sequence leading to the full and effective establishment of international control of atomic energy. In order that the transition may be accomplished as rapidly as possible and with safety and equity to all, this Commission should supervise the transitional process, as prescribed in the treaty or convention, and should be empowered to determine when a particular stage or stages have been completed and subsequent ones are to commence.

APPENDIX IV

PROPOSALS OF THE UNION OF SOVIET SOCIALIST REPUBLICS, JUNE 11, 1947[1]

THE following proposals were submitted:

1. For insuring the use of atomic energy only for peaceful purposes, in accordance with the international convention on the prohibition of atomic and other major weapons of mass destruction and also with the purpose of preventing violations of the convention on the prohibition of atomic weapons and for the protection of complying states against hazard of violations and evasions, there shall be established strict international control simultaneously over all facilities engaged in mining of atomic raw materials and in production of atomic materials and atomic energy.

2. For carrying out measures of control of atomic energy facilities, there shall be established, within the framework of the Security Council, an international commission for atomic energy control to be called the International Control Commission.

3. The International Control Commission shall have its own inspectorial apparatus.

4. Terms and organizational principles of international control of atomic energy, and also composition, rights and obligations of the International Control Commission, as well as provisions on the basis of which it shall carry out its activities, shall be determined by a special international convention on atomic energy control, which is to be concluded in accordance with the convention on the prohibition of atomic weapons.

5. With the purpose of insuring the effectiveness of international control of atomic energy, the convention on the control of atomic energy shall be based on the following fundamental provisions:

(*a*) The International Control Commission shall be composed of the representatives of states members of the Atomic Energy Com-

---

[1] Text from *Second Report* of A.E.C., p. 73.

mission established by the General Assembly decision of January 24, 1946, and may create such subsidiary organs which it finds necessary for the fulfillment of its functions.

(*b*) The International Control Commission shall establish its own rules of procedure.

(*c*) The personnel of the International Control Commission shall be selected on an international basis.

(*d*) The International Control Commission shall periodically carry out inspection of facilities for mining of atomic raw materials and for the production of atomic materials and atomic energy.

6. While carrying out inspection of atomic energy facilities, the International Control Commission shall undertake the following actions:

(*a*) Investigate the activities of facilities for mining atomic raw materials, for the production of atomic materials and atomic energy as well as verify their accounting.

(*b*) Check existing stocks of atomic raw materials, atomic materials, and unfinished products.

(*c*) Study production operations to the extent necessary for the control of the use of atomic materials and atomic energy.

(*d*) Observe the fulfillment of the rules of technical exploitation of the facilities prescribed by the convention on control as well as work out and prescribe the rules of technological control of such facilities.

(*e*) Collect and analyze data on the mining of atomic raw materials and on the production of atomic materials and atomic energy.

(*f*) Carry on special investigations in cases when suspicion of violations of the convention on the prohibition of atomic weapons arises.

(*g*) Make recommendations to governments on the question relating to production, stock-piling and use of atomic materials and atomic energy.

(*h*) Make recommendations to the Security Council on measures for prevention and suppression in respect to violators of the conventions on the prohibition of atomic weapons and on the control of atomic energy.

7. For the fulfillment of the tasks of control and inspection entrusted to the International Control Commission, the latter shall have the right of:

(*a*) Access to any facilities for mining, production and stock-

227

piling of atomic raw materials and atomic materials, as well as to the facilities for the exploitation of atomic energy.

(b) Acquaintance with the production operations of the atomic energy facilities, to the extent necessary for the control of use of atomic materials and atomic energy.

(c) The carrying out of weighing, measurements, and various analyses of atomic raw materials, atomic materials, and unfinished products.

(d) Requesting from the government of any nation, and checking of, various data and reports on the activities of atomic energy facilities.

(e) Requesting of various explanations on the questions relating to the activities of atomic energy facilities.

(f) Making recommendations and presentations to governments on matters of the production and use of atomic energy.

(g) Submitting recommendations for the consideration of the Security Council on measures in regard to violators of the conventions on the prohibition of atomic weapons and on the control of atomic energy.

8. In accordance with the tasks of international control of atomic energy, scientific research activities in the field of atomic energy shall be based on the following provisions:

(a) Scientific research activities in the field of atomic energy must comply with the necessity of carrying out the convention on the prohibition of atomic weapons and with the necessity of preventing its use for military purposes.

(b) Signatory states to the convention on the prohibition of atomic weapons must have a right to carry on unrestricted scientific research activities in the field of atomic energy, directed toward discovery of methods of its use for peaceful purposes.

(c) In the interests of an effective fulfillment of its control and inspectorial functions, the International Control Commission must have a possibility to carry out scientific research activities in the field of discovery of methods of the use of atomic energy for peaceful purposes. The carrying out of such activities will enable the Commission to keep itself informed on the latest achievements in this field and to have its own skilled international personnel, which is required by the Commission for practical carrying out of the measures of control and inspection.

(d) In conducting scientific research in the field of atomic energy, one of the most important tasks of the International Control Commission should be to ensure a wide exchange of information among nations in this field and to render necessary assistance, through advice, to the countries parties to the convention, which may request such assistance.

(*e*) The International Control Commission must have at its disposal material facilities including research laboratories and experimental installations necessary for the proper organization of the research activities to be conducted by it.

APPENDIX V

THE COMPTON AND FINLETTER REPORTS

IN MAY 1947 a report entitled "A Program for National Security" was issued in Washington by the President's Advisory Committee on Universal Training, of which the Chairman was Dr. Karl T. Compton. In January 1948 another report entitled "Survival in the Air Age" was issued by the President's Air Policy Committee, under the Chairmanship of Thomas K. Finletter.

The two documents provide a useful survey of American military and political thinking at an authoritative level. Both start with rather similar analyses of the military and strategic situation of America and lead on to recommending what steps should be taken by the United States Government to secure peace and to obtain security for the United States. The emphasis of the two reports is, however, somewhat different in that the *Compton Report* argues strongly that the most urgent need in the United States is for universal military training, while the *Finletter Report* comes to the conclusion that the first need is for a greatly expanded air force. The analysis of the existing and future strategic situations covers much of the same field that we have surveyed in this book. The conclusions are not, however, in all cases the same as those that we have reached. On the whole the analysis of the *Compton Report* is closer to that of this book than is that of the *Finletter Report*.

Both reports see as the main danger to the United States a sudden attack on the centers of population mainly by long-range weapons, aided by fifth-column activities and sabotage. The

229

Compton Report observes: "The 'sneak attack' of the type delivered upon our forces at Pearl Harbor is made vastly more probable by the increased range of aircraft and the enormous destructive capacity of atomic weapons. For a period estimated by responsible scientists at not less than four years and not more than ten years, we can expect immunity from such an attack because we alone possess the atomic bomb. After that the signal for the start of a war against us will, it is to be expected, be a large-scale, long-distance onslaught with atomic explosives against our principal centers of population and production.

"Every form of warfare has become more highly mechanized. The prospect is for a steady, and perhaps perpendicular, decrease in the number of troops physically exposed at the fronts and an increase in the number required in the rear as technicians and supply components and for home-defense duty.

"Fifth-column activities would become an even more important factor in the plans of an aggressor than they were under Hitler. The enemy would seek, as a preliminary to attack, to undermine the confidence of the people in the virtues of our form of government; to inhibit our defense preparations through disunity and sabotage; and to spread defeatism in the hope that the first major blow will bring surrender."

The author appears not to notice anything contradictory in the notion that the enemy would annihilate with atomic bombs a considerable fraction of the population which it has supposed to have successfully encouraged to form a subversive movement on a mass scale. We note also the view that America might *surrender* as a result of a first major blow; no indication is given that the enemy could follow up the blow by invasion of America.

On the other hand, when an American attack on the enemy (Russia by implication) is discussed, invasion is considered necessary. "We must contemplate also the possibility that the final outcome will not be determined by superiority in weapons of mass destruction. To defeat our enemy, we may in the future, as always in the past, have to rely on the cutting of supply lines, the systematic elimination of military objectives, and finally the invasion and occupation of enemy territory. We must not leap to the conclusion that Japan's surrender, without physical invasion and with a large part of its army intact, represents final proof that armies are obsolete. Japan's will to fight and her ability to fight had both been largely destroyed before the bombs were dropped on Hiroshima and Nagasaki. Her allies had been beaten, her outposts eliminated, her factories levelled. Russia's active entry into the war increased the hopelessness of her position."

Incidentally this passage admits the lack of overriding military necessity for the atomic bomb attack on Japan.

The myth that push-button war has already arrived is severely dealt with: "The only comfort we can extend in the contemplation of such an attack is that the era of push-button warfare, in which inter-continental rockets with atomic war-heads wipe out tens of millions overnight, has not yet arrived. It is extremely unfortunate that the mistaken idea has been planted in so many minds that that era is now present. Even the V1 and V2 rocket bombs that were used so terrifyingly against London in the last war have a very limited application in their present form. London presented an easy target and the distance across the Channel was short. It is true that weapons of similar or somewhat greater range and capable of being delivered with much greater accuracy than were those used by the Germans can soon be developed, if this has not already been done. But when it comes to trans-oceanic or trans-polar ranges, there is little immediate prospect that a weapon of this type can be produced and used effectively."

Scientists are quoted as holding that push-button war might be possible in twenty-five years. The limitation of atomic weapons is emphasized. "Moreover we must recognize certain practical limitations on the use of the atomic bomb. If an enemy were to seize Western Europe in a sudden 'blitz,' utilize its industrial plants. and occupy its principal cities as advance bases, we would be confronted with the knowledge that an atomic attack against these centers would destroy millions of people who are our friends and with whom we have had the closest of ties. One need only consider the possibility that the enemy might establish London and Paris as his forward bases to realize how serious a problem we would face."

A strong warning against over-emphasizing the possibility of long-range war is given. "To those who might urge that our security can be assured best by concentrating our defense, money and effort on preparation for retaliatory atomic bombing, we would point out an additional weakness in relying exclusively on this solution, at least in the foreseeable future. Experience thus far gives very little evidence about the ability of the United States to deliver atomic bombs in decisive numbers against targets in enemy territory at a great distance. An attempt to do so would have to meet the hazards of interception by combat planes and anti-aircraft fire, and would also have to meet the uncertainties of navigation over unfamiliar territory and unknown weather conditions and visibility at the target.

"To shut our eyes to the continued necessity of these functions and to place our complete trust and confidence for the preservation of our lives and liberties in the distant and vague prospect of guided missiles, complete aerial destruction of a possible enemy, and so-called 'push-button' atomic war, would, in our opinion be criminally negligent. We do not have faith in any early realization of such an easy, complacent way of bringing war to an attacking enemy. The United States cannot continue to be the only major power without any system of military training for its citizens, as it is today."

The arguments of the *Compton Report* make it crystal clear, but without explicitly saying so, that in the world of today there is no possibility of quickly and cheaply defeating a Great Power without a long-drawn-out war, so no possibility of inflicting "condign immediate and effective penalties" against a major power which violates a future scheme of international control of atomic energy. Dr. Compton's Committee has therefore implicitly destroyed the keystone of the Baruch Plan, expressed in his statement: "It would be a deception, to which I am unwilling to lend myself, were I not to say to you and to our people, that the matter of punishment lies at the very heart of our present security system."

The explicit conclusion of the analysis is, however, as follows: "So long as any great nation has power to stop by veto any proposed United Nations action against it as an aggressor, the United Nations cannot act to protect against such aggression. So long as there is no operating system of inspection whereby the United Nations can thoroughly check on the atomic energy activities of every nation, there is no guarantee that preparations for atomic war are not going on in secret, and there can be no certain security and no absence of suspicion and fear. Without such safeguards the United States must not only retain the atomic bomb, but must proceed actively with its further development and production."

The dominant theme of the *Finletter Report* is that the invention of devastating weapons of mass destruction, particularly atomic bombs and biological warfare, has made the defense of the United States impossible. It is argued therefore that the United States can only achieve security by building up a very strong offensive strength in the air so as to be able to destroy utterly any power which attacks or threatens to attack her. This is to be achieved by an increase in total arms budget and by a marked increase in the fraction going to the Air Force. "We can be supreme in the air by the weight of our air power. The United States can build a Military Establishment which will keep up with any nation and be a powerful force for peace. . . . In our opinion this Military Establishment must be built around the air arm. Of course an adequate Navy and Ground Force must be maintained. But it is the Air Force and naval aviation on which we must mainly rely. Our military security must be based on air power."

Much emphasis is given to the fact that there are other weapons of mass destruction, in particular biological warfare, of comparable destructive power to atomic bombs.

The keynote of the report is the importance of offensive as opposed to defensive measures.

"We emphasize again, however, that no plans for defense should be made in derogation of the striking counter-offensive air arm in being."

Perhaps the most striking feature of the *Report* is the superficial, even perfunctory character of much of the military analysis. No detailed or numerical arguments based on the actual events of the second World War are mentioned. It is almost as if the main thesis of the *Report*, which is that the evidently expected third World War will see devastating attacks on American cities unless the American Air Force is ready and able to inflict a still more devastating attack on enemy cities, is so obvious as to need no argument. Certainly none is given. No serious attempt is made to discuss from what bases the attacks on American cities will be made, nor what the supposed enemy (Russia) would do afterwards, except in so far as an airborne attack is to be expected.

"Indeed if we were not fully prepared, a mass destruction attack might be followed by airborne land troops for the purpose of taking advantage of the first confusion to seize strategic points in the United States and to destroy utterly the country's resistance."

It seems hardly complimentary to the people of America that the supposed landing of a few thousand enemy troops near their cities would "destroy utterly the country's resistance." Owing to the inherent vulnerability of airborne operations, the only conditions in which such an operation could be conceivably feasible would be one of complete surprise or with complete air superiority.[1] Since obviously Russian air superiority over the territory of the United States could not exist, complete surprise remains the only possibility. Once one abandons the conception deduced so erroneously from Hiroshima that a major nation can be defeated and induced to surrender by a single initial blow, and on the contrary admits that a follow-up by invasion on a major scale would in general be essential, then the danger of such a surprise attack becomes very small. For it would be completely impossible for an enemy to conceal its invasion plans, even if it could conceal the preparations for an atomic bomb and airborne attack. Without concealment of the invasion plans the airborne operations could not expect to achieve surprise and so would not be feasible.

The only possible condition for the decisive use of airborne troops far inside enemy territory would be when air superiority had been achieved and when the country under attack was in a near civil war condition, so that a substantial fraction of the population would be ready to cooperate with the airborne invaders. But in these circumstances it is reasonable to assume that atomic bombs would not be used on the cities.

It is worth, however, noting that the plan for the invasion of France in 1944 did not include airborne operations more than a

[1] Air Chief Marshal Lord Tedder, Deputy to General Eisenhower during the invasion of France, has recently written: "There are, I think, certain characteristics of airborne operations which it is important to appreciate. In the first place an airborne force is extremely vulnerable while in the air, both to air and ground defenses. Without complete local air superiority it is literally not feasible." Tedder, *Air Power in War*, p. 70.

few miles from the landing beach, in spite of the fact that the mass of the population were on the side of the invaders.

In general the discussion in the *Report* of the expected enemy attack on America is carried out in quite vague and unquantitative terms, with little or no regard to facts of geography, of manpower or air power resources, or of the real political situation in the world; it includes no vestige of an analysis of what the Soviet strategy might really be. As has been pertinently expressed, "What the American Air Force is really talking about is its own strategy, but described in reverse."[2]

In general, the Committee's explicit discussion of the American Air Force strategy of staging devastating atomic bomb attacks on Russian cities, in order to defeat Soviet aggression against America, is characterized by an extreme superficiality, particularly with regard to what happens next. For instance from the promising start, "moreover, we must not think that the atomic bomb alone will win a war," we go on to read:[3] "What we need during this Phase is an integrated Military Establishment, (1) capable of an atomic attack, (2) stronger in air power than that of any other country, and (3) capable of a sustained and powerful air counter-offensive, either directly or by the way of intermediate bases." Apparently invasion of Russian territory after the devastating atomic bomb attacks, is not envisaged.

In one passage the importance of bases is stressed: "What we must have and can support is a reasonably strong defensive establishment to minimize the enemy's blow, but above all a counter-offensive air force in being which will be so powerful that if an aggressor does attack, we will be able to retaliate with the utmost violence and to *seize and hold the advanced positions* from which we can divert the destruction from our homeland to his." But this point is not followed up except by the bold statement: "The task of securing advanced bases rests on all three services, with the Navy having a large sphere of the responsibility for establishing the troops and air force on shore." Nowhere in the *Finletter Report* is the possibility envisaged that major land forces might be necessary to seize and hold the atomic bomb bases. Clearly the

[2] W. Walton, *New Republic*, Feb. 2, 1948.
[3] *Finletter Report*, p. 22.

provision of such forces is inconsistent with the advocacy in the *Report* of the preeminence of the Air Force over the land forces. Perhaps, however, we have been unjust to the Committee. Its members may not have been unaware of the necessity of large land forces to hold their atomic bomb bases, but they may have been restrained by a natural tact from mentioning that they were relying on other nations to provide these forces. What bases the Committee had in mind is not clear, but were they in Scandinavia, Western Germany, France, Italy, Greece, Turkey, Persia, or the Near East, they would want protection from the Soviet land forces. Since the *Report* nowhere suggests that adequate American troops and the transport to get them to these places would be available, it is clear that they are relying on the land forces being provided by the local populations. The political problems of insuring that this support will be forthcoming are nowhere mentioned.

Taking the military analysis of the *Finletter Report* as a whole, it is hardly possible to resist the conclusion that it was not so much intended to be taken as a serious appreciation of the pattern of future wars, as to frighten the American public, in which task it has no doubt succeeded. But the report had clearly another serious purpose, that of remedying the present disastrous position of the American aviation industry. Two-thirds of the *Finletter Report* deal in a very interesting and objective manner with these difficulties. "A parade of witnesses has testified as to its current productive weakness as an industry, its general lack of preparation for rapid expansion, and its general financial instability. . . . The air lines, the most important element of civil aviation, are passing through one of the most serious crises of their history. The domestic trunk lines of the country suffered an operating loss of approximately $22,000,000 in the fiscal year ending June 30, 1947."

That this latter consideration is one of the main objects of the *Report* is shown by the witnesses called to give public testimony. According to a published analysis these comprised "seventy-one representatives of the aircraft industry, nineteen officials of Government departments, sixteen military and naval witnesses and one lone representative of labor."[4]

[4] Walton, *loc. cit.*

BIBLIOGRAPHY

ARNOLD, GENERAL HENRY H., *Second Report to the Secretary of War*. Included in *The War Reports* (J. B. Lippincott Company, Philadelphia, 1947).

ATOMIC ENERGY COMMISSION, *Scientific and Technical Aspects of the Control of Atomic Energy* [*First Report*] (United Nations, Lake Success, 1946).

ATOMIC ENERGY COMMISSION, *Second Report to the Security Council* (Reproduced for the United States Mission to the United Nations, New York, 1947).

BARUCH, BERNARD M. [United States Representative] *The International Control of Atomic Energy: Scientific Information Transmitted to the United Nations Atomic Energy Commission, 1946* (Washington, 1946-1947).

BLACKETT, PATRICK MAYNARD STUART, *The Atom and the Charter* (Fabian Society, London, 1946).

BRODIE, BERNARD (Editor), *The Absolute Weapon* (Harcourt, Brace and Company, Inc., New York, 1946).

BULLETIN OF ATOMIC SCIENTISTS (The Atomic Scientists, Chicago).

BULLITT, WILLIAM C., *The Great Globe Itself* (Charles Scribner's Sons, New York, 1946).

CHURCH ASSEMBLY, *The Church and the Atom* (London, 1948).

COALE, ANSLEY J., *The Problem of Reducing Vulnerability to Atomic Bombs* (Princeton University Press, Princeton, N. J., 1947).

COATES, WILLIAM P. and ZELDA K., *The Soviet-Finnish Campaign, Military and Political, 1939-40* (Eldon Press, Ltd., London, 1942).

COMMITTEE ON SOCIAL AND POLITICAL IMPLICATIONS OF ATOMIC ENERGY, *Franck Report, June, 1945* [Reprinted in *B.A.S.*, May, 1946].

COMPTON, DR. ARTHUR H., Substance of an Address before the American Philosophical Society and National Academy of Sciences [Reprinted in *Nature*, London, November, 1945].

DICKENS, ADMIRAL SIR GERALD C., *Bombing and Strategy* (Sampson, Low, London, 1947).

FALLS, CYRIL B., *The Second World War* (Methuen & Co., Ltd., London, 1948).

FLORENCE, PHILIP S. and BALDAMUS, W., *Investment, Location and Size of Plant* (Cambridge University Press, London, 1948).

HARRIS, SIR ARTHUR T., *Bomber Offensive* (Collins, London, 1947).

HIS MAJESTY'S STATIONERY OFFICE, *Effects of the Atomic Bombs on Hiroshima and Nagasaki* [*British Report*] (London, 1946).

KJELLBERG, SVEN H., *Russland im Krieg, 1920-1945*. [Translated from the Swedish into German] (Europa Verlag, Zurich–New York, 1945).

KNIGA, *Science at the Cross Roads* (London, 1931).

LEE, ASHER, *The German Air Force* (Harper & Brothers, New York, 1946).

LIDDELL HART, B. H., *The Revolution in Warfare* (Yale University Press, New Haven, 1947) and *Why Don't We Learn From History* (George Allen & Unwin, Ltd., London, 1944).

LIPPMANN, WALTER, *The Cold War* (Harper & Brothers, New York, 1947). Material originally appeared as a series of articles in the *New York Herald Tribune*.

MARSHALL, GENERAL GEORGE C., *The Winning of the War in Europe and the Pacific* (Published for the U. S. War Department by Simon and Schuster, Inc., New York, 1945).

MARTEL, GENERAL SIR GIFFARD LE Q., *The Russian Outlook* (Michael Joseph, London, 1947).

MASTERS, DEXTER and WAY, KATHERINE (Editors), *One World or None* (Whittlesey House, McGraw-Hill Book Company, Inc., New York, 1946).

NAMIER, LEWIS B., *Diplomatic Prelude, 1938-1939* (Macmillan & Co., Ltd., London, 1947).

NEWMAN, JAMES R. and MILLER, BYRON S., *The Control of Atomic Energy* (Whittlesey House, McGraw-Hill Book Company, Inc., New York, 1948).

PRESIDENT'S ADVISORY COMMITTEE ON UNIVERSAL MILITARY TRAINING, *A Program for National Security* [*Compton Report*] (Government Printing Office, Washington, D. C., 1947).

PRESIDENT'S AIR POLICY COMMITTEE, *Survival In the Air Age* [*Finletter Report*] (Government Printing Office, Washington, D. C., 1946).

RIECKHOFF, HERBERT J., *Trumpf Oder Bluff?* [In German] (Europa Verlag, Zurich–New York, 1945).

ROOSEVELT, ELLIOTT, *As He Saw It* (Duell, Sloan & Pearce, Inc., New York, 1946).

ROYAL INSTITUTE OF INTERNATIONAL AFFAIRS, *Atomic Energy* (London, 1948).

SHILS, EDWARD A., *The Atomic Bomb in World Politics* (National Peace Council, London, 1948).

SHULMAN, MILTON, *Defeat in the West* (Martin Secker & Warburg, Ltd., London, 1947).

SPAIGHT, JAMES M., *Bombing Vindicated* (Geoffrey Bles, Ltd., London, 1944).

STIMSON, HENRY L., *The Decision to Use the Atomic Bomb,* Harper's Magazine, New York, February, 1947 [Reprinted in *B.A.S.*, Feb. 1947].

TEDDER, LORD, *Air Power In War* (Hodder & Stoughton, Ltd., London, 1948).

THIRRING, JOSEF H., *Die Geschichte der Atombombe.* [In German.] (Vienna, 1946).

UNITED STATES SENATE, *Report of the Committee on Atomic Energy* (Government Printing Office, Washington, D. C., 1946).

UNITED STATES STATE DEPARTMENT, *A Report on the International Control of Atomic Energy* [*Acheson-Lilienthal Report*] (Publication No. 2948, Government Printing Office, Washington, D. C., 1946).

The International Control of Atomic Energy, Growth of a Policy (Publication No. 2702, Government Printing Office, Washington, D. C., 1946).

UNITED STATES STRATEGIC BOMBING SURVEY:

1. *Overall Report, European War* (Government Printing Office, Washington, D. C., 1945).

2. *The Effect of Bombing on Health and Medical Care in Germany* (War Department, Washington, D. C., 1945).

3. *The Effect of Strategic Bombing on the German War Economy* (Government Printing Office, Washington, D. C., 1945).

4. *Summary Report, Pacific War* (Government Printing Office, Washington, D. C., 1946).

5. *The Effect of Atomic Bombs on Hiroshima and Nagasaki* (Government Printing Office, Washington, D. C., 1946).

INDEX

A. E. C. (*see* Atomic Energy Commission)
Absolute Weapon, The, 5n., 52n., 64n.–65n., 78n.
Acheson, Dean, 118n.
Acheson-Lilienthal Plan, 97, 118–124, 144, 184
"Air Force in the Atomic Age," 50n., 53n.
Air power, 4, 9; in European War, 9–32; German use of, 12–13; importance of, 30; in Pacific War, 32–39; Russian view of, 13
Air Power in War, 11n., 16n., 216n., 234n.
Air raids, 11, 13–14; atomic, 61–65; civilian casualties from, 14, 18
Air strategy, 14–15, 31–32
Air supremacy, 31, 35, 47, 66–67
Aircraft, speed of, 55
(*See also* kinds of aircraft)
Aircraft engine design, 57
Aircraft production, German and British (chart), 25
Allied bombing offensive in Europe (table), 214–219
America (*see* United States)
American Association of Scientific Workers, 70
American Atomic Energy Commission, 107
American Chiefs of Staff, 80
Amery, L. S., 161
Area bombing, 10, 17–18, 26, 28–29, 36–38
Army-Navy Journal, 50n.
Argentina, 108–109
Arnold, General Henry H., 50n., 54n., 67n., 88n., 134
As He Saw It, 131
Association of Edison Illuminating Companies, 102
Association of Scientific Workers, 96n., 191
Atlantic Monthly, 129
Atom and the Charter, The, 96n.
Atomic bomb, actuating mechanism of, 51; compared with ordinary, 45, 48n., 52, 60, 88; damage to property by, 44; defense measures against, 43–58, 62–64, 68, 87; destructive power of, 48; diplomatic reasons for use of, 138–141; expense of, 61–62; future technical developments of, 49–73; and future wars, 3–6, 49; increased power of, 50–51; moral objections to use of, 127–128;

Atomic bomb, relative effectiveness of, 3, 59–60; relative value of, 48–49; stock pile of, 74, 93; strategic use of, 73; tactical use of, 49, 62, 65–68, 87, 90, 93; technical problems of, 73; as threat, 90; time factor of, 60–61; and UN, 91–97; as a weapon, 39, 65; weight of, 52, 67
Atomic energy, conditions for future negotiations concerning, 210–214; control of, 1, 8–9, 88, 114–115, 172–194; control of, first steps toward, 114–117; control of, national or international, 118–127; control of, Russian proposals for, 161–162, 226–229; control of, Russian proposals rejected, 193–194; economic aspects of, 104, 106–114; importance of to unindustrialized nations, 97–114; industrial aspect of, 7–8, 97; military dangers of, 104–106; nonmilitary application of, 97–114, 149; power from, 7–8, 97–114; technical possibility of, 120
Atomic Energy Commission (A.E.C.), 5, 7–9, 54, 104–106, 117–118, 143–144, 148–149, 154, 165, 168, 172–193, 197, 209, 211–214; *First* and *Second Reports,* 173–174, 177n., 185–186, 190, 221–225; suspension of, 194
Atomic Scientists Association, 190–191
Attlee-Truman-King statement, 117, 187, 212
Austin, Warren R., 183
Australian attitude to atomic power, 106, 173n., 183
Austria, 82, 209
Axis Powers, 5

B29's, 39, 46–49, 51, 64, 67
B36's, 55, 67
B50's, 55
Babbage, Charles, 1
Bacteriological research, 69–70
Baker, Newton D., 189
Baltimore Sun, 127
Barnard, Chester I., 118n.
Baruch, Bernard, 8–9, 144, 169, 172n., 173, 182n., 184–185, 188
Baruch Plan, 3, 9, 97, 143–160, 171, 173, 179, 183–185, 209, 211, 213; international comments on, 148–149; reasons for failure of, 158–160; supported by Great Britain, 190
Bases, for atomic warfare, 78–80, 82–85

241

Langmuir, Irving, 101
Lapp, R. E., 54n., 89n.
Lawrence, E. O., 98n., 129
Lee, Asher, 13n., 31
Lenin, V. I, 101
Lilienthal, David, 101, 118, 209
Lilienthal Plan, 3, 27, 114–127, 143–144, 150, 157, 159, 173, 189, 191–192, 209
    (See also Acheson-Lilienthal Plan)
Lincoln, Abraham, 145
Lippmann, Walter, 81–82, 157, 167, 198, 204–205
Lithium-helium reaction, 50–51n.

MacArthur, General, 128
McCloy, John J., 50n., 118n.
McCormick newspapers, 161
McMahon, Senator, 6, 121, 195n.
McNaughton, General, 148
Manchester Guardian, 9n., 97, 196n., 198n., 200n., 210n.
Manchuria, Russian offensive in, 131
Manhattan District Committee on Declassification, 123
Marianas, offensive against, and defeat of Japan, 38
Marshak, J., 102
Marshall, General, 9, 78, 96–97
Marshall Plan, 199, 201
Martel, General, 15, 65
May-Johnson Bill, 121–122
Menke, J. R., 72n., 100n.
Merck, G. W., 69–70
Mexico, comments on Baruch Plan, 142
Miller, Byron S., 121n.
Monsanto Chemical Company, 107
Moral objections and justifications to use of bomb, 127–128
Morrison, Dr. Philip, 107
Mott, N. F., 191
Mussolini, 87

Nagasaki, 4, 37, 39–47, 49–50n., 52, 71–72, 138–139, 142, 202
Namier, R. B., 11n.
Nature, 91n., 99n.
"Navy Department Thinking on the Atomic Bomb," 83n.
Nazism, 7
Netherlands (see Holland)
Neutrons, 41
New Mexico, static test in, 129, 135, 137, 196n.
New Republic, The, 107, 142, 198n., 235n.
New Statesman and Nation, The, 2–6n.
New Times, 163–164
New York Herald Tribune, 14, 56n.
New York Post, 196n.
New York Times, 54n., 136, 182n.
Newman, James R., 121n.
New Chronicle, 142n.

Nitze, Paul, 41n., 134
Normandy landing, allied bombing before, 27, 65, 80
Norway, 11
Nuclear Fission as Source of Power, 72n., 100n.

Oak Ridge Laboratory, 107–108
Observer, 161, 205n.–206n.
One Thousand Americans, 189
One World or None, 50n., 54n., 134, 163–164
Oppenheimer, Ernest, 72–73, 181n., 196–197
Oppenheimer, Dr. J. R., 6, 72–73, 88n., 98n., 107, 118n., 126n., 129n., 140, 142n., 169, 172, 181n., 207
Orr, Sir John Boyd, 125
Osborn, F. H., 187–188

Pacific War, 32, 39, 67
Pakenham, Lord, 192
Papagos, General, 19n.
Parsons, Rear-Admiral, 54
Passive defense measures, 43, 68–69
"Pathfinder" force, 28
Patterson newspapers, 161
Peaceful use of atomic power, 97–114, 149
Pearl Harbor, 33–34, 65
Persia, 80
Pilotless aircraft, 53–54
Plutonium, 41, 44–46, 71–72, 113
Poland, 81–82, 173n., 204
Potsdam Conference, 131–132
Power from atomic energy, 97–114
President's Air Policy Committee, 6
President's Advisory Committee on Universal Training, 6
"Push-button war," 79, 141

Quo, Dr., 149

Radar, 29, 31, 57, 65
Radiation, 41, 44, 71
Radioactive isotopes, 97–98
Radioactive poisons, 69, 71–73, 87, 180, 207
Radioactive tracer elements, 97
Review of Economic Studies, 29, 216
Revolution in Warfare, The, 6n., 13n., 17n.
Rieckoff, H. J., 13n.
Robertson, Archibald, 2–6n.
Rockets, 52, 65, 84
    (See also V2 weapons)
Roosevelt, Elliott, 131
Roosevelt, President, 89, 126
Rostas, Dr. L., 98
Royal Institute of International Affairs, 191
Rubinstein, Professor Modest, 101, 161
Ruhr, The, 16
Rumania, 82, 204